THE WORLD

OF THE

GOLDEN COMPASS

THE OTHERWORLDLY RIDE CONTINUES

Edited by Scott Westerfeld

Developed for Borders, Inc., by BenBella Books, Inc.

Send feedback to feedback@benbellabooks.com

Printed in the United States of America

10 9 8 7 6 5 4 3 2 1

Library of Congress Cataloging-in-Publication Data is available for this title.

Proofreading by Emily Chauvier, Paige Kimmel, and Yara Abuata

Cover art by Ralph Voltz

Cover design by Laura Watkins

Text design and composition by Laura Watkins

Printed by Victor Graphics, Inc.

THE WORLD
OF THE
GOLDEN COMPASS

CONTENTS

Introduction   1
His Dark Materials and the Idea of North
   SCOTT WESTERFELD

Pants on Fire   5
   CAROLE WILKINSON

Bushidō Bear   15
   LINDA GERBER

The Dangerous Worlds of Pullman's His Dark Materials   23
   CINDA WILLIAMS CHIMA

Lord Asriel: Dad from Hell or Heroic Rebel?   31
   SOPHIE MASSON

Hot Sex and Horrific Parenting in His Dark Materials   43
   MAUREEN JOHNSON

The Mysterious Mrs. Coulter   55
   ELLEN STEIBER

Shedding Light on Dark Matter   71
   ELLEN HOPKINS

Dæmons and the Hunt for the Human Soul   83
   SUSAN VAUGHT

Ghost in the Machine   93
   DIANA PETERFREUND

Where You Lead, I Will Follow   103
    DEB CALETTI

Dear Soul   111
    JULIET MARILLIER

Tempest in a British Tea Cup   121
    O.R. MELLING

Pullman's Dark Materials   131
    ALISON CROGGON

God Is in the Stories   143
    NED VIZZINI

Dancing with the Dust   155
    JAMES A. OWEN

Losing My Religion   165
    NANCY HOLDER

Unreal City   179
    ELIZABETH E. WEIN

A Short History of Hell and the Crabby Old God
    Who Sends You There   189
    HERBIE BRENNAN

Philip Pullman and the Loss of Joy   199
    KATHLEEN JEFFRIE JOHNSON

INTRODUCTION

HIS DARK MATERIALS AND THE IDEA OF NORTH

Here's a secret about us writers:

Many of us dread the question, "Where do you get your ideas?"

It's just too complicated to answer, and at the same time too simple—both silly and sublime. I've probably been asked it a thousand times, and yet I still don't have a real response.

Phillip Pullman has also admitted difficulty with the question. Not only with answering it, but with why anyone would ask. As he puts it: "I can't believe that everyone isn't having ideas all the time."

Now *that* answer makes sense, at least in Pullman's case. He's got more ideas than most of us.

As this anthology began to take shape, one complaint became constant among the contributors: Pullman had provided them with an embarrassment of riches. Or perhaps a *confusion* of riches. His Dark Materials simply contained too many ideas. There were talking bears to be wrangled, poetic allusions to analyze, and a canvas that stretched across "ten million other worlds . . . as close as a heartbeat" (*TGC* 164–165). And on top of that, the characters' souls were flitting around outside their bodies. Where was the humble essayist to start?

As Maureen Johnson fumes within these pages: "His Dark Materials is a kind of symbol scrap yard. . . . There are even symbols imprinted on symbols (the golden compass itself)." And just as with the alethiometer, the symbols are layered with meanings that change every time the needle stops.

Luckily, our intrepid essayists weren't dissuaded by this multitude of ideas. As you will read, they've plunged into the scrap yard boldly and with scintillating results. But perhaps it should be unsurprising that even when the needle stops in the same place, the answers change. For example, our three essays about dæmons conclude that:

1) We might one day have our own dæmons to talk to.
2) We wouldn't really *want* to have dæmons if we could.
3) We *already* have dæmons here in our own world.

1

It's up to you to decide who makes the strongest case, or to conclude that these contradictory claims can somehow coexist, all as close as a heartbeat.

As the essays rolled in, here's a question I started to ask myself:

If His Dark Materials lends itself to so many interpretations, how does it all hang together as one novel? Why doesn't the story just fly apart under the weight of its many, many ideas?

Well, I have my own personal theory about that, which I'll give you now, before I throw you into the scrap yard.

For me it all starts in the arctic, with the idea of North.

First, you need a little history.

Back in the early 1800s, here in our non-fictional world, the globe was getting warmer. A centuries-long period called the Little Ice Age was ending, ancient icebergs breaking up. With the sea lanes clearing in the far north, a new age of arctic exploration was about to begin.

It wasn't just scientific societies and scholars who found this new age exciting. In Victorian England, crowds waited in line for hours to see arctic cycloramas (huge painted landscapes that wrapped around the viewer, an early form of virtual reality). Expeditions were followed closely by newspapers and explorers feted as heroes on their safe return. Adventure novels set in the far north were immensely popular. Following this vogue, even Mary Shelley's *Frankenstein* (1817) heads north in the end, with the tragic monster disappearing across the glaciers toward the pole.

So what was so fascinating about a bunch of ice?

For one thing, the environmental extremes in the far north seemed to create a kind of magic. Explorers saw apparitions in the arctic sky, ghostly projections of floating mountains and cities. We know now that these visions weren't really magic, they were just ice crystals suspended in the air. The floating icy layer acted as a reflective surface, mirroring islands that were still over the horizon. But for a long time sailors believed their ships had actually gone *inside* the Earth, discovering another upside-down world inside our own. (Imagine yourself on the inside of a balloon, looking "up" at the other side!)

And floating cities weren't the only tricks the arctic played. Even the sailor's trusty compass can turn traitor in the arctic. The Earth's magnetic poles don't match up with the geographic ones, alas. So as explorers pushed farther and farther north, they found their compass needles pointing in strange directions, even swinging in lazy, uncertain circles. The simple notions of north, south, east, and west were suddenly up for interpretation. . . .

And then there's meteoric iron, the kind favored by armored bears.

About 10,000 years ago, five giant meteorites fell in Greenland. They were eventually discovered by ancient arctic dwellers, who harvested iron from them, creating metal tools that revolutionized their stone-age culture. By the time European explorers arrived, this magical sky-metal had become the ultimate status symbol in arctic culture, linking a huge community in trade.

And the iron to be found in the far north wasn't just in meteors. In the 1870s, an explorer named Nils Nordenskjold became obsessed with "cosmic dust." He discovered an almost-invisible layer of iron falling from space onto the arctic snows, and theorized that this cosmic rain played an important role in the formation of our globe. He wasn't totally crazy. These days, many scientists believe that the building blocks of life on our planet were brought here by meteors—intelligence arising from so much cosmic dust (NASA).

So let's review: cosmic dust, meteoric iron, needles swinging lazily on compasses, and floating cities that augur hidden worlds. Does any of this sound familiar?

This can't all be a coincidence, can it?

In *The Golden Compass* our first glimpse of the arctic comes near the start, during Lord Asriel's slide show at Oxford. He shows the Scholars (and Lyra, hidden in the wardrobe) a photograph of a floating city, just like those glimpsed by sailors two centuries ago in our world.

Intriguingly, this second chapter of *TGC* is entitled "The Idea of North." And perhaps that's a clue to how Pullman's symbol scrap yard all hangs together. He's taken arctic mysteries that modern-day science has explained away—cosmic dust, meteoric iron, floating cities, even wobbling compass needles—and reinvigorated them with wonder.

In Pullman's world, the floating city in the slide show is no illusion; by the end of the book, Lyra is stepping across onto its streets. It's an old "idea of North" made real again.

Of course, that's just my reading, partly formed out of my own obsession with the arctic. And it doesn't explain witches, anbaric lights, the Oblation Board, and Magisterium, or those all-important dæmons. But my theory does hint at answers to that classic question: where ideas come from. Pullman makes his fictional world from out-of-date pieces of the real one. His symbols hold together because they all lived together in the past of our own world, before scientific explanations made floating cities and iron from the sky mundane.

Within these pages you will find more answers to that question we started with, explanations for those witches, anbaric lights, and dæmons—*lots* of talk about dæmons, and the Magisterium, too, I promise. But this isn't a book of answers, really. It's a book of readings, full of signposts for your own journeys into the scrap yard of symbols that is His Dark Materials. So don't look for simple answers here; any compass with a wandering needle remains open to interpretation.

As the early arctic explorers learned, true north becomes trickier the closer you get to it.

—SCOTT WESTERFELD

REFERENCES

NASA. "Organic Molecules Fall to Earth in Meteors." 9 July 2007.
<http://astrobiology.arc.nasa.gov/news/expandnews.cfm?id=597>
Pullman, Philip. "About the Writing." 9 July 2007.
<http://www.philip-pullman.com/about_the_writing.asp>

The world of The Golden Compass *is full of secrets, deceptions, tall tales, fibs, and outright propaganda. In a word: lies. And yet, in Lyra's hands, the golden compass itself promises the truth. But is it the whole truth, and nothing but? Wilkinson tries to untangle the webs of deceit that weave through His Dark Materials.*

PANTS ON FIRE
Truth, Lies, and Deception in The Golden Compass

CAROLE WILKINSON

I tell lies.

Philip Pullman tells lies.

He's an author. So am I. Philip and me, we lie for a living.

The Golden Compass is all about lies. Truth and lies are at the heart of the His Dark Materials trilogy. Ultimately this book, this trilogy, is a vehicle for Pullman to expose lies, to tell the truth. But whose version of the truth is it?

There are different kinds of lies. There are "good" lies—the ones we tell children to keep them innocent; the ones we tell our friends so we don't offend them; the ones we tell our bosses so we don't lose our jobs. We call them "white lies" and they're about being polite, not wanting to hurt anyone's feelings. They're about protection: protecting children, protecting friends, and most importantly, protecting ourselves. And then there's just telling stories. Whether it's writing a novel or embroidering an anecdote to amuse dinner party guests, all good stories need improvement. It's all harmless stuff.

There's "bad" lying, too. Those are usually the lies that other people tell us, as opposed to the ones we tell. The ones that cause pain and misery, even death. The ones based on greed or maliciousness or cowardice. These lies are pitch black; they aren't harmless.

Often in works of fiction, it's easy to tell the goodies from the baddies, because the goodies tell the truth, whereas the baddies lie through their teeth. Philip Pullman doesn't make it that easy for us. In *The Golden Compass* everyone lies. All the adults in Lyra's life lie to her. Some tell

5

the good sort of lies, like the Master of Jordan College, who has told her she is an orphan when she isn't. He told her what he thought was best for her. Then there are her parents. They're both liars. Neither of them own up to being her parents, for a start. Lord Asriel lies to the Jordan Scholars about the severed head—but he's only lying so that he can get money to fund his expedition. Most of us have exaggerated in job and funding applications. We can relate to that. He is, after all, searching for the truth. Lord Asriel is not so bad.

It's Mrs. Coulter who's really the bad guy, isn't it? She's a nasty piece of work. Elegant and sweet-smelling, she's crueler than Cruella de Vil. This woman is no cartoon or caricature, though. She's three-dimensional; living and breathing and absolutely ruthless. She doesn't snaffle puppies for their pelts, she lures deprived children from the slums with the promise of food and hot chocolate so that she can kidnap them and use them for her evil purposes. Mrs. Coulter is deceit personified. As Will says, "'[S]he just loves lying too much to stop'" (*TAS* 128). Lying is so much a part of the way she functions that the thought of telling the truth is such a novel idea that it makes her laugh. She lies "in the very marrow of her bones," and she only does it for her own benefit (*TAS* 184). Her lies are jet black. That's what makes her so bad.

But Pullman doesn't stop there. His heroine lies, too. Lyra is a practiced liar (even her name is practically an anagram of the word). She's a storyteller. She lies to amuse her Oxford playmates, inventing fabulous adventures for Lord Asriel involving Tartars and death stares or Turks and serpent venom. She lies to stay out of trouble. Lying comes to her "as naturally as breathing" (*TAS* 152) but she's a kid. That's what kids do, so it's okay, isn't it? "'I'm the best liar there ever was,'" she says (*TSK* 91), and she's not bragging, it's just a fact. She's so good at lying that the bear Iorek Byrnison names her Lyra Silvertongue.

Then there's the Church. Lyra's whole world is dominated by an all-powerful and oppressive Church that actively suppresses the truth. Any scientific discovery that might contradict or disprove the "truth" of the Bible is called heresy. In particular, the Church wants to wipe out knowledge of Dust and deny the existence of other worlds. The holy fathers of the Church eradicate the truth using inquisition, exorcism, and torture. Scientists researching heretical subjects are threatened with execution if they persist. The Church is very successful, it seems, as Lyra's world, though so similar to ours, has an archaic feel, as if it's stuck in the past. The representatives of the Church are perpetuating a huge lie. Now they're *really* bad.

There is just one island of honesty in this sea of lies that surrounds Lyra: her relationship with her dæmon, Pantalaimon. She doesn't lie to him. She can't. Between them there is a bond of complete trust and truth.

Exactly when lies turn from white to black is difficult to discern. In between the two extremes, there's an ocean of gray. As with all polarities, everyone wants to draw the line in a different place. At what age do those cute stories that kids tell (*"I have an imaginary friend called Twinky who lives in the bathroom cupboard"*; *"A monster ate the missing cake"*) stop being childish fantasies and become adult deceit (*"Tayla broke your favorite mug, not me"*)? Somehow we expect that children will learn the difference at the right time (say, when they become teenagers). We might have told them a million lies (*"Fairies exist if you believe in them"*; *"If you eat up all your crusts/broccoli/tofu, you'll grow up big and strong"*), but once they start leaving the house on their own, parents demand truth from their offspring at all times.

At the beginning of *The Golden Compass*, Lyra is eleven years old. Not quite young enough for her lies to be completely harmless fantasies, but not yet old enough for them to be called deceit. No one gets harmed because of her lies, but I was uneasy about her effortless lying. Pullman tells us again and again that she's a liar. There's something of the Artful Dodger about Lyra-in-Oxford, a sense that her lying could soon lead to a more adult dishonesty.

Into this world of lies comes the alethiometer, a device that tells the truth. It's a very cool machine. I want to own one. Not just because it could tell me what I need to know, but because it's a beautifully crafted object, lovely to behold and suitably arcane. It looks like a large watch, made of brass (not gold). Instead of numerals, it has thirty-six symbols around its face. Instead of two hands it has four—three short ones, which the reader positions to frame his or her question, and one longer thin one, which points to the symbols to give the answer.

At first, Lyra doesn't know how to use the alethiometer. There are only six alethiometers in Lyra's world. A few scholars have learned to operate them, but only after years of study and reference to a detailed handbook. Lyra discovers that she can operate her alethiometer intuitively. In next to no time, the long needle has stopped its aimless wandering and provides her with detailed answers. This is the uneducated Lyra's special skill. She doesn't need a manual to explain the multiple levels of meaning that each symbol has. "'I kind of see 'em,'" she says. "'Or feel 'em rather, like climbing down a ladder at night, you put your foot down and there's another rung. Well, I put my mind down and there's another meaning'" (*TGC* 133). When Lyra reaches the correct level of meaning, her mind focuses, just as our eyes focus on a close object. The alethiometer tells her everything she wants to know about the here and now, but it doesn't foretell the future, it can only predict possibilities; it warns. The actual outcome of events is still in the hands of humans (and bears, witches, angels, etc.).

Like King Arthur, Lyra's specialness is foretold in a prophecy. Just like every orphaned, pig-keeping, womp-rat-shooting, pipe-weed-smoking soon-to-be-hero, Lyra doesn't have a clue, but the alethiometer has found its way into her hands because she is the Chosen One. She's got the gift. Pullman has given the task of saving the world to a child, but not because she's an innocent. He's entrusted the alethiometer, the truth-measure, to a born liar. Neat. Little lying Lyra is the one who's going to help save the world(s) through truth.

Lyra has guts and guile aplenty, what she lacks is knowledge. It's the alethiometer that gives her the knowledge she needs to fulfill her destiny. It's no get-out-of-jail-free card though. It doesn't give Lyra superpowers, it doesn't shield her from attack, it doesn't teleport her to where she needs to be. It just tells her the truth. It points her in the right direction. Our girl has to do all the dirty work herself. She has to travel miles and miles on foot, exhausted and hungry. She has to devise her own methods of escape from different prisons in different worlds. She has to confront everything from bears to witches, from creepy scientists to harpies. To overcome adversity and adversaries, she still has to draw on her own inner resources of strength, courage, and sneakiness.

The alethiometer is not a symbol of childish virtue. Lyra is not an innocent child who is going to save the world from the evil grown-ups. If anything, the device takes away what little innocence she has. She doesn't use the alethiometer to amuse herself or others, or to get out of scrapes. She discovers the truth to eliminate her enemies.

Like all heroes, Lyra has allies. But there is only one accomplice who

Lyra meets on her quest who she can trust to tell her the complete truth; to not withhold anything. It isn't a person, it's a bear. Iorek Byrnison is the *panserbjørn* who Lyra releases from servitude and who is her champion, the bear in shining armor who saves her on more than one occasion.

Bears can't lie. And that's their most effective weapon against humans, more important than their six-inch, dagger-sharp claws, their vicious teeth, or their huge paws, capable of crushing a skull with a single blow. It's precisely because they lack the human art of lying that they are human beings' deadliest enemy. People cannot trick bears. "'We see tricks and deceit as plain as arms and legs,'" Iorek tells Lyra. "'We can see in a way humans have forgotten'" (*TGC* 199).

Yet Lyra is such a skillful liar that she defeats the usurper bear king, Iofur, with lies. He yearns to be human, and in imitating humans he has lost his native bear-ness. Lyra promises to give him the one thing that sets humans apart from all other creatures—she offers him a dæmon: herself. Using the alethiometer, she discovers truths about the bear so that she can lie to him. She pulls the fur over his eyes. Is this Pullman's message? To lie is to be human? Lies can be bad, but used against evil they're okay?

Even now that she's the holder of the truth, lying is still an integral part of Lyra's strategy. It's a familiar weapon that she pulls out and uses with consummate skill, as other heroes might use a wooden stake, a lightsaber, or a summoning charm. Lyra never uses a conventional weapon. She doesn't need one. She has that uniquely human weapon. Lies. She's inherited the skill from her parents, just as a mythological hero might inherit a flaming sword or a magic ring. Lyra is the offspring of powerful representatives of opposing forces. Her father is a scientist and a heretic. Her mother is a zealous defender of the Church. Just as Aragorn's sword is forged from the shards of his failed father's broken blade, Lyra's skill at lying is forged from her parents' flaws, pieced together to create a weapon to be used for good.

By the end of *The Golden Compass*, Lyra has complete control over the alethiometer. She leaves Oxford. She thumbs her nose at the Church by walking off into the distance and into heresy—into another world.

Eventually, Lyra finds her way to a world that is both familiar and unfamiliar to her. We know it well; it's our world. There are no alethiometers here, but I know for a fact that people in our world have been obsessed with finding out the "truth" for thousands of years. Divination, prophecy, fortune-telling, whatever you want to call it— nothing any sci-fi or fantasy writer has ever invented can outdo the weirdness of the techniques that humans have come up with over time. The ancient Romans decided that the answers to all their questions lay in the entrails of sacrificed animals. In later times, poring over animal innards gave way to the less gory practices of reading the lines on hands, dealing cards, and studying the patterns in just about anything—from oil in water to the ashes of burnt offerings, from the flight of birds to tea leaves in the bottom of a cup. There's apparently even a method involving cheese! Our desperation to control our lives knows no bounds.

I scoff at most of these methods ("'What, are we into fortune-telling now?'" [*TSK* 80]), but I have to confess, I have been known to use the I Ching. I've allowed the fall of three coins to make major life decisions for me when I have been overcome by that terrible paralysis of mind that makes you incapable of taking a leap into the unknown or of deciding between the best of two (or more) evils.

In *The Subtle Knife*, scientist Mary Malone has an interest in the I Ching and how it works. She has just made a breakthrough; she has discovered the existence of new subatomic particles and begun to realize that they are conscious. "'[T]hey know we're here. They answer back'" (*TSK* 78). She hasn't made a truth reader yet, she's getting close, but in the meantime she has to make do with the I Ching. (Her preferred technique is the rather clumsy method involving the division and counting of a bundle of fifty yarrow stalks.)

Pullman isn't content with creating a divination device; he also invents a scientific theory to explain how it works. And his theory works just as well for the I Ching in Mary's world as it does for the alethiometer in Lyra's.

It's all to do with Dust. The elementary particles, which Lyra calls Dust and Mary calls Shadows, are what makes the alethiometer work. And what is Dust? It's dark matter, the dark materials of the trilogy title; that mysterious stuff that we can't see or measure. As Pullman says, "It's just a wonderful gift for a storyteller to discover that most of the universe is made of this stuff called dark matter that nobody knew about until very recently. Astronomers don't know what it is. Nobody knows. That gives you a license to imagine anything" (Renton).

These particles are conscious. They interact with our thoughts. "'The Shadows flock to your thinking like birds,'" Mary says (*TSK* 78). But you can't receive them unless you're ready to believe in them. The alethiometer operator, after creating her query by positioning the three moveable hands, must enter a trance-like state. Then the Dust "reads" the operator's query and provides the answer by manipulating the alethiometer's long, free-floating hand.

But does Dust always tell the truth? And whose truth is it telling, anyway? Or is Lyra just interpreting the symbols to fit her own needs? If it's anything like using the I Ching, it's all about interpretation. I can remember, after a terrible argument with my husband, when I threw the I Ching half a dozen times asking it if I should leave him. It never said yes. But was I receiving a universal truth, or was it just how I wanted to interpret it? Let's face it: "The fifth nine undivided shows its subject amidst the appliances of a feast" isn't a clear-cut answer. Should we trust Philip Pullman when he tells us that Lyra is learning the truth? Does she just read what she wants to? Or, for that matter, does the Dust lie to get its own way? Dust has its own opinions. Lyra senses that it is rebuking her when she asks the same question twice. And sometimes it tells her things she doesn't ask for. What exactly does the Dust want?

As the story continues to unfold, we grow so used to lies and deceit that they become normal. Lord Asriel and Mrs. Coulter change their spots so many times that we don't know who to trust. Pullman waits until the final book of the trilogy before he introduces the last, shocking level of deceit. The Authority himself is a liar. Pullman has waited until we're all totally immersed in the story, completely entranced by his worlds, desperately concerned about Lyra. That tail-end deception doesn't just sting, it whacks you in the face and knocks you off your feet. God lied when he said he was the creator of the world. He's just another angel. He lied when he said Heaven is a paradise. The afterlife is, in fact, a terrible prison camp where harpies are constantly flapping around the dead people's heads, reminding them of their worst mistakes. Even for an atheist like me, that's pretty breathtaking stuff.

The hard thing about having the ability to lie is deciding when to use it and when to tell the truth. Like many normally truthful parents, I cheerfully fed my daughter the Holy Trinity of childhood lies (Father Christmas, Easter Bunny, Tooth Fairy) with a completely clear conscience. I enjoyed leaving the rabbit paw prints in the garden, encouraged her to write to Santa and leave him a beer and a sandwich on Christmas Eve. But then one day, out of the blue, at age seven, she came to me and said, "Tell me if there really is a Father Christmas . . . and don't lie." I had it in my power to give her at least another two or three years of innocence. All I had to say was, "Of course there is, darling. You saw the teeth marks in the sandwich crusts." But I didn't. Lying to her face when she asked me a question was different than inventing a fantasy for her. I chose to tell the truth. She wasn't happy with the truth; she wanted to believe. I think she resented me for telling her. But at least she knew that I told her the truth. She's twenty-six now. She still has that knowledge.[1]

Gradually, truth takes the place of lies as Lyra's most effective weapon. When she meets scientist Mary Malone, she immediately tells this stranger everything she knows about Dust. It's a gamble. She knows what Scholars are like. It's "difficult to tell them the truth when a lie would [be] so much easier for them to understand" (*TSK* 75). Lyra doesn't lie, though. She tells the truth, because the alethiometer has led her to Mary. Lyra's strategy works. Mary is convinced.

In *The Amber Spyglass*, when Lyra is confronted by the hideous harpies, it's telling the truth that saves her. At first she falls back on her trusted weapon—lies. She tells the harpy No-Name her story, but it's a complete fabrication, the sort of story she would make up to amuse the kids in Oxford. Her lies enrage No-Name, and Lyra is aghast. She thinks she's lost the knack of lying. The skill that she's honed and polished all her life has left her. But when Lyra tells the true tales of her life in Oxford to the ghosts in the World of the Dead, the harpies are held spellbound. They're nourished by the truth, human truth. Instead of feeding on "the worst in everyone" (*TAS* 283), the harpies ask for a payment of truth from each ghost, and in return for those "true stories" the harpies guide them through the terrible, barren underworld and allow them to die, to disintegrate, their molecules returning to the earth.

Even Lord Asriel and Mrs. Coulter find the center of truth in themselves and sacrifice themselves for their love of Lyra (though they achieve this with lies and deception).

---

[1] And I'd like to acknowledge that my daughter, Lili Wilkinson, helped me a lot with this essay (the title was her idea).

Lyra and Will learn to trust each other and to tell the truth, to reveal things they have kept secret from others. This honesty is essential for them to be able to unite their powers and save the world(s). Ultimately it's that special human truth, the declaration of love, which enables them to do that.

Finally, the power to read the truth is taken away from Lyra. She reaches puberty. She is no longer a child. The ability to follow the alethiometer's swinging needle, to plumb the levels of meaning for the symbols, gradually slips away until she's no wiser than anyone else as to its operation. Now if she wants to use it, she must do it the hard way. She must embark on years of study and memorize the many levels of meaning the symbols hold, or she must learn to recognize the truth herself, unaided.

On her epic journey, Lyra learns the value of truth and the power of lies. She learns truths about herself—she's loyal, she's brave, and she's capable of love. Lies have a place, Pullman tells us. But ultimately, it's truth that is important, particularly inner truth, being truthful to yourself.

"'You must tell them true stories,'" a ghost tells Mary Malone, "'and everything will be well'" (*TAS* 386). This is the truth for Philip Pullman.

He has taken us on a long journey through lies to truth. For him, truth is everything. Stories are fiction, authors are a type of liar, but if the stories have that core of truth, then they're a force for good even if they are a tissue of lies. He lies so that we, like Lyra, learn the value of truth.

And there's one particular truth that Pullman wants to leave us with. Being independent from any sort of "authority," including God, is another kind of self-truth. "'We've had nothing but lies and propaganda and cruelty and deceit for all the thousands of years of human history. It's time we started again'" (*TSK* 282). He's ready to throw out the concept of the Kingdom of Heaven and replace it with the Republic of Heaven, where everyone gets to think for themselves. We shouldn't let God, or anyone's idea of a god, or any representative of a god, tell us what is true and what is a lie.

In the world of His Dark Materials, Dust particles know the truth, the universal truth, but in the end it's just Philip Pullman's truth, the only truth he knows. "Truth" isn't something that can be captured or quantified. It isn't fixed, nor is it universal. Truth has as many shades as lies do.

Truth comes from within, not from holy books and not from works of fiction.

Philip Pullman is up there on his pulpit. He's telling us his version of the truth and he's shouting it out loud. I admire him for that. He's a brave man to voice this opinion in these times, though he denies that he's preaching to us.

"I'm not making an argument," he said in a 2002 interview, "or preaching a sermon or setting out a political tract: I'm telling a story" (Spanner).

I don't believe him, not for a minute.

He's lying.

CAROLE WILKINSON is an Australian children's author and sci-fi/fantasy fan. She is best known for her multi-award-winning historical fantasy series Dragon Keeper, set in Han dynasty China.

REFERENCES

Renton, Jennie. "Philip Pullman Interview." *Texualities*. 2005.
   <www.textualities.net/writers/features-n-z/pullmanp01.php>
Spanner, Huw. "Heat and Dust." *Third Way*. 13 Feb. 2002.
   <http://www.thirdway.org.uk/past/showpage.asp?page=3949>

Pullman's armored bears are both magnificent and terrifying, oversized animal counterweights to Lyra's slight physical presence. But Iorek Byrnison is not all brute strength: he lives by a code more strict and honorable than most of the human characters in the series. Gerber compares the code of the armored bear to those of warriors past, and looks closely at what all of us stand to gain (and lose) when we let ourselves be constrained by honor.

BUSHIDŌ BEAR
The Constraint of Honor

LINDA GERBER

Iorek Byrnison: *panserbjørn*, exiled king, larger-than-life character. He's the embodiment of machismo, a real he-man (or in this case, he-bear). Tough. Strong. Huge. And double cool points for being a renegade.

From our first glimpse of Iorek Byrnison behind Einarsson's Bar, we know he's something special. He's mysterious. He's dangerous. He's powerful. Even better, as Lyra notes, his power is controlled by intelligence. He's the perfect hero-in-the-making.

But alas, poor Iorek! This hero comes with a tragic flaw: he's hobbled by more than his weakness for raw spirits or his temporary loss of armor—Iorek Byrnison is afflicted by honor.

Yes, you read that right—afflicted. Rhymes with convicted. Iorek's idealism cages him as surely as if he were behind bars.

But wait, isn't honor a good thing? Sure, if you want fair maidens to swoon at your feet and poets to write epics about your virtue. But in reality? Maybe not so much.

In Iorek Byrnison's case, a little flexibility with the whole honor thing could have saved him a world of trouble. Like when he got exiled from Svalbard for unwittingly killing the judgment-impaired bear. Sure, the *panserbjørne* code mandates exile for any bear who kills in such a way, but couldn't Iorek Byrnison have argued that his actions were justified? After all, he was provoked, and his opponent should have backed down before the fight got out of control. That has to count for *something*.

Not to Iorek, though. He's such an honor fanatic that he condemns himself for breaking the code of conduct. He willingly allowed his armor—his soul!—to be taken away from him and accepted exile as right and just. It's ironic, isn't it, that the very thing that's supposed to protect one's soul—honor—is the thing that causes Iorek Byrnison to lose his? His soul, that is. He's still got his honor, for all the good it does him once he gives up his rightful position as king.

You might think Iorek would do anything to get his armor back. But no. He can't let go of his warrior's code. Under its constraints, he wound up in Trollesund, tricked and trapped by unscrupulous men who got him drunk and took away the armor he made to replace the first set he gave up. Under the circumstances, he'd have been completely justified if he bent a few rules . . . but he didn't.

Even when Lyra tells him where his armor is hidden, he refuses to go look for it until sundown because he had promised he would work until then. Armored bears keep their word. No exceptions. It isn't until Lyra astutely observes that, from where she's standing, the sun has already set that Iorek is able to leave without departing from his beloved code.

He does, however, appear to appreciate her creative interpretation of his promise. Later, when he finds that Lyra has tricked Iofur Raknison by lying to him, he proudly calls her "'Lyra Silvertongue'" (*TGC* 305). He seems to admire her flexibility with the truth. Too bad he couldn't take a page from her book and learn the art of a well-placed lie.

But that's the one thing the *panserbjørne* code will not allow. He might rip an opponent to shreds with his claws, he might fight for whoever offers the most gold, but an armored bear will never speak untruth. Imbalanced as that may seem, strict obedience to that code sets the *panserbjørne* apart. It defines their actions and allows their reputation to precede them.

That's what warrior codes of conduct are supposed to do: distinguish the warrior by holding him to a higher standard than his non-warrior counterparts. At least in theory. In reality, many of the ideals are overly romanticized. They sound great in poetry, but how realistic are they in practice? Sure, being honest and loyal and chivalrous toward women, for instance, is fine at court, but how many warriors are really going to be able to maintain that in the heat of battle?

The answer to that question could very well be why warrior cultures from this and alternate worlds have developed elaborate codes of behavior for their fighting elite. Give a warrior a cause and it justifies war. Teach him that death is honorable and it normalizes the killing. Give him an ideal and it elevates his actions from barbarism to heroism.

Most codes of honor not only spell out how warriors are supposed to act when they're fighting each other, but define the warrior's role in society (French). This makes sense. Out on the battlefield he's got to be tough. Brutal. Powerful. But polite society prefers a kinder, gentler he-man, not someone who might be tempted to use his might to intimidate or control anyone weaker than himself. Without some kind of guideline to define what's honorable and what's not, societies could get stuck with a bunch of fighter types running amok.

Take a look at Japan, for instance. Their early feudal years saw a lot of battles between clans as families jockeyed for territory. Amid all the fighting, a kind of proto-samurai warrior class developed. This warrior class was made up of rustic, brutish farmer types, and each clan's warriors followed their own set of rules. It was chaos until someone got brilliant and decided to get philosophical about how all this fighting should be done.

The concept of *budō* emerged. Translated literally, *budō* means the way (*dō*) of war (*bu*). What's interesting is that if you look at the Chinese characters for *budō*, you see that *bu* actually means "stop conflict" (Kesshin No Rekishi). War, ironically, was defined as keeping the peace, and as such, it became an honorable institution.

From the *budō* "way of war" came the philosophy of *bushidō*, the samurai "way of the warrior." Beyond requiring mastery of specialized fighting techniques, the samurai established strict codes of conduct and assigned virtues that were meant to elevate warriors to an elite status.

These early samurai were much like the *panserbjørne*—feared and respected, fierce and armor-clad. Both were bound by a strict code of conduct, the violation of which could mean exile, or more honorably, death.

Meanwhile, oceans away, the concept of chivalry, or knightly virtue (or nightly virtue for those knights who had taken a vow of chastity), emerged. Like *bushidō*, chivalry embraced the ideals of honesty, loyalty, and courage.

In fact, across the globe, each culture logically adapted codes that would work within the framework of their unique society. Even the Mongols under the leadership of Genghis Khan, who many consider to be barbarians, lived by a strict honor code called the great *Yasa*. Sure, they could hack their Chinese counterparts to death, but they weren't supposed to lie, steal, or commit adultery. They also had some really weird rules, like a ban on urinating into water or ashes, the violation of which was punishable by death (Oestmoen). Point is, Genghis Khan's men, though far from perfect, were true warriors.

The *panserbjørne* probably fall more into this Mongol warrior category than the self-righteous knightly category. According to Tony Costa, the *panserbjørne* are "'like mercenaries. . . . They sell their strength to whoever pays.'" Further, "'They're vicious killers, absolutely pitiless.'" But, as warriors, the *panserbjørne* live by a code: "'[T]hey keep their word. If you make a bargain with a *panserbjørn*, you can rely on it'" (*TGC* 96).

The assurance with which Tony Costa can say that is exactly the kind of confidence these warrior codes were supposed to foster. A true warrior universally embraced honesty, loyalty, fealty, and death before dishonor.

Plutarch illustrated that last one rather vividly in his *Moralia*, quoting a Spartan mother's admonition to her son as he headed off to battle: "*E tan, e epi tan*," which, depending on which scholar you ask, is roughly translated as, "Come back with your shield or upon it." Now, those Spartan mamas might have been particularly big on the tough love, but the saying represents the kind of honor most warrior classes are familiar with.

A Spartan warrior's heavy shield protected not only the warrior, but also the man next to him in formation. Consequently, if a warrior lost his shield through carelessness (or worse yet, dropped it on purpose so he could high-tail it off the battlefield unencumbered), he not only endangered himself, but let down his comrade.

Hence the mother's earnest advice: Come back with your shield so that we will know you fought honorably. Come back carrying your shield, or else carried by your shield (in which case, you're injured or dead). Otherwise, don't come back at all, you bloody coward.

Sound extreme? How about the Rajput practice of *Saka*? The Rajput were an elite warrior caste hailing from the Indian subcontinent. They also held fast to a stringent code of conduct that they would abide by to the point of laying down their lives. When a Rajput community found itself surrounded and outnumbered, the warriors prepared for *Saka*—literally a fight to the death. They entered into battle knowing they would either obliterate or be obliterated; there was no other option. Death was preferable to captivity or surrender. In fact, before the fight, Rajput warriors clothed themselves in saffron robes, to show their absolute commitment to the battle and acceptance of their possible demise (Ziegler).

Compare the resolve of these Spartan and Rajput warriors to that of Iorek Byrnison as he returns to Svalbard to rescue Lyra. He knows full well that, according to the *panserbjørne* code, his status as outcast has degraded him to less-than-bear. As Professor Santelia puts it, "'Iorek might as well be a seal now, or a walrus, not a bear. . . . They wouldn't fight him honorably like a bear; they'd kill him with fire hurlers before he got near'" (*TGC* 291).

Though his comrades and former subjects no longer recognize his status as a fellow warrior, Iorek Byrnison's sense of honor will not allow him to deny his responsibility and to act accordingly. Perhaps this sense of honor is more important than all the codes of conduct in all the warrior cultures in the world. People may differ in motivation and in whatever codes they adhere to, but if they truly know who they are, that knowledge is the thing that drives their actions. Warrior or not, honor lies in being true to oneself no matter the circumstances. So perhaps honor is not such a constraint after all.

Take Lyra, for instance—she of the silver tongue. She may be adept at trickery and lying, but she is fiercely loyal and does not hesitate to act on what she believes to be right. She has somewhat of a warrior mentality, having waged many wars within and without the walls of Oxford, and she knows the value of forming quick alliances and redefining enemies. Her honesty, however, is malleable. This may give her more flexibility than Iorek, but it also leaves her to navigate life's challenges with only her conscience to guide her.

However un-bear-like the idea of doing so may be, Lyra earns Iorek's respect by remaining true to who she is. When the stakes rise beyond territorial play-fighting to the reality of kidnapped children and severed dæmons, Lyra's character really shines. She's brave, she's clever, and though she may lie and deceive when it suits her, at least her purpose is pure.

Compare her with another of Iorek's friends, American aeronaut Lee Scoresby. Whereas Lyra is driven by a strong sense of right and wrong as she searches for Roger, hunts down the Gobblers, and struggles to get the alethiometer to Lord Asriel, Scoresby says he's in it for the money. As he explains to Serafina Pekkala, "'I do my flying in exchange for cash. . . . Flying is just a job to me, and I'm just a technician. I might as well be adjusting valves in a gas engine or wiring up anbaric circuits'" (TGC 271).

But Lee Scoresby is more warrior-like than he'd like to admit. Though his initial motivation for involving himself in the gyptian's quest to find the missing children may have been monetary, it could be argued that his loyalty to his old friend, Iorek Byrnison, is a greater influence by the end. He and Iorek go way back. As Scoresby says, "'I fought beside him in the Tunguska campaign. Hell, I've known Iorek for years'" (TGC 169). Though he may not view it as a code-of-honor thing, Lee Scoresby's loyalty to an old comrade mirrors the loyalty demanded in most warrior cultures.

Scoresby doesn't hesitate to employ methods of deceit to help his friends—for instance, he distracts the gyptians in a game of cards so that his dæmon can direct Pan and Lyra to where Iorek's armor is being held, before it can be moved somewhere else. But this deceit, like Lyra's, is born of honorable intentions.

Contrast these characters with Iofur Raknison. While Iorek Byrnison, Lyra, and Lee Scoresby are true to who they are, Iofur is not content with his lot in life. He loses his bear self to his obsession with becoming human and, in so doing, becomes a sad parody of what he could have become.

Not satisfied with his armor, Iofur covets the dæmons the humans have. He even takes to carrying about a little doll dæmon, which is ironic (and foretold), given that Iorek explains to Lyra earlier, "'A bear's armor is his soul, just as your dæmon is your soul. You might as well take [Pantalaimon] away . . . and replace him with a doll full of sawdust'" (TGC 172).

Though Iofur Raknison tries to humanize Svalbard by building a palace and a university and dressing himself and his subjects up in fine array, he is discontented without a dæmon to call his own. He may learn to be "'clever in a human way'" (TGC 277) but it does him no good. No matter how much he wants it, he can never be human.

His discontent and frustration drag him down, and he pulls his bear subjects with him. He's their king, after all, and they are supposed to follow him, but as his actions become less and less bear-like, the other bears can't help but be confused. Even if they ape his actions—add a little bling to their dress and carry around their own little fake dæmons—the charade does not bring them any closer to being human. They may have the marble halls of human learning, but they don't know how to take care of them. They become caricatures. They become weak.

In the end, Lyra is able to use this weakness against them, both in manipulating the guard to take her to the king, and in getting Iofur Raknison to agree to duel Iorek Byrnison. Had they been bears acting as bears, they could not have been tricked, but as it was, bears acting as humans are all sorts of gullible.

This brings us back to Iorek Byrnison, the constrained hero. Having held fast to his code of honor, he is about the only one who remains "pure and certain and absolute" (*TGC* 303). When he meets up with Iofur Raknison again, a comparison is inevitable. Two different roads have led them to that moment in time and two different futures will follow.

Iofur and Iorek look completely different as they face each other, the former all proud and polished in his fine armor and the latter looking scruffy and dented in his. But, as Lyra observes, Iorek's "armor was his soul. He had made it and it fitted him. They were one. Iofur was not content with his armor; he wanted another soul as well. He was restless while Iorek was still" (*TGC* 306–307).

In the end, perhaps that's what the whole honor thing comes to after all—not some obscure ideal or a provision of protection for society, but a means by which a warrior can stay true to himself.

For all its constraints and limitations, his sense of honor defines and distinguishes Iorek Byrnison: *panserbjørn*, rightful king, true and honorable hero.

Linda Gerber recently ended a live-in love affair with Japan, birthplace of the *bushidō* way of the warrior. She is the author of two S.A.S.S. novels: *Now and Zen* and *The Finnish Line*. Her mystery novel, *Death by Bikini*, will be released Spring 2008. Gerber currently lives the way of the writer in Dublin, Ohio.

References

French, Shannon E. *The Code of the Warrior: Exploring Warrior Values Past and Present*. Maryland: Rowman and Littlefield, 2003.

Kesshin No Rekishi. "Budō Defined."<http://www.kesshin-no-rekishi.org/Budo.html>.

Oestmoen, Per Inge. "The Yasa of Chingis Khan: A Code of Honor, Dignity, and Excellence." *The Realm of The Mongols*.

<http://www.coldsiberia.org/webdoc9.htm#General%20Precepts,%20from%20Yasa.%20Further%20quotations%20from%20Vernadsky>

Plutarch. *Moralia*. Whitefish: Kessinger, 2005.

Ziegler, Norman. "Action, Power and Service in Rajasthani Culture: A Social History of the Rajputs of Middle Period Rajasthan." Diss. U of Chicago, 1973.

All parents worry about the journeys their children take without them, even excursions into works of fiction. Chima examines the fears raised by His Dark Materials, wondering if perhaps books are alternate worlds, and reading is the subtle knife that all ages get to play with.

THE DANGEROUS WORLDS OF PULLMAN'S HIS DARK MATERIALS

CINDA WILLIAMS CHIMA

In Philip Pullman's His Dark Materials trilogy, young protagonists Will Parry and Lyra Belacqua acquire the magical ability to cut doorways into neighboring, parallel worlds through the use of a magical tool called the subtle knife. Once there, their actions create a cascade of changes that affect the world around them while they, in turn, are changed by their experiences. They aren't just observers—they are players.

While Will and Lyra are specially chosen for this task of inter-world travel, we as readers of fiction have our own magical tools. Each time we open a book, we cut our way into another world and step through—temporarily, at least. This, to me, is what makes reading so compelling, compared to other media—readers immerse themselves, participate, react, and shape the action.

Pullman's trilogy has been reviled and extolled, praised and pilloried. It has been called "amazingly wonderful" (Ruiz) and "loaded down with propaganda" (Hitchens).

What is going on? Are these people reading the same book?

Maybe not.

Reading is a collaboration between the writer and the reader in which each contributes to the final story. The reader has as much to do with it as the author, and it is the reader who delivers one of the most important parts—the theme.

Theme evolves out of story and the reaction of the reader to the words on the page. It's like the fairy that disappears when you look straight at it. You have to come at it at a slant. And if you spend all your time looking for fairies, you miss the story. And story, after all, is what keeps the reader reading.

Some authors claim that they have no idea what the theme of their work is until it is finished and a reader (or critic) reveals it to them. Then they say, "Oh, yes, how perceptive of you. That's what I meant all along."

Other writers are very intentional about theme, but the author's intention—whatever it is—may or may not match what the reader takes away. The take-away depends largely on what the reader brings to the story: his own experiences, biases, convictions, and principles.

Good writers leave room for the reader's contributions, just as good picture book or graphic novel writers allow room for the illustrator to enhance the story. Some of the early action in HDM takes place in an alternative Oxford. The reader who's been to the British Oxford will conjure a different setting than the one who has not. Neither is incorrect.

As a writer of fantasy novels for young adults, I often receive e-mails from readers eager to discuss the worlds they've entered by way of my books. I'm always amazed by where readers end up and who they meet when they get there. It's often very different from what I envisioned—and that's okay.

As authors, we might want to hang over the shoulders of our readers and say, "No, no, no, what I meant was. . . ." Or "You see, what she's trying to do here is. . . ." Or "You can't blame Hastings for that, when you think of what happened when he was just a boy. . . ." Or "Actually, as I see it, the castle has *three* crenellated towers and the postern gate is on the *left* side."

But that's not the way it works. Explanation is the death of story—it's like somebody telling you about a movie he saw. A work of fiction must stand on its own. Once a book is launched, we writers lose control of it. We put it into the hands of readers, and we have to trust them. If authors have to trust readers with the words they bleed onto the page, then censors and critics should, too.

Book group discussions are like a reunion of travelers to some exotic place who reconvene to view each other's slides. Our images and memories of the journey are different, depending on the baggage we bring along. When I was in college, my girlfriend and I traveled to Italy. I came away smitten with Michelangelos and Medicis. She came away complaining that she was taller than most of the men.

The importance of reader participation has resulted in the evolution of genres targeted at specific audiences: so-called "women's fiction," for example. The success of a romance requires active participation by the reader—stereotypically a woman. It's likely that the different audiences that have read the Pullman trilogy are what account for much of the controversy that surrounds it.

In HDM, whenever the subtle knife is used to cut between worlds, it makes Specters, horrible creatures that feed on the souls of the living. Not only that, Dust, a kind of conscious dark matter, leaks out if these holes are left open.

In our world, books that cut holes into alternate worlds of science and faith have often been banned by political and religious authorities, as if such books might result in either a leaking out of grace or the leaking in of harmful ideas.

In an article in *The Catholic Herald*, Stratford Caldecott (what a great name!) takes Pullman to task for "shoddy thinking and anti-Christian fanaticism that spoils these admittedly fascinating tales."

Rupert Kaye, Chief Executive of Britain's Association of Christian Teachers, says, "As a Christian teacher I find it particularly odious that Pullman's bitter and twisted trilogy has been marketed and sold as *children's literature* and desperately sad that so few Christians have taken the time to see Pullman's work for what it is—anti-Christian propaganda."

The Harry Potter books have also come under fire for containing references to witchcraft and wizardry. But *The Catholic Herald* defended Rowling's books—by comparing them to Pullman's more insidious work.

Pullman himself expresses amazement that Rowling's books have been vilified by some religious authorities because of their magical content, while his own more subversive books have received less notoriety. (One has the sense he's disappointed.) But conservative columnist Peter Hitchens went so far as to call Pullman "the most dangerous author in Britain."

It seems that, just as the religious enforcers in Lyra's world consider it blasphemous to posit the existence of multiple worlds, there are those in our own world who view it as heresy to delve into Pullman's universe.

Not everyone shares this opinion. Rowan Williams, the Archbishop of Canterbury, has suggested that works like HDM can play a useful role in discussions about faith and the nature of God. In his book *Dark Matter: A Thinking Fan's Guide to Philip Pullman*, Christian writer and commentator Tony Watkins admits to being a fan of the books while taking issue with Pullman's anti-religion point of view.

Literary critics have been largely enthusiastic. William Flesch in *The Boston Globe* says, "The work is thrilling—in some ways perhaps the most electrifying piece of literature of the past twenty years." Polly Shulman of Salon, calls it "one of the most resonant fantasies of our time." Margo Jefferson of the *New York Times Book Review* says, "His prose has texture and flexibility, like excellent fabric."

And all three volumes have received multiple literary honors. Most notably, *The Golden Compass* received the Carnegie Medal, and *The Amber Spyglass*, the third and perhaps most criticized volume in the trilogy, was awarded the prestigious Whitbread Prize.

These critics, commentators, and church officials all read the same books, but they encountered different worlds, shaped by their own purposes, convictions, and expectations. Some found heresy or dangerous nihilism, others a world of enlightened rationalism; still others encountered the simple dream of fiction—a good story well told.

"He knows perfectly well what he is doing," Hitchens says of Pullman. "He openly and rightly believes storytelling can be a form of moral propaganda." No doubt Pullman's outspoken criticism of C. S. Lewis for his Christian themes has encouraged his detractors.

No one familiar with Philip Pullman's atheism would argue that the themes emerging in HDM—criticism of religion and of the church hierarchy—are accidental . . . but dangerous? It depends on what the reader brings.

The very best books are layered creations that can be read on many different levels. The first and most important job of a novelist is story. In his acceptance speech for the Carnegie Medal, Pullman said, "What characterizes the best of children's authors is that they're not embarrassed to tell stories."

Any work of fiction must succeed first as story. A sermon thinly disguised as a novel will appeal only to the already converted. I recently gave up reading an epic high fantasy series after slogging through nine volumes because I grew tired of being lectured by the author.

First and foremost, HDM is a really good story with compelling characters. This actually fuels the debate, since the trilogy was published as a work for children. Cagy and cynical adults have enough experience to identify and resist seductive ideas, the reasoning goes, but Pullman's work—because it is so good and compelling—might exert undue influence over the minds and hearts of children and teens.

Rupert Kaye describes HDM as "a honeyed trap," and suggests that it be removed from every primary school in England.

I disagree.

Growing up, I was allowed to read pretty much anything I was capable of finishing. My mother never saw danger between the covers of a book—only opportunity. My aunt's *True Romance* magazines might have been a head-turning education to a child of eight, except that certain key concepts soared right over my head.

For instance, I couldn't understand why the adults in those stories were so anxious to go to bed together. For me, bedtime brought the curtain down on the most interesting part of the day and my goal was to put it off as long as possible. Looking back from an adult perspective, I assume that I cut into a different world than my aunt when I picked up those magazines.

It's like the time in fourth grade when I gave a lecture to my class on guppy sex. My teacher's reaction was memorable, but I didn't understand it until years later.

I first read the Chronicles of Narnia as a child, totally unaware of its Christian allegorical themes. It was an exciting story, full of interesting fantasy imagery and intelligent talking animals. The religious element lent a rich new dimension when I re-read it later on. When I was a young teenager, I read Marion Zimmer Bradley's *Mists of Avalon* as a romantic fantasy, only later picking up on its feminist themes and criticism of the patriarchal church.

I don't think I was a particularly dull child. If anything, my reading ability outstripped my larger knowledge of the world and the subtleties of sociopolitical and religious symbolism. There's a chance that all those radical ideas are festering somewhere deep inside, a suppurating wound on the soul that will one day surface, but I doubt it.

As readers, we enter different worlds at different times in our lives. As an adult, I read *Huckleberry Finn* to my eight-year-old son—not as a searing social commentary on slavery and mid-nineteenth century society, but as a fast-paced adventure story. He read it again in high school to a different purpose. I would argue that the book he read in high school was a different book—because he was a different reader. He was ready to participate on that level.

I've had parents write me to praise my books for their themes of "class struggle and oppression" (!), for their appeal to teenage boys, and for promoting a non-violent approach to solving problems. Teens write to thank me for the fighting scenes, others to request a little more "romance." One parent wrote to criticize implied "sexual tension" and a scene of teenage drinking (by bullies and street thugs). These readers brought different sensibilities to my stories, and had different take-aways, for sure.

Books can change history in profound ways—positive and negative. I recently found an online list of the "Most Harmful Books" of the nineteenth and twentieth centuries. The list included *Mein Kampf, Das Kapital, The Kinsey Report, The Origin of Species, The Feminine Mystique,* and *Silent Spring.* These are books that created converts, convinced or repelled the wavering, and engendered active opposition by others (including the creators of the "Most Harmful Books" list). At the time they were published, the world was receptive to them. Otherwise, they would have faded into obscurity.

Abraham Lincoln famously accused Harriet Beecher Stowe of causing the Civil War with her book *Uncle Tom's Cabin. Uncle Tom's Cabin* inflamed abolitionists, but probably had little effect on the slaveholders themselves.

Thomas Jefferson read voraciously from Thomas Paine and other philosophers' writings about the rights of man. He drew heavily on their ideas in writing the Declaration of Independence. All the while, he continued to hold slaves himself. He could articulate an idea, and yet fail to act on it.

The Church Pullman describes in HDM is an evil and repressive power that does not hesitate to torture and murder children and others in furtherance of its aims. Some have seen this as an assault on faith or at least on religious authority. Christian writer Tony Watkins says, "Something about the passion with which Pullman denounces it, and the fact that the Magisterium has not one single redeeming feature, leaves one feeling that the contempt is still directed at the real-world Church, even if the specific criticism is only within the realm of fiction."

That may be true. Should we assume, then, that the international popularity of HDM among readers of all ages represents a massive movement away from religion and a new antipathy to the institutional church as it exists in our world? I think not. HDM has a mixed audience: fans of fantasy fiction and children's literature; readers who favor strong female protagonists; history buffs; polar bear lovers; seekers of controversy; agnostics; atheists; and yes, Christians.

I suspect that if there is one thing that HDM readers do agree on, it's that they are totally on Will and Lyra's side and hope they escape the bad people who are out to murder them. And that dæmons are totally cool. That's it.

There's no need for religious authorities to pick up the gauntlet in defense of the Church that Pullman describes in HDM. As Watkins says, "His Dark Materials is *fantasy* literature. The Church Pullman describes is in another world; it is not the Church in our world."

If asked, defenders of faith should simply say, "That's not *my* church, thank God," and shudder a little at the very idea. I think of faith as being too robust to be threatened by an author of fantasy fiction with an axe to grind. The faithful have been inoculated by their own positive experiences with the church. They bring with them the tools to examine, shape, and interpret Pullman's worlds accordingly. The faithful, in effect, enter a different world than the skeptic does when they open the book.

That's not to say that they won't be changed. Great novels tell great stories. Some may also cause readers to examine their beliefs—which, if those beliefs are worthwhile, should be able to withstand the scrutiny. Some readers will leave Pullman's world better prepared to articulate what they've always believed. Some may begin a new journey of discovery. Others will not participate in the debate at all.

Great books are one component of a rich mental humus from which ideas and principles grow. Mission on the part of the author is not enough. Exposing readers to new ideas is necessary, but not sufficient. Character and action derive from multiple influences: family, society, secular education, religious teaching, the media, and our own hardwired proclivities.

I'm unqualified to serve as spokesperson for either side in the battle over Pullman's work. It is not my intention to position myself as a defender of faith nor as a promoter of skepticism. I am a defender of books and our right to participate in the marketplace of ideas.

Ignorance doesn't lead to salvation, nor does knowledge pave the way to sin. Each reader meets the author at a different place. Each reader shares with the author the responsibility for the story's theme. No two readers enter identical worlds—and no author can transport you to a place that you refuse to go.

CINDA WILLIAMS CHIMA is the author of contemporary young adult fantasy novels *The Warrior Heir* and the recently released *The Wizard Heir* (Hyperion Books for Children). *The Warrior Heir* was named to VOYA's Best Science Fiction and Fantasy 2005–2006, is a 2006 Booksense Summer Reading Pick, and was named to the 2007–2008 Lone Star Reading List. *The Wizard Heir* received a "Perfect Ten" from VOYA. Her third novel, *The Dragon Heir*, will debut in 2008.

REFERENCES

Caldecott, Stratford. "Phillip Pullman's Day of Judgment." *The Catholic Herald*, 21 Jan. 2005, pg. 13.

Hitchens, Peter. "This Is the Most Dangerous Author in Britain." *The Mail on Sunday*, 27 Jan. 2002, pg. 63.

Jefferson, Margo. "Harry Potter for Grown-Ups." *New York Times Book Review*, 20 Jan. 2002, sec. 7, pg. 23.

Kaye, Rupert. Rev. of His Dark Materials trilogy, by Philip Pullman. Association of Christian Teachers. < http://www.christian-teachers.org.uk/newscomment/31>

Ruiz, Gina. Rev. of His Dark Materials Omnibus, by Philip Pullman. *BlogCritics Magazine*. < http://blogcritics.org/archives/2007/05/15/022043.php>

Shulman, Polly. Rev. of *The Amber Spyglass*, by Philip Pullman. Salon. <http://archive.salon.com/books/feature/2000/10/18/pullman/index.html>

Watkins, Tony. *Dark Matter: A Thinking Fan's Guide to Philip Pullman*. Southampton: Damaris, 2005.

Flesch, William. "Childish Things." Accessed at <http://www.boston.com/news/globe/ideas/articles/2004/06/13/childish_things/ July 13, 2007>

Lord Asriel is one of the most contradictory father figures in children's literature: cruel, malevolent, uncaring . . . yet somehow charismatic, even heroic. Masson finds this mix—this "destructive glamour"—strangely reminiscent of her own grandfather. She considers the haunting effects that a man at war with Authority can have on his own family for generations to come.

LORD ASRIEL: DAD FROM HELL OR HEROIC REBEL?

SOPHIE MASSON

Beyond ideas, themes, or controversies, the test of a great novel is in the quality of its *life*: the richness of the imagined world created or re-created for the reader, and the vitality of the characters who inhabit that world. Generally, it is on the richness of the imagined world, or rather, worlds, created within *The Golden Compass*, *The Subtle Knife*, and *The Amber Spyglass* that most attention has been focused. The sensual reality of Lyra's world in *The Golden Compass*, with its gorgeous mixture of Dickensian, Gothic fairytale, and steampunk atmospheres, is particularly attractive. The sheer verve of the author's inventiveness, his vivid, muscular language and exquisite sense of timing, sweep the reader along on an irresistible tide of storytelling delight and terror. What is there *not* to love about dæmons and armored bears and truth-telling compasses? What is there *not* to fear about a mysterious order of child-stealers known as the Gobblers, or a hideous silver guillotine that separates not heads but souls from bodies? But to just discuss the richness of that imagined world without reference to the characters that inhabit it is like employing that silver guillotine to excise soul from body.

Characters are the soul of story. Without character, there is no story; there is only description. It is the interaction of characters—good, bad, and indifferent—that creates and drives the plots of stories, providing their twists and turns. Many writers will testify to the fact that very often it is a character, rather than an idea or a plot, which is the inspiration for a story.

That seems to have been the case with *The Golden Compass*: Philip
Pullman has said in several interviews that he started with an image of
Lyra hiding in the wardrobe, overhearing things she wasn't meant to
hear. He also knew there was someone there with her in the wardrobe.
Someone who turned out to be Lyra's dæmon, Pantalaimon.

There is a very rich panoply of characters in *The Golden Compass* and
its sequels: human, superhuman (such as angels), para-human
(dæmons), and non-human (armored bears, *mulefa*).

And every reader will have his or her favorite characters: those we
love or hate, who fascinate or even repulse us; those who, as readers, we
can't be indifferent to. Instinct is often the dictator of whom we trust and
don't trust, like or don't like, in literature as well as in life. But when you
try to analyze why that is, some surprising things can come out.

So it's been for me, in thinking about the character that stands out
above all the others, especially in *The Golden Compass*, but also in its
sequels: the dark star of the trilogy is Lord Asriel—Lyra's father, Mrs.
Coulter's lover, the tireless general leading the rebel forces against the
Authority, the ruthless, courageous Luciferian hero who trails his sulfurous glamour behind him. He is the character who, throughout the
trajectory of His Dark Materials, seems to be both more than (and less
than) human, yet whose unpredictability and complexity exemplifies,
for me, Pullman's great skill as a creator of unforgettable characters.

We first meet Lord Asriel at the beginning of *The Golden Compass*,
seeing him as Lyra does, through the crack in the door of that heavy oak
wardrobe in the Scholars' Retiring Room. And what do we see? A harsh-
voiced, extraordinary man of fierce power, "yawning like a lion" (*TGC*
10), whose dæmon is a gorgeous, dangerous snow leopard named
Stelmaria; a man Lyra believes to be her uncle, whom she both fears and
admires; a man involved in "high politics, in secret exploration, in distant warfare" (*TGC* 5); a man so dangerous the Master of the College is
prepared to attempt to murder him. As befits such a legend, his very
physical presence is imposing:

> Lord Asriel was a tall man with powerful shoulders, a fierce
> dark face, and eyes that seemed to flash and glitter with

savage laughter. It was a face to be dominated by, or to fight: never a face to patronize or pity. All his movements were large and perfectly balanced, like those of a wild animal, and when he appeared in a room like this, he seemed a wild animal held in a cage too small for it (*TGC* 12).

Elsewhere in the book, we are told that he is a "'high-spirited man, quick to anger, a passionate man'" (in the words of John Faa [*TGC* 108]), that he is "haughty and imperious," a "prisoner acting like a king" (as Soren Eisarson, one of the older armored bears tells Lyra), so much so that he even dominates the powerful Iofur Raknison (*TGC* 318). He is very brave, both physically and intellectually; we are told he thinks things most people wouldn't dare to. We learn that he is highly intelligent but considered heretical and dangerous, and that he is not only Lyra's real father, but the killer of her mother Marisa Coulter's husband, Edward. It was ostensibly for this crime that he had his property confiscated and was sent to exile in Svalbard, with the Church no doubt hoping they were rid of a dangerous troublemaker. But as authorities have learned to their detriment throughout the ages, the exile only honed this rebel's determination to prevail, and he used the time in the North to prepare the way for his first step into full-blown war with the Authority.

We also learn that he is on the opposite side of his erstwhile lover Mrs. Coulter, that her golden power matches his dark one, but that when the two of them meet, sparks still fly, as they embrace with a greedy passion that seems to Lyra more like cruelty than love. And we learn that he is unbelievably hard and ruthless; he appears to have no qualms at all about sacrificing the helpless and gentle Roger, Lyra's friend, in order to open the door into other worlds. He also appears to have no qualms about the fact that his lust for revolution, no less than his lover's lust for power, has robbed Lyra of her parents and her history. As Lyra fiercely accuses him toward the end of *The Golden Compass*, he appears quite bereft of normal, warm human parental love:

> You en't human, Lord Asriel. You en't my *father*. My *father* wouldn't treat me like that. Fathers are supposed to love their daughters, en't they? You don't love me, and I don't love you, and that's a fact (*TGC* 323).

He responds to what any other man might see as a devastating tirade with a contemptuous, "'If you're going to be sentimental, I shan't waste time talking to you'" (*TGC* 234), before going on to calmly discuss the theological and political ramifications of his crusade with her, and explaining things that have been puzzling her.

At this stage, he still considers Lyra to be of little importance, a meddling child, and sees himself as the savior of the worlds against the tyranny of the Authority. Later, in *The Subtle Knife* and *The Amber Spyglass*, he becomes convinced of Lyra's central importance in the revolt, and changes his attitude toward her. He protects her from Mrs. Coulter and the Oblation Board because he knows that as "the second Eve" she must survive if the revolution is to succeed. But we never really get the feeling that he loves her for herself, as his daughter, as a human being. His destiny is inextricably bound up with hers, not because he loves her, but because of what she represents. Even his final fight to the death with Metatron at the Abyss is part of that. It is what everything in his life had led up to—his own manifest destiny, the last grand gesture.

If Asriel actually ever really loved anyone, it was Marisa Coulter, and their death together is symbolic of that. Yes, their deaths also help to protect Lyra, and enable her and her friends to finish the thing once and for all, but it's hard to escape the conclusion that neither of her parents ever considered Lyra a precious, irreplaceable person as most parents would have. Self-sacrifice is, in this case, part of these characters' prides. Both of them suffer from a massive overdose of pride, ambition, and conviction, but Asriel is by far the more monstrously endowed with these characteristics, and it empties him of all humanity, even an attachment to his own life and family. In this, he is not so far removed from a being like Metatron, and one can't help being rather concerned about the nature of the Republic of Heaven he was planning for.

In this reading, he is the Dad from Hell, the destroyer. Lyra is lucky indeed not to have been brought up by him, and to have been ignorant of her true parentage until she was old enough to at least be able to cope. Much better that she should be a half-wild, half-civilized urchin running loose amongst vague Scholars and busy servants than to be groomed from birth by a man who felt he had Destiny in his hands and a woman who is always on the side of Power. Asriel had the last word on Mrs.

Coulter's influence as well before he went into exile: he made sure that Lyra's mother would never have her. He did not want her to be brought up in the world of the Church, of course, but little did he care that she not only missed out on ideological indoctrination, she also missed out on having a mother.

Or is that too harsh? Is the truth of the matter that, like so many revolutionaries, Asriel has deliberately burnt away all traces of gentler feeling in order that he may survive and fight another day, and perhaps also so that his daughter can survive as well? He must have some feeling for her that isn't ideological, or else why does he look so horrified when she comes into his house in Svalbard, and he thinks she is the child who must be sacrificed so he can cross into other worlds? And keeping her from her mother may not have had a solely ideological purpose; he may have recognized the emotional and spiritual harm Mrs. Coulter could have done to her daughter. In this reading, Asriel is a heroic rebel who gives up all that makes life worthwhile for most people, for the benefit of the "greater good." Life will be better in the "Republic of Heaven" than it was in the old tyrannous Kingdom, or so he firmly believes. And that means for his daughter, too.

Many commentators have pointed to the fact that the trilogy is not only inspired by Milton's *Paradise Lost*, it is also a kind of anti-*Paradise Lost*, in which God, or the Authority, becomes the enemy, and Satan, or the Rebel, becomes the hero. They've also pointed to Blake's insight that Milton was of the Devil's party without knowing it, because at least to post-Puritan sensibilities, Milton's Satan appears to be the more heroic figure—or in any case the most interesting, and most accessible of the two, God being too arbitrary, tyrannous, remote, and unknowable. Paraphrasing Milton, Pullman himself has said that, "I am of the Devil's party, and I know it" (Vulliamy).

But although Asriel could be seen in many ways as a Satanic figure, interestingly, his name does not have a Luciferian ring. It is not one of the Devil's many names that the author chose to riff on, but rather that of Azrael, as he is known in Hebrew lore, or Izrail, as he is known in Koranic lore: the Angel of Death.

In the Koran, Azrael/Izrail (whose name means, ironically enough in our context, "whom God helps") is depicted as the biggest of the angels, with a pleasing shape that differs according to the beholder. His *raison d'etre* is to separate souls from bodies at the moment of death. This occurs kindly, almost seductively, in the case of believers: the fourteenth-century Sufi mystic Abdul Karim Jili says that the Angel of Death appears to the soul in a form provided by its most powerful metaphor. In the case of unbelievers, however, Azrael acts violently, carrying off their souls after striking their bodies on the face and back.

It's interesting that the name Asriel owes much to the name of the Angel of Death, when Lord Asriel himself appears to be in a crusade *against* Death as one of the cruelest weapons in the Authority's armory; he even makes the statement to Lyra that, "'Death is going to die'" (*TGC* 331). But the name of the Angel of Death may not be the only angelic influence in Asriel's name. Two other important figures in angelology could be associated to him by allusion.

Azazel ("God strengthens") is chief of the *Grigori*, or Watchers, rebel angels who, Prometheus-like, came down to Earth, lived amongst humans, taught humanity all kinds of previously forbidden skills and knowledge, and were duly exiled for their pains. Some of these areas of knowledge included herbs, astrology, constellations, war and weaponry, writing, cosmetics, enchantments, minerals, and more. A good deal of Asriel's philosophy (and the trilogy's) centers around the idea that the Authority does not want us to know things, so the Watchers connection is apt.

And finally, a third angelic figure that may well have had an influence, conscious or not, on Asriel's name is the angel Ariel. His name means "lion of God"; he is often shown with a lion's head, is ranked among the seven princes of Heaven, and is associated in Gnosticism with the Creator God (note that the Authority who is destroyed in *His Dark Materials* is said not to be the Creator, but an impostor and usurper).

But Asriel's strength as a character does not lie in such fascinating byways, or in the notion that as a literary creation he has angelic or Satanic influences and aspects. Despite the fact he obviously believes he has a manifest destiny—that he is predetermined to be the great Rebel who will tear down the roots of the Kingdom of Heaven and utterly eradicate the Authority—he still acts, often despite himself, in a very human and unpredictable way. But it's not that which struck me so forcefully when I read the trilogy, and especially *The Golden Compass*. It was a sense of familiarity. I felt I knew Lord Asriel instinctively. I didn't *identify* with him; if anything, I identified much more closely with Lyra, peering out of that wardrobe. But I *recognized* him, at some level.

I didn't really think about it, not until I was asked to contribute to this book of essays, and one of the first topics that leaped into my head was Lord Asriel, and the conundrum of his character. Why him? Why did I have such a strong emotional reaction to him—so much anger and defiance against him and all his works, but also so much fascination? And why that nagging sense of familiarity?

It didn't take long to work out. Lord Asriel, in his elegance and arrogance and feline ferocity, his violence and contempt for the ordinary and the sense of danger that hovers around him, reminded me of the man who haunted my childhood, and whose restless ghost even now stalks through my family, generations on. Not my father, but *his* father.

My grandfather was a man of the same handsome physical type as Asriel, though with very light brown eyes, rather than black. Tiger's eyes, I used to think as a child. Or eagle's eyes. He had the face of a majestic predator, too, all sharp angles and strong features. He scared me and fascinated me in equal measure, not only because of his imposing presence, but because he trailed a dark and sulfurous history. Of wealthy *grand bourgeois* (upper middle-class) origin, educated in France and England, he had been one of the "'gilded youth" of the '20s and '30s, living a life of reckless and effortless glamour. In his late twenties, he married my beautiful golden-haired grandmother after a whirlwind courtship. He worked for a while for Pathe Films as a cameraman but retired at the ripe old age of twenty-eight when he inherited his father's large fortune. That was in 1932, the year his eldest child, my father, was born. He had impeccable manners, and dressed elegantly; he was adept at all kinds of sports, graceful, generous, quick-witted and sardonic, and brave to the point of recklessness.

But he was also cruel, ruthless, and selfish. An adventurer by instinct and a natural rebel for whom morals meant very little, he was also a violent man who craved excitement and for whom fighting, allied to political causes, became his *raison d'etre*. He became involved in political street violence in the 1930s, and got started on a ghastly trajectory that would end up disgracing and ruining him, and almost destroying his family. Physically, mentally, and socially, he was punished very severely for the path he took, but never, when I knew him, did he show any trace of self-pity or even attempt to justify himself. Here is not the place to tell his entire story, though one day I plan to do just that. Here is the place to note the devastating effect that his Asriel-like personality had on his three children: his son, my father, and his two daughters. Add to this the fact that their ambitious, subtle, narcissistic, lovely mother had more than a touch of Mrs. Coulter about her and it's no wonder I felt that shock of recognition.

My father was deeply affected by his childhood and the shame and pain his father's choices inflicted on the family. As a child, he both admired and was terrified of his father. But during the years in which his father was absorbed in "high politics and secret exploration and distant warfare," and his mother was swept up in her own edgily glamorous world, my father was sent away with his doting nanny to his kind, feisty maternal grandmother. It was these two women who lent at least some normality to his childhood. And it was perhaps during this time that, away from his parents' destructive glamour, he was able to hone his spirit to a Lyra-like *farouche* toughness and defiance.

Unlike Lyra, however, he was always aware of his parentage, and deeply riven by it, especially when his parents became passionate enemies, fighting ruthless battles over the children's future and their own version of history. At one time, taking his mother's side, he hated his father enough to literally consider killing him. At another time, finding out some of his mother's own secrets, he despaired so much of his family that he wished he'd never been born. He escaped his family by eloping with my mother at a very young age and going to live and work abroad, refusing any offer of help or money from his parents. He was determined to be "self-created," to forge an entirely new life, out of whole cloth, with my mother. But he did not find it easy. And neither did we, his children, having to live with the unpredictable moods of a father still haunted by his childhood.

But I didn't know my grandparents only through Dad's memories. I was born in Indonesia, when my parents were working there, and because I fell very ill as a baby, I was sent back to France to live with my grandmother and aunts for the duration of my parents' posting there. That turned out to be four more years. So my earliest memories are not tied to my parents, but to my grandmother and my aunts. And my grandfather, when he came to visit. By this time, he and my grandmother had separated, but he would still turn up fairly regularly, impeccable in his smart English suits, his handsome profile as hawk-like as ever, his tiger's eyes unmellowed by age, and his ramrod poise unbowed by his dark past or his difficult present. He took a liking to me, for some reason, and brought me presents and defended me, often harshly, against my grandmother's admonitions to behave more like a little lady and less like a little savage. I was a rather *farouche* child myself: self-sufficient, imaginative, quick-tempered, observant, and quietly determined. But I was wary of him, scared stiff of the verbal and occasionally physical violence that would flare up unpredictably and of the cruel wit (usually turned against his ex-wife and his daughters, never me), but also fascinated by the undiminished aura of masculine power and glamour.

He was dismissive of my father but also strangely obsessed with him. Looking back on it now, I suspect his son's rejection of him as the Dad from Hell who was forever damned hurt my grandfather far more than his proud, dark heart would, or could, ever admit. However, I suspect he also secretly admired my father's stiff-necked defiance of him; like many authoritarian rebels, he was intensely contemptuous of compliant people. But nothing could make him say that he loved his son, just as his son could never be made to say he loved his father; such things would be dismissed by my grandfather as sentimental tomfoolery, and by my father as a weakness that would put him again in his father's power. Meanwhile, my aunts feared him and humored him when he was there, and criticized him volubly with my grandmother when he was not.

I watched him from a metaphorical crack in the door, not as engaged emotionally as my father, of course, but close enough to feel more than just a surface fascination. And strangely, when it came time for my parents to come back, I reacted to my own father in much the same way. I remember the very first time I saw him—remember hiding behind a curtain and peeping out to watch this man, a younger version of my grandfather, with the same handsome, sharp features, the same light brown eyes, the same elegance, look around for me, the daughter he hadn't seen for four years. I didn't remember him at all except as a word—*Papa*—and suddenly there he was, looking so like his father it was uncanny.

I soon came to learn he was both very different—his whole, anxious life-focus was on his family and on attempting to create a haven of loving security for us—*and* very similar, in those unpredictable dark moods, cruel wit, overbearingness, and outbursts of violence.

I think now, is that what Lyra would have been like, grown up? Like my father, she thinks she can make her own life, be her own person, and you can imagine she'll succeed, to some extent. Yet, like him, she'll surely never completely escape the pull of the past, of her strange, tumultuous, painful childhood and adolescence, and of her father and mother's characters, which help also to make up her own. It won't make things easy for any children she might have. Was I, then, in a similar position to Lyra's child? And what does that mean?

The experience with my grandfather, and those early years away from my parents, had taught me to be wary, and also to be more detached than otherwise might have been the case. The most savage family wars and feuds raged unabated, but I was not as affected as I might have been, because I had discovered my way out. The "'wardrobe" of imagination became a favored hidey-hole, and through it I discovered all kinds of wonderful other worlds, especially through stories, those I read and those I created for myself. Stories were very early on both an escape and a discovery for me, a way of understanding the world and its perplexing people as well as a glorious holiday from real problems and ambiguities.

Lyra herself is a girl of action—at heart, an adventurer like her father, though less ruthless. Like *my* father, she would be an adult of independent mind, and probably not an easy person to live with. Like him, perhaps, she'd also never have the sense of distance from her own past and her own parentage to be able to write about it. *But Lyra's child might.* Lyra's child, fascinated, but at one step removed from the dark and dangerous glamour of his or her grandparents, might be able to body the story forth again in words. Lyra's child might become a writer, like me.

Writers are born with a curse and a blessing. We are like other people, and yet not. We act, and yet we also observe. Early on, we learn to view life through the crack in the door, not necessarily because we're afraid, but because we are incurably curious. It is that curiosity that drives literature: the curiosity about other people, about the characters that loom large in our lives and our imagination. But it isn't only writers who are driven by curiosity. Readers are, as well. We want to know not only what happens how and to whom but *why*. Reading, and especially reading a great novel, is an act that can produce all kinds of unexpected results. It can make us see things we never would have otherwise seen, like my own imaginative kinship to Lyra and her terrible, extraordinary father.

And if in the end, we still don't come to an answer, if we still can't answer the question, was Lord Asriel Dad from Hell or heroic Rebel, does it really matter? Surely not. It doesn't even matter if you don't feel that the author himself has resolved those tensions, one way or the other, any more than the reader has. What matters is that a work of art like *The Golden Compass* has engendered that haunting shock of recognition, that passionate engagement of emotion and intelligence, both positive and negative, which is the mark of a truly great novel, a work that will last.

Born in Jakarta, Indonesia, of French parents, SOPHIE MASSON came to Australia at the age of five and spent the rest of her childhood shuttling between France and Australia. She is the author of many novels for children, young adults, and adults, which have been published in many countries. Her latest U.S. publication is a fantasy adventure novel, *Snow, Fire, Sword* (HarperCollins 2006), set in a magical, alternative-world version of modern Indonesia. Just out is *The Maharajah's Ghost* (Random House Australia 2007), a comic fantasy adventure set in an enchanted version of modern India.

REFERENCES

Vulliamy, Ed. "Author Puts Bible Belt to the Test." *The Observer*, London, 26 Aug. 2001.

It's a lucky orphan who discovers that her true parents are still alive, isn't it? Except that in Lyra's family, reunions turn out to be the wrong kind of tearful—not surprising, given that Lord Asriel and Mrs. Coulter are a pair of neglectful, amoral, protagonist-abandoning child-nappers. Johnson contemplates exactly what makes two of literature's most appalling parents so appealing.

HOT SEX AND HORRIFIC PARENTING IN HIS DARK MATERIALS

MAUREEN JOHNSON

Heroes. What's with them? Always running toward danger like lemmings and making the rest of us look bad. Thankfully, in most stories you get maybe one or two of these numb-nuts. Not so in the His Dark Materials trilogy. Philip Pullman (in keeping with the general spirit of giving us *more* of everything) stuffs them into every corner. Lyra, Iorek, Lee Scoresby, Serafina Pekkala, John Faa, Ma Costa . . . all irritatingly brave, honest, and consistent.

And that's just the first book.

Normally, I would have given up all hope on a story like that. That many do-gooders in one book . . . well, it's like having too many goats; they just chew the scenery and flatten the landscape.[1] Luckily for us, Pullman introduces two oddballs to the mix and has them knock around the story, smacking everyone and everything else out of place. As soon as they walk on to the scene, the world lights up. London glows with a million anbaric lights; I can see the zeppelins, and the Aurora sways overhead. I'm left guessing, flipping pages, dragged along on the sledges and riding the bears. Lyra may be the main character, but she spends the story running away from or toward them. They made her, and they set the pace. Their personal feud is the rock upon which the story is built.

I'm talking of course about those ever-squabbling former lovers, Lord Asriel and Mrs. Coulter. The couple-at-war scenario is hardly unknown.

---

[1] Sorry for all the animal references. You're going to think this is some kind of zoological essay. It's not. I'll stop. (Dæmons don't count.)

From Kate and Petruchio in *The Taming of the Shrew* to Han and Leia in *Star Wars*, we know the drill. But Pullman imbues these two with something the others don't have: real charisma that leaps off the page. They are one of the sexiest couples in children's literature, and certainly some of the worst parents. Gorgeously unlikable, justifiably conceited—they are the stars under which all the other characters glow. Because of them, even the elements that trouble me seem *right*: the seriousness, the jumble of information. Myths are frequently insane, but if the mythic figure is big enough, we can go with it. Lord Asriel and Mrs. Coulter are at that level. Their faults are so huge, they seem like virtues.

Good Entrances Are Everything

The very first impression we get of Lord Asriel is his voice, which is described as "harsh" (*TGC* 10). The very first thing he does is break a rule: he invites himself into the retiring room, even though the Master's permission is needed to enter it. Lord Asriel is a man used to giving commands, and answers only to his own authority.

Though Lord Asriel is sitting in a quiet room in a college, he is a beast, and Pullman does not want us to miss that. He sort of gets out his hammer in the next page or two and pounds the fact into our heads. He yawns "like a lion" (*TGC* 10). He is "savage" and "fierce" (*TGC* 12). His dæmon, a snow leopard named Stelmaria, is a fairly large wild mountain cat—though she looks tame and submissive by his side. Pullman gets so wound up trying to tell us what a brute Lord Asriel is that he repeats the key phrase: "All his movements were large and perfectly balanced, like those of a wild animal, and when he appeared in a room like this, he seemed a wild animal held in a cage too small for it" (*TGC* 12).

Did you get that? He's a wild animal. Thunk, thunk, thunk.

So far, it's all pretty heavy-handed. But then, we see him encounter his niece-daughter for the first time in the story, and within three lines, he is threatening to break her arm. He relents a little when he finds out that Lyra is risking her own skin to save his life, but he's not exactly appreciative. As soon as there is a knock on the door, he dismisses her. "'Back in the wardrobe. If I hear the slightest noise, I'll make you wish you were dead'" (*TGC* 13). The first time there's a glimmer of affection is when Lyra stands up to him and demands to be taken North—and also to see the dead man's head. Lord Asriel can only respect people who challenge the rules. He considers her request briefly, and turns it down with a gentle threat that if Lyra doesn't shut up, Stelmaria will sink her fangs into her neck.

Really, this should not work. This man just strode into the story, insulted the help, and immediately started smacking around a child. I should dislike him. But I don't. It's the charisma. Everyone does exactly what Lord Asriel says, even though he has no real power, and no money, and isn't even properly dressed. He makes a glancing remark that they might try to fine him a few bottles of wine for his transgressions, but that never comes to pass.

It's also immediately clear that whatever Lord Asriel has shown up with is a ticking time bomb, far beyond anything the half-dead Scholars can handle. The steam train is waiting to take him to London, the Master is trying to kill him . . . the weight of the world is on this wild man, this explorer, politician, scholar. So we forgive him, already sensing that he is working on something so huge that smacking Lyra around and abusing the staff is perfectly excusable.

It's hard to come up with an equal to that, but Pullman manages it in Mrs. Coulter. While most of the other characters remain on arrow-straight courses, Mrs. Coulter swings like the needle of the golden compass itself, ruthlessly aware of her every step and yet completely in the dark about her own role in the Big Picture. She goes from being the ultimate villain to the savior of mankind.

The first time Mrs. Coulter is seen, she is standing in the doorway of St. Catherine's Oratory, swaddled in furs, looking fabulous, clutching a jeweled prayer book. She is watching a poor child eating a stolen pie, and she will soon lure that child to a fate worse than death with the promise of chocolate. This is pure Brothers Grimm stuff—the lovely woman luring the children with sweets. It also has an immediate connection to another prominent children's tale: Narnia.[2] Mrs. Coulter makes her entrance in a similar fashion to the White Witch, who rolls up on a sled, bearing Turkish Delight. The flash of the jewels is a nice Mae West, diamonds-are-a-girl's-best-friend touch, except she doesn't

---

[2] The relationship between His Dark Materials and Narnia must be well known if even *I've* heard about it. If you haven't, and it's okay if you haven't, Narnia is the Christian allegory, and HDM is seen as the secular reply.

wear them on her fingers. The bling goes on the book.

That Mrs. Coulter is framed in the doorway of a church with a bejeweled prayer book is certainly no accident. She is a Church official, one of the highest. The Church is where the power is in this world, and Mrs. Coulter likes power. She had tried other means of attaining it, but none had worked. She had been a Scholar, which didn't really get her anywhere. (As Lyra herself notes, female Scholars "could never be taken more seriously than animals dressed up and acting a play" [*TGC* 59].) She married a politician, but that gave her nothing directly. And though women had no real place in the Church power structure, she forged one for herself. Mrs. Coulter saw that the Church needed her as an anti-mother, a collector of children. Her femininity, her air of respectability, her charm, her apparent warmth, her willingness to go to any length necessary . . . all these things come in handy in the child-stealing and dæmon-cutting business.

While Lord Asriel's entrance involves busting in, inappropriately dressed and barking out orders, Mrs. Coulter's is the opposite. Everything she does is completely correct, and she plays the status game like a grand master. She pretends to be docile and confused when meeting Lyra. "'I hope you'll sit next to me at dinner,'" she says. "'I'm not used to the grandeur of a Master's lodging. You'll have to show me which knife and fork to use'" (*TGC* 59).

Of course she knows which knife and fork to use, but she deliberately gives Lyra what seems like the upper hand. She and Lord Asriel use opposite tactics: he always radiates dominance and begs confrontation, she pretends to be docile and quietly extracts what she requires. This is a trick Mrs. Coulter will pull time and time again, using it the final time to lure the Metatron to his demise. It works beautifully in Lyra's case. She spills the beans about her entire life (her entire "half-wild life" [*TGC* 59], another nod to that "wild animal" who contributed half of her DNA). Within five minutes, the untrappable Lyra belongs to Mrs. Coulter, and by the end of the night, she calls her "'the most wonderful person [she's] ever met'" (*TGC* 61).

His Dark Materials is a kind of symbol scrap yard. They're everywhere. We could spend weeks on the dæmons alone, as each one speaks to the character it is connected to. Then we have the subtle knife, the armor, the oil, the lights, the seeds, the spyglass. . . . There are even symbols imprinted on symbols (the golden compass itself). The more you read, the more everything in the book develops an iconic feel, like *everything is supposed to mean something*. Having said that, I think the golden monkey is the hardest-working symbol in the book. Sometimes, a tamarin is just a tamarin, but that monkey means a lot more to me than the gibberish pictures on the compass.[3] He is evil itself. He is fear. He is uncertainty. You might forget some of the other dæmons, but everyone knows the Monkey.

The monkey stands out among dæmons, not only because of his awesome golden helper monkeyness,[4] but because he is the only major unnamed dæmon. He is the Monkey. He's gold, just like the compass. His color is constantly mentioned and described. While Pan chatters away and Stelmaria offers grave counsel, the monkey is silent but never inactive. Oddly, he's also one of the most adept liars in the book . . . except he lies in action. In mime! He lures other dæmons to their doom, acts coy, playful, whatever Mrs. Coulter requires. When Lyra is planning her escape from the London apartment, she isn't worried about Mrs. Coulter noticing; it's *the monkey* that concerns her. And when Lyra and Pan are happily nestled in the sledge going North under the lights of the Aurora, it's the monkey they imagine swinging from tree to tree, following them. Lord Asriel can smack you around, but Mrs. Coulter gets into your head.

MOMMY AND DADDY DEAREST

Lyra should really be doomed. She's a downtrodden "orphan," abused and manipulated by two parents who are very much alive. Lyra is the product of passion, not marriage. This was never meant to be a functional family unit—this is a family of gods. Even the most casual reading of the Greek myths or the Bible[5] shows us that characters of this level make atrocious parents. But their self-absorption also makes them intriguing lovers.

Before they were manipulating Lyra and threatening to snap off her arm, there was a romance, and a birth. One of my chief complaints with

---

[3] Fruit bats, lawnmowers, hamsters, combine harvesters. . . . I never followed what was on it. And it can't just be me.

[4] Claim whatever you want. Say you only want a happy family or a successful career or a big house. I say: no, that's not what you want. You'll settle for those things, but you really want a monkey that does your evil bidding. Pullman is a genius just for this.

[5] And mine is *exceedingly* casual.

the book is that we don't get to hear more about this golden period. Most of the story comes via John Faa, whose tale-telling style is of the stiff, hard-ened-sailor-who-is-also-the-local-wise-man school. He is exactly the kind of person who would leave out the *really* good bits, and I think that Mrs. Coulter and Lord Asriel had some really good bits to dish about.

We learn that when Mrs. Coulter met Lord Asriel, she was married to Edward Coulter, a politician. The evidence of this previous connection remains in her name; she is almost always identified in exactly that way.[6] All we know about the relationship is that they "'fell in love as soon's they met'" (*TGC* 108). Sadly, that is all we get in terms of the affair. Mrs. Coulter wound up pregnant. When little Lyra was born and was clearly not a Coulter, she decided that the best thing to do was let a gyptian fam-ily take care of the baby, and tell everyone that the girl had died. Mr. Coulter found out about Lyra's existence and went to kill her in a rage, but Lord Asriel (who had been out hunting, like a *wild animal*) got there first and killed him instead.

That could have been the moment when the two came together, the obstacle removed. But this is not a couple who can work together. Lord Asriel doesn't seem to get this, but Mrs. Coulter knows the score. They require struggle, friction. After a protracted legal battle, Lord Asriel was stripped of his massive wealth but allowed to remain free. Mrs. Coulter "'wanted nothing to do with it, nor with [Lyra]. She turned her back'" (*TGC* 109).

This betrayal of their relationship is what turned Lord Asriel against Mrs. Coulter. If you aren't with him, you are against him. "[A]ll the anger in his nature had turned against her now," John Faa says (*TGC* 109). Lyra is merely a byproduct that can be used as a pawn. Mrs. Coulter apparently put up no resistance when Lyra was placed in a con-vent. Lord Asriel, in a characteristic move, needed to exert his power and break a rule. He defied the law and had her relocated to Jordan

---

[6] Apropos of nothing . . . Mrs. Coulter's moniker is reminiscent of Emma Peel in the British television classic *The Avengers*, who was almost always known as Mrs. Peel. Mrs. Peel's husband was forever away, lost on a mission, leaving her attached, yet single and free to do karate in tight bodysuits, drive around in little sportcars, outwit bad guys, and shoot guns. Her mysterious husband handily canceled out any opportunity for romance between her and her spy partner John Steed. They could flirt, but it never went further. Her name was a constant reminder of the barrier that kept the sexual tension going. Until I saw Nicole Kidman in the role of Mrs. Coulter, I always mentally cast her as Diana Rigg in her Mrs. Peel bodysuit, her dark hair in a flip.

College, to grow up under the care of Scholars. Then he ignored her for most of her life, dropping by only infrequently. The only thing he seemed to care about was that Mrs. Coulter was not allowed to see her.

Mrs. Coulter's ultimate role, of course, is of mother—mother of the mother of the world. By the third book, it's explicitly stated that Lyra is the new Eve, which is the reason everyone has been going so crazy trying to catch her. After all, if Lyra is going to bring about the end of death and press history's "restart" button, that puts the Church out of a job and a fair amount of cash.

Mrs. Coulter is the worst mother-material ever, considering that she runs what's essentially a child-killing factory. At first, Mrs. Coulter seems to want Lyra just because Lord Asriel doesn't want her to. She takes her to her home and keeps her around like a strange little pet. The truth is up North, but the windows of her London apartment face south, and it is as pretty as she is:

> [T]he walls were covered in a delicate gold-and-white striped wallpaper. Charming pictures in gilt frames, an antique looking-glass, fanciful sconces bearing anbaric lamps with frilled shades; and frills on the cushions too, and flowery valances over the curtain rail, and a soft green leaf-pattern carpet underfoot; and every surface was covered, it seemed to Lyra's innocent eye, with pretty little china boxes and shepherdesses and harlequins of porcelain (*TGC* 67).

You can feel the padding and opulence of Mrs. Coulter's house. Like any good Victorian, Mrs. Coulter lays it on thick, with decorations on top of decorations. Everything is delicate, feminine, plush . . . and, I always get the feeling, soundproof. She knows what image is expected of her, and she plays it out in every aspect of her life. But no china boxes and delicate flounces can hide the truth.

We get a hint as to what Mrs. Coulter is like on the inside through her smell—there is a metallic undertone to Mrs. Coulter's overall odor. At one point, she seems ready to burst forth and reveal her true fembot nature: "Mrs. Coulter seemed to be charged with some kind of anbaric force. She even smelled different: a hot smell, like heated metal, came off her body" (*TGC* 81). This may be a result of Mrs. Coulter's experiments with dæmon-cutting and her exposure to the resulting energy. Perhaps.

But I choose to believe it is simply Mrs. Coulter's full-blooded power, an excess of iron.

Lyra frustrates this most controlled of women; Mrs. Coulter finally cracks over the white shoulder bag that Lyra insists on wearing inside of the house. Mrs. Coulter can lure children, but she has no idea how to deal with them in the long term except to take them down with brute force. She herself does nothing—she arranges flowers for her party. But the monkey coolly pins Pantalaimon to the floor until Lyra submits. When the maternal feelings finally do stir, she *still* has no idea how to cope. Her solution for the entire first section of *The Amber Spyglass* is to drug Lyra and keep her asleep. It's much easier to play mommy when the baby is as insensible as a bag of potatoes.

Lord Asriel isn't much better in the paternal skills department. *The Golden Compass* contains my all-time favorite parental reveal. Poor little Lyra has escaped from London, taken a ship North, broken out of the experimental station, reestablished the king of the bears, and gotten all the way to Lord Asriel's polar prison. When she finally gets to confront Lord Asriel and ask him if he is her father, his reply is beautifully direct: "'Yes. So what?'" (*TGC* 323).

Lyra emotes a bit, as is her right. She expresses her fury that he never told her this himself and that everyone else seemed to know. But he's simply not interested in the "very special episode" part of the story.

> "Who did tell you?"
> "John Faa."
> "Did he tell you about your mother?"
> "Yes."
> "Then there's not much left for me to tell. I don't think I want to be interrogated and condemned by an insolent child. I want to hear what you've seen and done on the way here" (*TGC* 323).

And there you go. No long, drawn-out hugging sequence. No heartfelt explanation. No tears of remorse at all the years missed. Darth Vader was more sentimental than this.

Even by quasi-Victorian standards, this is a bit harsh. I feel like a Victorian would have defended himself a bit, said a few words about propriety, given the child a rough pat on the head. The last thing Lord Asriel cares about is propriety. He's also not all coldness. His pained reaction at the doorway when he thinks Lyra has been sent to him as the sacrifice to open the door between the worlds is palpable. He is rendered speechless with relief when he sees that she has another child with her. Another child to kill. Awkward moment resolved!

How is it possible that this can all be explained, even excused? Her murderous mother kidnaps her, so she runs to her father, who promptly kills her best friend. But these violent gestures are necessary in the cycle of creation and destruction the books describe. Yet Lord Asriel and Mrs. Coulter will, in time, atone . . . and they go out in breathtaking style.

THE BIG BANG

Lord Byron said that tragedies end in death and comedies end in marriage. In Pullman's world, marriages end in explosions. They are the Big Bangs.

Despite their lack of sentimentality all three novels use love as the driving force. It is not the sticky love of your average romance, it is volcanic in force, Earth-shaping in nature, and sex is an essential part of it. However, in this world, love (or marriage) is also not very good for you. It can, in fact, kill your ass. There isn't a single character in any of the books (with the possible exception of Iorek Byrnison, and he's a bear, so maybe I am better off saying there isn't a single *human* character) who isn't warmed and burned by love. When you see a happy couple, beware. Pullman likes nothing better than to attack the joyful tie with the literary equivalent of flamethrowers and claw hammers. In the His Dark Materials universe, the message seems to be that when you mate, do it big, then separate as quickly as possible. You'll live longer and get more done when you're single.

The casualty list is long. There's Mr. Dead Coulter, for a start. All of the witches, who are destined to outlive their lovers and can only watch helplessly as they grow old and die. Baruch and Baltamos, who after thousands of years of companionship are wrenched apart. Mary Malone, who gets a taste of it then wisely bails and remains on her own. Lyra, after accidentally sending her first "boyfriend" to his death, experiences the full flush of love in her relationship with Will. They probably bear the worst of it, in the magnum force breakup that made everyone cry and throw the final book across the room. They are forced into their own worlds to be apart forever.[7]

The bang that starts it all, of course, is between Lord Asriel and Mrs. Coulter. Lord Asriel and Mrs. Coulter are unique in that they are apart by choice, both violently repelled by and attracted to each other. They spend the entirety of *The Golden Compass* at war, yet the moment they actually meet face to face—the very second they set eyes on each other—the monkey extends a paw and Stelmaria bows in acceptance. After a classic "come with me, we can rule the world together" speech (and its refusal), there is some excellent making out. Light that looks like "sparks and beams of intense anbaric power" (*TGC* 346) flies around them; the monkey and leopard wrestle and claw each other. Neither of them notice that their daughter is standing not too far away with her dead friend in her arms. This is truly bad parenting, but it's pretty sexy.

When we last see them in *The Amber Spyglass*, they are standing on the edge of the eternal abyss, out of which even ghosts cannot escape. They reconcile as they plot against the Metatron. There is a final embrace, and then we get a full-on battle to the death, during which they have their heads bashed with rocks, their bodies crushed, and their eyes bloodied, before they pounce on the angel together and willingly fall into the never-ending darkness. As she goes, we see that Mrs. Coulter is filled with love and is transformed:

> *"Marisa! Marisa!"*
>
> The cry was torn from Lord Asriel, and with the snow leopard beside her, with a roaring in her ears, Lyra's mother stood and found her footing and leapt with all her heart, to hurl herself against the angel and her dæmon and her dying lover, and seize those beating wings, and bear them all down together into the abyss (*TAS* 365).

---

[7] Apart, but not alone, because they have their dæmons. I can't quite figure out what the human-dæmon relationship is. I was hopelessly baffled by the weird dæmon separation and wandering a la *The Incredible Journey* that happens near the end of the trilogy. There's definitely a romantic/sexual element. All those "Pan, darlings," those loving human-to-dæmon clutches, the dæmon-touching taboo, the fact that Pan is instructed to look away when Lyra is bathing. . . . If you take this to the terminal, it's both beautiful and just a step beyond incest. No matter what, if you can read the scene of Lee Scoresby and Hester's final shootout and their goodbye without shedding a tear, you are a cold-hearted snake.

Now, *that's* the way you end a relationship! The only man in the world strong enough to fight the Authority calls out to the only woman with the strength to do the same. She is Marisa now, and Lyra's mother, and Lord Asriel is her lover—all knots retied at the moment of death.

Or close to it. That's a really deep hole. Who knows what happens to them as they fall? There are no dead bodies, no scenes of mourning. Their fate is as unknown as Schrödinger's cat's. This is either romantic, heroic, or deeply annoying, depending on your mood. If you are me, however, you believe that they all land on a ledge, somewhere fairly far down, and despite the limited chances of survival (given the infinite nature of the hole, their multiple traumatic head wounds, and the angry angel who landed on top of them) they manage to crawl out. They fight all along the way, of course, and now hate each other again. That is the way it should be.

MAUREEN JOHNSON is the author of *The Key to the Golden Firebird*, *The Bermudez Triangle*, *13 Little Blue Envelopes*, *Girl at Sea*, and the Norton Award-nominated *Devilish*. Her work has earned starred reviews in *Publishers Weekly*, *School Library Journal*, and *Booklist*, as well as recognition by the American Library Association, the New York Public Library, the Chicago Public Library, Borders Original Voices Program, and Book Sense. She hopes to use the profits from this book to purchase a helper monkey, so please buy as many copies as you can. Good monkeys are expensive (but worth it). To read more about Maureen, visit www.maureenjohnsonbooks.com.

Despite stiff competition, Mrs. Coulter proves herself to be the worst parent in His Dark Materials, and often threatens to take the worst villain category as well. And yet she is endlessly seductive and fascinating, one of the few creatures in Pullman's universe able to spellbind not only the reader, but Lyra Silvertongue herself. Steiber delves into the literary antecedents of Mrs. Coulter's glamour, and discovers a smidgen of fairy dust among the tufts of golden monkey fur.

THE MYSTERIOUS MRS. COULTER

ELLEN STEIBER

There's something fascinating about a great villain.

It's easy to identify with a story's hero or heroine. That's what we're meant to do. And yet, when an author creates a truly evil villain, that's often the character who we can't forget. It's the villains who often have the power to make us dread turning the page. They force us to enter the shadows, to confront the absolute worst we can imagine. They speak to our deepest fears.

It's been more than ten years since I first read *The Golden Compass*, and in those years I'd forgotten many details of the story. But I never forgot Mrs. Coulter. She and her golden monkey remained as vivid in my mind as a nightmare. Although the Authority and his regent Metatron are responsible for the big evil forces in Pullman's world—they are, in a sense, the evil overlords—it's Mrs. Coulter who is by far the most frightening of his villains. Part of this may simply be that Mrs. Coulter is given the most attention; she's the villain we come to know best. But she's also the most complex, the most intriguing of Pullman's evil-doers. How is it that she can be simultaneously repulsive and fascinating? And why is it that she is able to grab the reader by the throat and hold on for years?

What I love best about His Dark Materials are the dæmons. The idea of an animal soul is not only irresistible, especially for all of us who've had strong connections with animals, but somehow familiar. It's almost as if we've always suspected that we had dæmons; we just needed Philip Pullman to properly describe them. Mrs. Coulter, too, is somehow familiar—as if she already existed in our imaginations, just waiting for

Pullman to give her form.

On the most basic level, Mrs. Coulter is the bad mother, the one who neglects, damages, and wants to destroy her young. I suspect she also draws on ancient literary archetypes, characters we've seen in fairy tales. My first guess was that she's a new version of the wicked stepmother, a witchy, selfish creature bent on destroying the young heroine. But that idea didn't quite work. Mrs. Coulter's evil doesn't grow out of either jealousy or anger at being slighted, which are so often the stepmothers' motives in the fairy tales. Besides, her evil is much bigger than that of the classic fairy-tale stepmothers, who tend to focus their nefarious deeds on the unfortunate stepchild. In Pullman's trilogy, Lyra is only one of many whom Mrs. Coulter harms. More to the point, Mrs. Coulter is not Lyra's stepmother. She's her mother, her blood kin, which turns out to be an essential difference.

The more I thought about Mrs. Coulter, the more she seemed rooted in another creature from the realm of folklore: the fairy queen. I realize that the idea of Mrs. Coulter as a fairy may seem like a weird notion. Nowadays, fairies show up on decals, lunch boxes, and at birthday parties for four-year-olds. They often seem to be no more than sweet, pretty girls with wings. But in the old stories, fairies weren't always pretty and they were far from sweet. They were tricksters, predators, shape-shifting creatures with dark and frightening powers.

Almost every culture has its own version of fairies. Our Western notion of the fey comes mainly from Europe, where fairy lore was found in folktales, ballads, and poems. Because there are many sources for these tales, there are many ideas about who fairies really are and how they came to be part of our world. Some scholars say fairies are actually old pagan gods and nature spirits (such as dryads and nymphs) who changed in the retelling of the tales into the "little people," who lived under the earth and were capable of hindering or helping mortals. Other theories say that fairies were originally the spirits of the dead, or fallen angels or demons.

Whatever their true origin, fairies became symbols of the forbidden and even the terrible. During the Middle Ages, the Church ruled every aspect of life. Sex was forbidden unless you were married—and even then, it was only allowed in order to have children. So when husbands and wives strayed from each other, they often blamed the carnal sin on an irresistible fairy lover who tempted them. In later stories, infants who sickened and died were considered fairy changelings, and everything from insanity to a poor harvest was blamed on the spells of vengeful fairies.

With all this bad press, the interesting thing is that fairies were never completely rejected and hated the way witches were. They were not depicted as ugly old hags who deserved to be burned or hung. They had too much power, too much beauty. Fairies were ageless, elusive, unpredictable creatures, who could help as well as harm. They were known for breaking all rules and crossing all boundaries. Fairyland (or Fairy) was a place of illusion and the elves lived charmed lives. Mortals, especially those who had hard lives toiling in the fields or mines, envied these fey creatures, who seemed to have no conscience and no responsibilities beyond dancing in a moonlit ring. If humans have always been half afraid of fairies, the other part of the equation is that we've also been half in love with them.

And so we come to Mrs. Coulter. We first hear of her indirectly, just the rumor that children are disappearing. This is, of course, one of the prime evils that has been assigned to fairies: they're notorious child-nappers. The idea behind fairy changelings is that fairies would steal healthy human infants and replace them with their own sickly get. But there are also stories in which children just vanish, because the fairies have taken them to their realm. Pullman even writes that one of the rumors about the missing children is that they are being taken to Fairyland. At the heart of these stories is an even darker belief that probably traces back to old ritual sacrifices: it was believed that fairies needed humans, that they fed on their energy. This, too, aligns with what we learn about Mrs. Coulter.

Pullman introduces us to nine-year-old Tony Makarios, a hungry street urchin who sits down on the chapel steps to eat some food that he has stolen. We're told, in the creepiest fashion, that as Tony devours his stolen treat with his little dæmon at his side, they are being watched by a beautiful young woman who emerges from the chapel with a jeweled prayer book in hand. Tony is unaware of being watched. The first hint of evil comes in the description of the woman's dæmon, an extraordinary monkey with a black face and shining golden fur. What follows is a chilling dance between the monkey and the boy's dæmon, in which Tony's dæmon (in sparrow form) finally hops onto the monkey's outstretched hand. The monkey's hand closes around it. Pullman tells us, "And then Tony turns. He can't help it" (*TGC* 38). In Mrs. Coulter's presence, people are helpless to resist her power. This is the beginning of the seduction. With the sparrow dæmon charmed by the monkey, Mrs. Coulter approaches the hungry boy, tempting him to follow her with the promise of chocolate. As Pullman tells us, the boy is already lost. He has been since the moment his dæmon lit on the monkey's hand.

Mrs. Coulter leads Tony to a warehouse, where he not only finds the promised chocolate but also other children similarly lured into her lair. Like Tony, they are all from the slums, all young, and all equally enchanted by the young woman with the dark, gleaming hair. She seems so kind that when she asks them to help her by going on a voyage, they all readily agree. She even offers to let them write notes to their parents, so that their families won't worry. Since the children are all illiterate, she takes dictation, carefully copying down their messages. Then she and her dæmon tenderly release them to the sea captain who will take them to the North. Pullman stays with her for a moment after they've left and if we have any doubts about her nature, he erases them with an act of breathtaking callousness: Mrs. Coulter takes the children's letters and tosses them into the fire.

Pullman doesn't pull any punches. He never tries to disguise her nature. We're told almost at once that Mrs. Coulter is the one behind the disappearance of the children. We know from the moment we meet her that she's evil. Part of the tension in *The Golden Compass* is waiting to see how long it takes Lyra and the other characters to understand the truth about her, which the reader has known from the start. This is a classic plot device, in which the reader, who has vital information that the characters don't have, is put into the role of a helpless god. The characters tread ever closer to danger, and you can only keep reading, praying that somehow they'll learn what you know—and survive.

Fairies have the trick of knowing exactly what it is that a person most deeply desires and then giving that thing—or the illusion of it—at a terrible price. That is Mrs. Coulter in a nutshell; we'll see her do it again and again. Here, in her very first appearance, she pulls that trick on its simplest level. Tony is hungry; she gives him not only all the food he can eat but that sweetest of foods, chocolate. This echoes the old stories that warned that those who ate fairy food never returned from the fairy realm (or if they did, they sickened and died). But Mrs. Coulter also seems to intuitively fill an emptiness in Tony. His own mother is so addled by alcohol that she barely recognizes him. And suddenly, he's being cared for by a kind, beautiful woman who seems positively angelic. Tony's experience mirrors other hapless mortals who've encountered fairies: he can't resist her because it seems she's offering what he wants most.

Lyra first encounters Mrs. Coulter when she is forced to attend what she assumes will be a boring Scholars' dinner at the Master's house. There, among the guests, is a beautiful young woman with a golden monkey for a dæmon. Pullman tells us that "Mrs. Coulter had such an air of glamour that Lyra was entranced" (*TGC* 59).

Fairies seek out and deceive their human victims, often through the use of glamour. Glamour, in the original sense of the word, didn't refer to beauty and style. It literally described an enchantment: a fairy spell cast over the eyes so that you saw only what the fairy wanted you to see and nothing else. In a way, it's not so different from the way the word is used today. Those who are considered truly glamorous—our actors, musicians, models, and athletes—often seem to hold large parts of our culture in thrall. People devour books and articles about them, dress like them, and buy the things they advertise. It's a matter of trading a bit of your own individuality for the hope that a bit of someone else's magic— their beauty, popularity, or success—will rub off on you. It's not that being glamorous is a bad thing. It's only dangerous when we fall under glamour's spell—when we give up our own powers of discernment and free will.

As Lyra does, at least for a while. She, and nearly everyone else who encounters Mrs. Coulter, falls under her very potent glamour. Beyond that, Mrs. Coulter's M.O. is seduction. In the old tales, the fairies' seductions were sexual. They lured wandering knights from their wives or young brides from their husbands. But while seduction always has an emotional element, it isn't always sexual. In this first meeting, Lyra can't stop looking at Mrs. Coulter and within minutes confides all her secrets. She becomes even more entranced when Mrs. Coulter admits that she is not really a Scholar but an explorer who, like Lyra's uncle, Lord Asriel, has been to the North. By the end of dinner, Lyra is convinced that Mrs. Coulter is the "most wonderful" person she's ever met (*TGC* 61). So when the Master later tells Lyra that Mrs. Coulter, a widow, has offered to take her in as her assistant, Lyra's answer is an instant yes.

Mrs. Coulter further sweetens the deal by telling Lyra that the work may be dangerous because they might have to go to the North—which thrills Lyra—and that she'll not only educate Lyra but buy her lots of pretty clothes because Lyra will be meeting lots of important people. This is the beginning of Lyra's seduction. She is being offered all that her heart desires and more. Lyra has been all but ignored during her years at Jordan College, and here's Mrs. Coulter, promising to transform her life and make her an important person. Beyond that is the unspoken assumption that by becoming so learned and going North, Lyra will become someone like, and hopefully of interest to, her impressive but distant uncle.

Like Tony, Lyra cannot believe her good fortune. There's a hint, though, that Mrs. Coulter might not be completely trustworthy. The Master gives Lyra the alethiometer, warning her that she must keep it secret from Mrs. Coulter.

Soon Lyra is living in Mrs. Coulter's flat. It's a fairyland of sorts, in that Lyra finds in it everything she could possibly want. The flat is filled with light and pretty things, all of it elegant and charming, graceful and feminine. It's a place that delights the senses, much as Fairy does. On their first day together Mrs. Coulter begins to fulfill all her promises. She takes Lyra to the Royal Arctic Institute, where she points out other explorers and tells Lyra thrilling stories. Next, she takes Lyra shopping and buys her beautiful new clothes. Mrs. Coulter is better than Christmas.

At night Mrs. Coulter bathes Lyra, and an interesting thing happens. Curious, Lyra's dæmon, Pantalaimon, watches this bath until Mrs. Coulter looks at him in a way that makes him turn away, suddenly conscious of Lyra growing up and needing privacy. This is the first time he's ever looked away from Lyra.

Although this is all part of Mrs. Coulter's seduction of Lyra, drawing her further under her power, it's also an indication that Lyra is growing up, separating a bit from Pan and moving into her own femininity. What this scene made me see is that seduction itself is an integral part of growing up. At some point we all get seduced—by friends or crushes, groups or styles, alcohol, drugs, other places, or even by what is right for us, our path or calling—and the act of growing up has a lot to do with whether or not we give in to those seductions, those influences. I don't think anyone can truly grow up without giving in to and surviving at least a few of them. Seduction is one of those inescapable and somehow necessary rites of passage that allow us to grow from a child into an adult.

At the end of this first magical day with Mrs. Coulter, Pullman describes Lyra in her new cozy bed, exhausted, and "too enchanted to question anything" (*TGC* 69). When you're under the spell of someone else's glamour, you blithely accept what's been put before you. You stop asking questions, you stop thinking for yourself, and that's when things get dangerous.

Fairy is famously a place where mortals get exactly what they desire. In particular, they're given all the food and drink they could want, and the food is always unimaginably delicious. But the delights never last. Either the fairy food gives the fairies power over the mortal or the sumptuous feasts vanish in an instant and the poor, deluded human who thought he was in a crystalline fairy palace finds himself sitting on a barren moor, gnawing on a stalk of heather. While you're there, though, before the enchantment breaks, you're happy. Think of Tony or Lyra in Mrs. Coulter's apartment. What saves Lyra? Perhaps it's the fact that she has Mrs. Coulter's blood in her, and so she's never fully taken in by the magic. Or she is, but Pantalaimon isn't.

It's Pan who sees the warning signs, who understands that the compass must be kept away from Mrs. Coulter. I think it's Pan who sees these signs first because he's the one who is attuned to Mrs. Coulter's dæmon. Six weeks into their stay, Pan tells Lyra that Mrs. Coulter has been lying all along, and Lyra believes him. When she later defies Mrs. Coulter, the golden monkey attacks Pantalaimon, nearly ripping off Pan's ear with a cold, dispassionate cruelty that terrifies Lyra.

The monkey doesn't release Pan until Lyra promises to do as Mrs. Coulter tells her, which includes kissing Mrs. Coulter's cheek. Lyra obeys and realizes that beneath Mrs. Coulter's scent, her flesh smells like metal. It's one more clue that Mrs. Coulter is not quite flesh and blood. Lyra now sees Mrs. Coulter's true nature: she's cruel and controlling, and beneath all her beauty is something like metal, unfeeling and unyielding.

Later, during a cocktail party hosted by Mrs. Coulter, Adèle Starminster, a journalist, begins questioning Lyra about her mentor. Mrs.

Coulter intervenes at once, and Lyra again smells something like heated metal coming from Mrs. Coulter, as if she's drawing on some sort of supernatural energy. The journalist's dæmon, a butterfly, collapses into a faint and poor Adèle barely makes it out the door. This, plainly, is Mrs. Coulter casting a spell of some sort. But the metallic scent vanishes so quickly that Lyra is left wondering if she imagined it. Fairy magic is always ephemeral.

We tend to think of the soul as something that each person hides deep inside him or her. In Pullman's world, every adult's true nature is clearly revealed by his or her dæmon. The golden monkey is menacing and frightening from the moment it appears. You almost have to wonder: How is it that so many people fall for Mrs. Coulter's act? How is it that everyone who sees the golden monkey doesn't run screaming in the opposite direction? The only plausible explanation is the force of Mrs. Coulter's glamour.

At this same hellish party, Lord Boreal approaches Lyra, and Lyra begins to piece together the real nature of Mrs. Coulter's work. Mrs. Coulter is involved in the Oblation Board, which is somehow sacrificing the missing children, and she intends to use Lyra to "bring in" more children. A horrified Lyra and Pan manage to escape, sneaking out while the party is still going on.

At this point, Mrs. Coulter drops out of the action for a while. Lyra is rescued by the gyptians, and as she travels North with John Faa and Farder Coram, Pullman gives us some background on Mrs. Coulter, allowing us to connect the dots to Lord Asriel and Lyra. We discover that Mrs. Coulter's first name is Marisa, and that she's studied black magic in Africa, specifically the sort of magic that creates zombis. John Faa explains that although she wasn't high-born, she married a politician, Edward Coulter, and became a society hostess, gaining entry to people of influence, wealth, and power.

While still married, she met Lord Asriel, and it was instant infatuation for them both. Each had met their equal. There's a lasting fascination and attraction between them that the reader sees whenever they meet: their dæmons can't resist each other.

Despite her marriage, Mrs. Coulter and Lord Asriel became lovers, and she became pregnant with Lyra. This is very much aligned with the medieval tales of fairies. Fairy was a realm of transgression, where the rules didn't apply, where taboos were broken and natural laws inverted. Mrs. Coulter clearly thrives in this realm, and I suspect it's this, not England, that's her native ground.

When Lyra was born, it was clear that she didn't look anything like Edward Coulter. So Mrs. Coulter concocted another lie, telling her husband the baby had died. Instead, the infant was taken to one of Lord Asriel's estates, in Oxfordshire, and given to a gyptian woman, Ma Costa, to nurse. Word of this reached Edward Coulter, and he went to Oxfordshire, determined to slay the child. Ma Costa fled the cottage where she and Lyra had been living and hid with the baby in the main house, where Lord Asriel found Mr. Coulter searching for Lyra. Much like a medieval knight, Lord Asriel fought the husband of his temptress lover, and killed him. Lord Asriel broke the law, and paid for it, by having his wealth and lands taken from him.

You might think at this point, with her husband out of the picture, that Mrs. Coulter would reclaim her baby and marry Lord Asriel. But like the fairy queen, she seems to have no conscience and no heart. She turned her back on her lover and her child. At Lord Asriel's insistence, Lyra was placed at Jordan College to be raised, with the condition that Mrs. Coulter not be allowed to see her. Mrs. Coulter remained a stranger to Lyra, but during all the years that Lyra was at Jordan, the gyptians kept an eye on her.

I don't think it's a coincidence that Ma Costa—Lyra's surrogate mother—and Mrs. Coulter have the same initials. They're two sides of a coin, the good mother and the bad. Mrs. Coulter is elegant, beautiful, charming. Ma Costa is poor, crude, and has none of Mrs. Coulter's worldly sophistication. But though Mrs. Coulter gave life to Lyra, Ma Costa was the one who nursed and nurtured Lyra, the one who kept her out of a murderer's hands, the one who made sure that someone was always looking out for her. Despite all Mrs. Coulter's brilliance and power, Lyra successfully lies to and tricks her. Ma Costa, however, can't be fooled. Ma Costa is the one who understands Lyra's nature and sees her for what she truly is: "'[Y]ou got witch oil in your soul. Deceptive, that's what you are, child'" (*TGC* 100). Lyra indignantly protests this characterization, but Ma Costa explains that she means it as a compliment, and it is. Lyra is later given the name Lyra "Silvertongue," acknowledging her ability to lie as one of her greatest gifts. It's worth noting that the witch oil in Lyra's soul and her talent to endlessly deceive are probably inherited from her mother. So despite her cruelty and her neglect of her daughter, Mrs. Coulter gave her child the skills and strength that would save her life and determine her future.

If Mrs. Coulter is a fairy who's left her child to be raised by humans, does that make Lyra a changeling? Yes and no. The infant Lyra wasn't wanted by her enchanter of a birth mother, probably because raising a child would have interfered with Mrs. Coulter's raging ambition. So, like a changeling, Lyra was given up, though unlike a changeling she was given to her father. When he left her with strangers and insisted that he was only her uncle, the abandonment was complete. Still, there was no swap involved, no mortal infant who was taken by Mrs. Coulter in Lyra's place (though Lord Asriel does do something very like this at the end of *The Golden Compass*). Unlike traditional changelings, Lyra isn't sickly or damaged. In fact, even under the benign neglect at Jordan College, she thrives. So she's sort of the inverse of a changeling, especially because she's got power of her own. And though Lyra chooses to use her power for good rather than evil, she turns out to be every bit as wily, strong, and extraordinary as her dazzling mother.

In *The Golden Compass*, Mrs. Coulter's most horrific crime is that she kidnaps children to sever their dæmons. This seems kin to all the tales in which fairies stole humans and sacrificed them to sustain their own existence. There are also echoes of the traditional fairy hunt, in which the fairy riders cross the countryside, hunting souls and brutally tormenting anyone who crosses their path. Mrs. Coulter's cruelty, too, is part of the traditional lore. During the late-nineteenth century, fairies became a subject of intense interest in England, and there were a great many Victorian artists who painted them. These fairies were, as you might expect, depicted as ethereal and beautiful. They were also frighteningly cruel. Painting after painting showed these exquisite, otherworldly creatures tormenting animals or humans for sport. They were perverse. They were sadists. They were even linked to vampirism.

Fairies liked to trick humans into breaking laws. They would lure a husband to leave his wife or children to leave their homes. It was well known that those who went with the fairies either never returned or returned changed, often damaged. It wasn't uncommon for those who entered Fairy to come back blinded or insane. In *The Golden Compass*, even more horribly, those who follow Mrs. Coulter lose their dæmons; they're trapped in an excruciating half-life without their souls. But the old stories hold out hope. You could be taken by the fairies and come back safely—if you were rescued by a mortal's love (the Scottish ballad of "Tam Lin" is an example of this kind of story). This means that there's a chance that Lyra, through her love and dogged determination, can rescue Roger and the others from her mother.

So Lyra, true to the old fairy stories, tries—but she is caught, and finds herself and Pan in the dreadful guillotine, about to be severed from each other. This is one of the most horrific moments in the entire trilogy, and Pullman uses it to reveal a new side of Mrs. Coulter. Just as the blade is about to fall, Mrs. Coulter enters the room. Seeming stunned by the prospect of Lyra being separated from Pan, she stops the intercision and takes Lyra to a safe room, where she gives her hot, soothing tea, and tucks her into bed.

In the midst of outright horror, the good mother surfaces. Or does she? Lyra asks Mrs. Coulter why she saved her, but Mrs. Coulter never gives a decent answer. Instead she reverts to lies and begins questioning Lyra about the alethiometer. This time Lyra sees through the spin. For her, the glamour is well and truly broken.

As Lyra and Pan escape with the alethiometer, Pullman leaves us wondering why Mrs. Coulter rescued Lyra. Did she just want the alethiometer? If she did, wouldn't it have been easier to get it from Lyra once her dæmon was severed, since that would have made her more obedient? One can only guess that either Mrs. Coulter needs the girl in some way . . . or perhaps the vicious Mrs. Coulter actually has a shred of maternal feeling for her daughter.

We next see Mrs. Coulter just after Lord Asriel sacrifices Roger and tears apart the Aurora Borealis, opening the way into other worlds. Mrs. Coulter is there with him, in his arms. For the first time Lyra sees her parents together, sees the passion that still exists between them and their dæmons. Mrs. Coulter refuses Lord Asriel's invitation to enter these new worlds with him, telling him to take the girl, that Lyra is more his daughter than hers. When he argues, reminding her that she took Lyra in, Mrs. Coulter dismisses that, saying she waited too long to try to mold her, that Lyra was already too coarse and stubborn.

This has got to be a devastating conversation for Lyra to overhear, but

I think that in an odd way it frees her. It's the undeniable proof that while her parents may be brilliant, they're both completely mad. Each cares only for their own ambitions. Neither seems capable of anything remotely like love. But when Mrs. Coulter casually dismisses the possibility that she cares about Lyra, Lord Asriel implies that she's lying. She never responds to this charge. The last that Lyra sees of her mother in *The Golden Compass* is her leaving Lord Asriel. And leaving Lyra and Pan with Roger's lifeless body.

For the greater part of the next two books, Mrs. Coulter remains Pullman's arch-villain. In *The Subtle Knife*, she doesn't really change. She's still lying to, seducing, and torturing people. We find that the intercisions are not even the worst of what she's done. We also find that Lord Asriel was right. Mrs. Coulter isn't nearly as indifferent to Lyra as she claimed to be. . . . In fact, she is quite obsessed with getting her daughter back and spends most of the second book pursuing her.

Beyond that, we discover that Mrs. Coulter is the one commanding the Specters of Indifference, who execute the adult version of intercision: they eat adult dæmons, leaving humans as empty shells. Mrs. Coulter is making a specialty of ripping out souls. She takes away free will and imagination, turning her victims into the equivalent of zombis, who can do nothing but obey. This, too, feels similar to the old stories, in which fairies would capture mortals to enslave them. More than one story tells of humans caught by the fairies who remain slaves because fairy magic has drained them of their free will.

The witches are out to get Mrs. Coulter, and seem to be the only ones who might succeed. Near the end of *The Subtle Knife*, in a heart-breaking scene, the witch Lena Feldt, who has come to kill Mrs. Coulter, instead finds herself Mrs. Coulter's captive. In the moments before she's caught, Lena is struck by Mrs. Coulter's tremendous force of soul, and I couldn't help wondering if she was always that powerful or if, like the fairies, Mrs. Coulter has somehow become stronger by feeding on the energy of those she has destroyed. We watch her use the Specters to torture Lena Feldt's dæmon, all the while calmly extracting information about Lyra. As Mrs. Coulter finally gets what she wants, a desperate

Lena asks what she'll do to Lyra now that she knows the girl's true destiny. Mrs. Coulter replies that she'll have to destroy her.

For most of the trilogy, Mrs. Coulter is somewhat two-dimensional: she's beautiful and she's bad. In *The Amber Spyglass* her character changes in a way that's unexpected and sometimes difficult to believe. When the book opens, we find that Mrs. Coulter has succeeded in stealing Lyra from the witches and has her hidden away in a cave in the Himalayas. Mrs. Coulter once again concocts a tale that deftly mingles truth and outrageous lies. She tells the locals that she's a holy woman and that the child she's caring for is her daughter, who's caught in the spell of an enchanter. Even more ironic, she claims that she is trying to heal Lyra when, in fact, she's drugging her, keeping her in a semi-conscious dream state.

A number of things seem to be going on here. We watch Mrs. Coulter tenderly caring for Lyra, comforting her in the midst of nightmares. She's acting like a loving mother, and there's a hint that this behavior might be genuine. Her dæmon doesn't like it. The golden monkey is contemptuous of this suddenly nurturing aspect, and his skepticism provokes a rare reaction: Mrs. Coulter actually doubts herself, wondering if she's going mad and suspecting that she's willfully blinding herself to the truth. The question is—what is the truth of her?

A young local girl, Ama, has been bringing food to the cave, convinced that the holy woman will bless her in exchange for these services. Ama, like everyone else, adores Mrs. Coulter and is eager to do anything that will grant her time in her presence. Ama, though, also develops a powerful curiosity about the enchanted child. When she secretly brings a remedy for sleeping sickness to Lyra, Ama witnesses the Mrs. Coulter we've come to know. Pan resists Mrs. Coulter's attempt to force more sleeping potion down Lyra's throat, the golden monkey attacks Pan, and Mrs. Coulter viciously slaps her nearly unconscious daughter. The truth of Mrs. Coulter is getting increasingly complex. Loving mother and cruel enemy: she seems to contain them both.

Will eventually makes it to the cave and even he, who's been told exactly how ruthless Mrs. Coulter is, finds himself inexplicably charmed by her. He has to keep reminding himself that she's evil, because all he can see is a woman who's beautiful, kind, brave, and very much like Lyra. The glamour is working full force, and he's nearly caught in it. Mrs.

Coulter explains that she's keeping Lyra in the cave because she loves her, that she's protecting Lyra from the Church, which seeks to kill the girl. Will manages not to be taken in. He returns to Iorek and reports that she's lying, that she loves lies too much to stop telling them. Will seems proof against her glamour, and yet when it comes time for him to free Lyra, Mrs. Coulter throws the one thing at him that he cannot possibly harden himself against. As he tries to use the subtle knife to leave the cave, Mrs. Coulter, with the fairy gift of knowing what his heart most desires, reflects an image of his mother's face. Will's mind leaves the knife, and the knife is shattered.

The only one who seems capable of fighting Mrs. Coulter is the Chevalier Tialys, one of the dragonfly riders. If you look at the traditional paintings and stories of the "little people," they're often depicted riding dragonflies. Perhaps the reason the Chevalier can successfully fight Mrs. Coulter is because he, too, has a good deal of fairy magic in him.

As Will finally escapes with Lyra, Mrs. Coulter sobs pathetically, pleading with Lyra not to leave her, claiming that this is breaking her heart. Is it? I didn't believe her at all, but when Lyra later tells Will about her time in the cave, she doesn't remember her mother drugging or hitting her. Her memory is of her mother being kind, caring for her. Even Lyra, who knows the worst of Mrs. Coulter, believes that her mother never wanted to hurt her.

The question really becomes: Has Mrs. Coulter had a change of heart? Has she somehow, beneath her mad, cruel grab for power, discovered a genuine love for her daughter? From this point on in the trilogy, everything she says and does seems to indicate that she has. Yet many readers are never convinced. It may be the "Boy Who Cried Wolf" syndrome: Pullman has created a character who's been lying so steadily and brilliantly that we don't believe anything she says, even when she's telling the truth. It doesn't help that whenever she declares her love for Lyra, she's actively manipulating someone else, whether it be Will, Lord Asriel, or even Metatron. She's always got a scheme, an angle, and this makes her protestations of love seem phony. I think there are two other factors that make this change hard to accept. The first is that the golden monkey remains as maleficent as ever. How can anyone love when she's got that vile creature for a soul? The second is that, if Mrs. Coulter *has* changed, the change has occurred off-stage, perhaps during those hours when she was alone with Lyra in the cave, somewhere in the chambers of her own heart.

The big, vital way in which Mrs. Coulter differs from the traditional fairy queen is that she's not barren. She gives birth to Lyra . . . and this will eventually be the undoing of her cruel fairy magic. Fairies, we're told, don't have human emotions, aren't capable of love. It's when Mrs. Coulter allows herself to love her daughter that she becomes vulnerable. Until this point, she is unstoppable, a horrific being who accumulates more and more power by sacrificing others. When she realizes that she loves Lyra, she becomes mortal.

Ultimately, I think we have to believe Mrs. Coulter's claims of love. She not only repeatedly risks everything for Lyra, but willingly and fiercely gives her life for her daughter. At the end she chooses love, and in this final act, I think Pullman grants her redemption. At the very least, he holds out hope that even people who've done the very worst can change by choosing to act from love. In the end, speaking through the character of Mary Malone, this is what Pullman tells us about the truth of a person:

> "I stopped believing there was a power of good and a power of evil that were outside us. And I came to believe that good and evil are names for what people do, not for what they are. All we can say is that this is a good deed, because it helps someone, or that's an evil one, because it hurts them. People are too complicated to have simple labels" (*TAS* 398).

Mrs. Coulter is far too complex to be merely evil, and it's her complexity that gives her so much resonance. We can't help being fascinated and thrilled by a character who so boldly embraces her own freedom and the forbidden. Unrestrained by conscience or law, she seizes what she wants, crosses every boundary, and manages to charm all the while. She is a fearless predator, a trickster, an enchanter, a character imbued with all the old magic of Fairy. Perhaps, strangest of all, she's a loving mother. Mrs. Coulter embodies the best and the worst that we're capable of: creativity and destruction, reason and madness, terrifying darkness and, ultimately, the redeeming light that is love.

ELLEN STEIBER lives in Tucson, Arizona, where she writes fantasy for teens and adults. Lately, she's been writing a lot about fairies and the power of gemstones. Her short story, "Screaming for Faeries," appears in *The Faery Reel: Tales from the Twilight Realm*, edited by Ellen Datlow and Terri Windling. She's currently working on the sequel to her novel, *A Rumor of Gems*. She thanks both Philip Pullman and the fairies for this chance to explore their worlds.

REFERENCES

Briggs, Katherine. *An Encyclopedia of Fairies.* New York: Pantheon Books, 1976.

——. *The Vanishing People: Fairy Lore and Legends.* New York: Pantheon Books, 1978.

Duffy, Maureen. *The Erotic World of Faery.* London: Sphere Books, 1989.

Keightly, Thomas. *The World Guide to Gnomes, Fairies, Elves, and Other Little People: A Compendium of International Fairy Folklore* (reissued). New York: Crown Books, 1978.

Purkiss, Diane. *At the Bottom of the Garden: A Dark History of Fairies, Hobgoblins, and Other Troublesome Things.* New York: New York University Press, 2003.

Silver, Carole G. *Strange and Secret Peoples: Fairies and Victorian Consciousness.* New York: Oxford University Press, 1999.

Astronomy and religion have one thing in common: both look to the heavens for answers about the origins of the universe. Astrophysics has its dark matter in the sky, and religions have their angels above. Pullman combines these two concepts, positing a kind of dark matter with Intelligence, called "Dust," from which the angels in His Dark Materials are created. Here, Hopkins takes a long look at angels, both in Pullman's cosmology and across several doctrines, and at the tensions between science and faith that the trilogy illuminates.

SHEDDING LIGHT ON DARK MATTER

ELLEN HOPKINS

In the wake of the His Dark Materials trilogy, author Philip Pullman has alternately been labeled brilliant, subversive, visionary, heretical, ingenious, and dangerous. The adjective used, to a large degree, has depended on the theological lean of the labeler. Pullman, a self-proclaimed atheist, takes great pride in dropping the jaws of "the faithful." But the religious theories presented in *The Golden Compass*, *The Subtle Knife*, and *The Amber Spyglass* are deeply rooted in the author's shunned Christian upbringing, and none more so than his concept of angels. One key element, however, is missing: belief. Much like religion, the supernatural relies on belief, and angels are, by definition, supernatural beings, as much at home in a fantasy novel as tiny spies riding dragonflies and anthropomorphized polar bears in heavy armor. But the HDM books are not only fantasy: they intertwine fantasy, science fiction,[1] and mysticism. As reviewer Craig Bernthal writes, "Pullman weaves together elements of modern cosmology, quantum physics, the I Ching, and especially, the Bible." Science often endeavors to divorce itself from belief, and this is where the HDM fusion fails for me.

If asked to choose one of the adjectives above to describe the HDM books, I'd have to write in, "none of the above." As a practicing (if not especially devout) Lutheran, I take more exception to Pullman's over-

---

[1] Webster's defines "science fiction" as "fiction of a highly imaginative or fantastic kind, typically involving some actual or projected scientific phenomenon." While the definition doesn't apply to Gallivespians, it certainly applies to the "dark materials" or "dark matter" on which these books rely.

inflated prose[2] than to his skewed, but not remarkably revolutionary, views on organized religion in general, and Christianity in particular.

In *The Subtle Knife*, we meet Dr. Mary Malone, a former nun who chose physical love over her calling. Mary echoes Pullman's own statement that "God is dead," (KidsReads.com) when she tells Lyra and Will, "'I thought physics could be done to the glory of God, till I saw there wasn't any God at all and that physics was more interesting anyway. The Christian religion is a very powerful and convincing mistake, that's all'" (*TAS* 393).

I could let myself be offended by Pullman's contention that God is dead, and by the way he disposes of Him in *The Amber Spyglass*.[3] And, yes, I suppose I could take umbrage at his description of God as the Authority. Pullman writes, "'The Authority . . . was never the creator. He was an angel like ourselves. . . . The first angels condensed out of Dust,[4] and the Authority was the first of all. He told those who came after him that he had created them, but it was a lie'" (*TAS* 28).

HDM's portrayal of the Authority as just another angel is somewhat in line with the Mormon view that God, angels, and men are relative equals. This is just an aberration within standard Christian doctrine; Pullman's portrait of the Authority as over-ambitious poser who lied his way into the role of Creator is a much larger perversion of Christian belief.[5]

The HDM ideology that angels were created at the same time as the universe, however, very much reflects traditional Western monotheistic views, which hold that angels were created before man but after whatever bang (most likely a big one, all things considered) jumpstarted the cosmos. It is not such a stretch to think they might have been formed from creation's "leftovers," the mysterious dark matter that scientists believe comprises 85 percent of the universe.

---

[2] Admittedly, this has everything to do with my personal passion for storytelling through verse. It is a poet's job to use as few words as possible to paint vibrant pictures. Where Pullman might utilize several paragraphs to describe a warm evening after a storm, I would choose a simple metaphor: *The night had hung a sultry black curtain, sequined gold* (from my book *Crank*).

[3] Many critics take particular offense at the idea that God might happily dissolve into atoms and lift off into oblivion, but I personally think if He was ready to leave this world behind, it might be in just such a fashion. I can only hope when I go, it will be as easy.

[4] Dust, as defined elsewhere in the books, is dark matter.

[5] More on this later.

Astronomers cannot see dark matter, which does not shine or reflect light. But they have deduced its presence in galaxy clusters by its gravitational effects on surrounding objects. The Hubble Space Telescope recently returned images that suggest a ring of dark matter, created by the collision of two galaxy clusters. Computer simulations indicated that when the two clusters collided and combined, dark matter fell toward the center, then radiated outward while slowing under the pull of gravity.[6]

Mankind has long turned its collective eyes toward the sky in search of otherworldly beings, from angels to fairies to aliens in UFOs. The Earth was the realm of the everyday, but for eons, the heavens were beyond man's reach and so belonged to the spirit world. Connection to that place has always been important to people, though often they can't say just why. Understanding the cosmos is the work of science. Transcending the heavens is the work of faith.[7]

Christianity was the first of the Western religions to embrace science and find ways to coexist with the laws of nature. But it is far from the only religion to look for messengers from the heavens. Judaism, Zoroastrianism, and Islam all share the Christian belief that the universe is tripartite. Each part—Heaven, Earth, and Hell—has its own inhabitants: angels, humans, and demons. The English word *angel* derives from the Latin *angelus*, which came from the Greek *angelos*, meaning "messenger." The closest Hebrew word is *mal'akh*, which also means "messenger" and, according to the scriptures, angels have two jobs: to praise and serve the Maker, and to act as His messengers.

The Bible does not offer a wealth of knowledge about angels.[8] But often, when they are mentioned, it is in the role of messenger. In the Old Testament, angels foretell the birth of Isaac and Samson, and the destruction of Gomorrah.

In one of the most famous New Testament stories, an angel appears to

---

[6] Before the arrival of "modern" science, Western theology proposed that angels moved the stars and elements. Gravity was not a law of nature, but rather a force of heavenly will and supernatural strength.

[7] Here, and elsewhere, I use "faith" and "belief" interchangeably.

[8] Most details of angelic existence have been gleaned from texts outside the orthodox scriptures. These include the three Chronicles of Enoch, which were declared apocryphal (not authentic) in the fourth century A.D. Before that, they were considered inspired canonical scripture, and the New Testament absorbed many of Enoch's writings, including the idea of fallen angels, a concept not mentioned in the Old Testament.

shepherds, and the night illuminates with the "glory of God."[9] The angel's message is, "Don't be afraid. I bring you the most joyful news ever announced, and it is for everyone! The Savior . . . has been born tonight in Bethlehem. . . . You will find a baby wrapped in a blanket, lying in a manger!" (Luke 2:10–12, *The Living Bible*).

Five hundred years before that night, a messenger angel named Vohu Manah delivered God's message to Zoroaster in Persia. A thousand years later, the archangel Gabriel dictated the Koran to Mohammed. And in the early 1800s, an angel named Moroni carried the message of the Book of Mormon to LDS founder Joseph Smith.

As messengers, Pullman's angels resemble traditional definitions. In *The Subtle Knife*, Joachim Lorenz tells the witch, Serafina Pekkala, that angels "'carry messages from [H]eaven, that's their calling'" (121). Mary Malone also has an exchange with angels, via a computer screen. Here again, Pullman informs readers that angels are creatures of dark matter, the same matter that makes up Mary's Shadows and also Lyra's Dust. Mary asks if Shadow matter is the same as what people call "spirit." The angels answer, "'From what we are, spirit; From what we do, matter. Matter and spirit are one'" (221).

But the angels have not come to Mary only to impart this knowledge. They have come as messengers, for she has a role in the coming melodrama: "'Find the boy and girl. Waste no more time. . . . You must play the serpent'" (221).

A large majority of Americans believe in angels,[10] and for many, the concept is synonymous with "guardians." Movies like *It's a Wonderful Life* and television shows like *Touched by an Angel* have reinforced this popular notion. The Bible does speak of angels as guardians: God sent an angel to protect the Hebrew people as they fled Egypt. An angel saved Daniel from becoming lion food. Another broke Peter out of prison. And Psalms 34 tells us, "For the Angel of the Lord guards and rescues all who reverence him" (Psalms 34:7, *TLB*).

Pullman sends a pair of angels, Balthamos and Baruch, to lead Will to Lord Asriel. When Will refuses to go without first rescuing Lyra, the two accompany him. Eventually, they are forced into the role of guardians,

---

[9] Traditionally, an angel's light source is God.
[10] According to a December 2005 Harris Poll, 68 percent.

when the evil angel Metatron[11] tries to kill Will. After the skirmish, Baruch goes to inform Asriel, and Balthamos stays on as Will's reluctant guardian. Near the end of the trilogy, in his most important role as guardian, Balthamos draws the assassin Gomez to the priest's own death, thereby saving the lives of Lyra and Will.

The likable angelic duo has generated much flak among hard-line Christian critics, who envision the pair as homosexual. That there is love between them is obvious,[12] but since they are beings without flesh, the question becomes how they might have sex at all. Without physical consummation, can same-gender love be considered "sexual"?

Can beings without flesh even have a gender? Though it seems unlikely, and the vast majority of theologians claim angels are definitely genderless, most references in the scriptures and other holy writings give angels male characteristics.[13] Most angel names we hear (Michael, Gabriel,[14] Lucifer, etc.) are guy names. And in languages with grammatical genders (including Hebrew, Greek, and Latin), the word for "angel" is always masculine.

When it comes to their duties, the trend continues. The archangel Michael is a mighty warrior, who destroyed 185,000 Assyrian soldiers in a single night. A cherub guards the Gate of Eden with a fiery sword. An angel of the Lord causes an earthquake when he rolls away the gigantic stone from in front of Jesus' tomb. These jobs—battalion destroyer, fiery sword-bearer, mega-stone mover/earthquake initiator—seem much more suited to the stereotypically masculine gender.

Angels in art do take on more feminine aspects. In paintings, the faces of angels are usually beautiful, their features finer, their bodies slender. In more modern art, some of them even get breasts![15] While some paintings depict angels in battle garb, most allow them the comfort of long,

---

[11] "Evil," as an agent of the Authority.

[12] In one of the most poignant scenes in the trilogy, Pullman tells us that Balthamos feels the death of Baruch the moment it happens. He takes wing, lifting his anguish into the air and sobbing into the clouds. Half his heart has been extinguished. It seems to me that love like this is a celebration, not, as some critics might call it, an abomination.

[13] Of course, across the board, the authors were men. Makes a girl wonder!

[14] It is interesting to note that many theologians believe Gabriel is, in fact, female. As such, she is the only female archangel, and the only one other than Michael mentioned in the Old Testament.

[15] Dirty old artists!

flowing robes, imparting a much more feminine demeanor.

Pullman gives readers angels of both genders, though still without flesh. Serafina tells Mary how she met a female angel named Xaphania, who told her that she "'and the rebel angels, the followers of wisdom, have always tried to open minds; the Authority and his churches have always tried to keep them closed'" (*TAS* 429).

Here, Pullman attempts to flip Western theology onto its proverbial head. "Rebel angels" refers to the fallen host, regarded by traditionalists as the veritable "bad guys." It's a simple game of role reversal and to a point this, the basis of the HDM ideology, works, at least in the context of Pullman's fictional universes.

The Old Testament makes no reference to fallen angels, or even a separate "evil." In Genesis, we do learn of "giants" who came to Earth and coupled with the "daughters of men." The word "giants" translates from the Hebrew *nephilim*, from the root word *naphal*, which means "to fall." Enoch tells us two hundred *bene ha Elohim* ("Watchers," or "Sons of God") left their first estate (Heaven) and came down (fell) to Earth to marry human women and have children with them.[16]

Apparently, these Watchers, or *Grigori*, did have flesh, for by all accounts they married and their wives bore them children. These, then, were no ordinary angels, and this has been explained[17] by making them angels of the "tenth order."[18] This places them outside the standard hierarchy of the host, which puts God at the top, followed in descending ranking by the first triad—1. Seraphim, 2. Cherubim, and 3. Thrones; the second triad—4. Dominations, 5. Virtues, and 6. Powers; and the third triad—7. Principalities, 8. Archangels, and 9. Angels.

It is easier to visualize the celestial hierarchy as a sphere, with God at the center, and also at the highest point (think North Pole). The host spirals outward and downward. Those closest to the pole are closest to God, and so directly receive His pure light and love. They serve as conduits,

---

[16] This story is echoed by Jude in the New Testament: "And the angels which kept not their first estate, but left their own habitation, he hath reserved in everlasting chains under darkness unto judgment of the great day" (Jude 1:6, *King James Bible*). Phew. Stiff punishment!

[17] By those voyeuristic sorts who need an explanation. Perhaps those who see Balthamos and Baruch as "gay" are students of angelology.

[18] An alternate explanation claims they were "angels of fire," transformed to flesh on contact with the Earth.

transmitting the energy of His light to the next lowest order, which in turn transmits it to the next lowest, and so on. Ultimately, a sort of filtered energy reaches mankind.[19]

Each angelic order has specific duties. The lower their ranking, the more direct dealings they have with humankind. The highest order, Seraphim, surrounds the throne of God, chanting His praises.[20] As we descend through the hierarchy, we find angels more and more concerned with the everyday goings-on here on Earth. Angels dispatched as guardians and messengers most often come from the ninth order.

Pullman remains true to this when Balthamos and Baruch tell Will, "'We are not of a high order among angels.'" He does deviate from the common view that angels are more powerful than humans, however, when Will asks his guardians if they are stronger or weaker than he is. "'Weaker,'" answer the angels. "'You have true flesh. We do not'" (*TAS* 10).

Either way, as followers of Lord Asriel,[21] the two are "fallen angels." Here, the term takes on the Christian definition of angels who have been exiled from Heaven because of actions taken against God. There are many versions of the Fall, and all are made possible only because God gave angels free will.[22]

One account[23] says simply that through free will many angels decided to check out the scenery beyond God's dwelling place. Those who didn't venture far remained in the celestial orbits of the first and second triads of the host. Those cursed with more daring and curiosity fell into the lower rings of the third triad. Of these, some remained angels. Others became humans or even demons.

Another take on the Free Will Fall tells us God gave angels free will, but decided He just might have made a mistake. What if His angels decided to give sin a try? As perhaps a great experiment, God deepened the devotion of some of His host through an act of grace. The rest did

---

[19] In his book *Angels, An Endangered Species*, author Malcolm Godwin takes this a step further, describing this energy as vibrations that slow as they travel away from the center, eventually condensing from light into matter.

[20] Seraphs are supposed to be creatures of pure thought who, by virtue of their proximity to God, are literally aflame with His love.

[21] In HDM, Asriel represents Lucifer, usually considered Fallen-Angel-in-Chief.

[22] People, too. You think He would have learned!

[23] This comes to us from Origen of Alexandria, a theologian of the early Christian church.

not receive God's grace and, as He feared, waded deep into the sin pit. God's right-hand archangel, Michael, led a legion of the enlightened into war against the others, ultimately driving them out of Heaven.

If angels are, indeed, vulnerable to sin, lust is often proposed as a reason for the Fall. This theory provides the explanation for the Grigori. Originally sent to help the archangels create Eden, the Watchers fell hard for the daughters of Cain.[24] While trying to impress the women, the Grigori revealed some powerful heavenly secrets, including the ins-and-outs (figuratively speaking, of course) of astrology and weapons production. They also wanted their women to be beautiful, and so told their fiancés how to enhance natural comeliness with perfume and makeup.

The Amber Spyglass provides an interesting twist on this tale when Mrs. Coulter tries to seduce Metatron.[25] Pullman has Metatron tell Mrs. Coulter how he was once a man, Enoch, but was transformed into the archangel Metatron at God's bidding. Standing close enough to Mrs. Coulter "to smell the perfume of her hair and to gaze at the texture of her skin," Metatron explains that as Enoch, he loved the flesh of his many wives (357). "'And I understood it when the sons of Heaven fell in love with the daughters of earth, and I pleaded their cause with the Authority. But his heart was fixed against them . . .'" (356–357).

At least one of the Grigori was female. She was called Lilith, and some theologians refer to her as Adam's first wife. Hebrew legends tell how God created her for the "first man," but obedience[26] was not Lilith's forte. Rather than submit, she took carnal pleasure with demons (and also Satan, as his bride), ultimately giving birth to one hundred offspring each day. Her daughters, the *Lilim*, were said to tempt faithful men[27] as they slept. The *Lilim* were also known as succubae or night hags.

HDM refers several times to Xaphania, the leader of the rebel angels led by Asriel. Balthamos tells Will that she was wiser than the Authority, and the one who uncovered His lie. The discovery led to her banishment

---

[24] When it came to sin, like father, like daughters, it seems.

[25] Pullman sides Metatron with the Authority and, if Enoch's tale is true, he was certainly chosen by God to be His representative. Elsewhere, however, Metatron is associated with Satan.

[26] "Obedience," in this context, means agreeing to marital relations in only the missionary position. The early church fathers, it seems, preferred their women submissive.

[27] These faithful men included monks, who tried to protect their celibacy by tying crucifixes to their unmentionables.

from the Clouded Mountain.[28] We see Lilith in Xaphania, though only as the general of Asriel's forces, not as his wife.

Beyond lust, the concepts of pride and disobedience creep into some versions of the Fall. Islam holds that no angel ever created loved God more than did Lucifer. After God created the angels, he commanded them to bow to no one but Him. And then he created man, whom he held in high esteem. Now God changed his mind and told the angels to bow before Adam. But Lucifer refused to kneel before anyone but his beloved Lord. God, says the Koran, expects obedience,[29] and Lucifer's refusal earned him expulsion from Heaven. While that was a blow, his real punishment was separation from the One he loved most.

An even more prideful Lucifer takes center stage in perhaps the most widely embraced vision of the Fall. As the story goes, Lucifer was beautiful, radiant, and second in power only to God Himself. Eventually, Lucifer decided he and God should be equals, and he raised his throne to the level of God's. Horrified at such impudence, the other angels cast Lucifer from Heaven. The New Testament records that Jesus saw Satan, a Son of God, plunging toward Earth as a lightning bolt. This is the fall of the "Bringer of Light."[30]

Pullmans often credits John Milton's *Paradise Lost* as inspiration for HDM's ideology. Milton writes of Lucifer's fall:

> Lucifer from Heav'n
> (So call him, brighter once amidst the host
> Of Angels, than that Star the Stars among)
> Fell with his flaming legions through the Deep
> Into his place (168).

Some stories have Lucifer and the other fallen angels wandering Earth until the Day of Judgment. Others cast them straight into Hell. The fallen then become demons, with Lucifer or Satan claiming the throne of the pit. Exactly what and where Hell is remains in the mind of the believer. Some see Hell as a fiery underground chamber. Others

---

[28] The Authority's realm, or Heaven. Also called the Chariot.
[29] The traditional meaning, not Lilith's.
[30] Lucifer, also known as "The Morning Star."

see it as frozen. Still others view Hell as right here on Earth.

In the HDM trilogy, Lucifer materializes as Asriel, who is more flesh than spirit.[31] When the story opens, he has been exiled in the frozen waste-lands. But he is gathering his fallen host, and readying them for battle with the Authority[32] and His followers. Asriel's forces include witches, Gallivespians, armored polar bears, men, and ghosts. But the core of his regiment consists of angels.

To this point, the HDM books work well as a nice blend of fantasy and mystic adventure. But then Pullman insists on incorporating science, and for this believer, that is where it falls apart. The problem isn't hovercraft you can control with your mind[33] or opening doorways between universes, something scientists keep looking for ways to do. What bothers me is a little problem with light.

In *The Subtle Knife*, Joachim Lorenz says he sometimes sees angels, "'shining like fireflies, way, way up high'" (121). He is talking to the witch, Ruta Skadi, who looks up to see a flight of angels as "a tiny cluster of lighted beings" (123). When she goes to speak to them, they surround her, "five huge forms glowing in the dark air, lit by an invisible sun" (124).

Later, Serafina Pekkala observes a gathering of angels and perceives them as "beautiful pilgrims of rarified light." She and Ruta Skadi watch them take to the air, "rising like flames into the sky . . . moving like shooting stars toward the north." Ruta Skadi agrees that these angels are much like the ones she saw before. "'Bigger, I think, but the same kind. They have no flesh . . . [a]ll they are is light'" (244–245).

In *The Amber Spyglass*, Asriel sees Dust[34] as "a stream of billions of tiny particles, faintly glowing. They flowed steadily down the tunnel like a river of light." As he follows the Dust fall, he thinks the particles look like "stars of every galaxy in the sky . . . melancholy light to see by" (358).

Pullman tells us that Lyra's Dust, Mary's Shadows, and angels are all made of dark matter. Science tells us dark matter does not shine or reflect light. How, then, can angels be creatures of light? When I first

---

[31] As we've seen, some believe angels who walk the Earth can "clothe" themselves in flesh.

[32] More accurately, the decrepit Authority's stand-in, Metatron.

[33] Who knows what those sneaky Area 51 guys have come up with by now?

[34] And therefore angels, who are made of Dust.

posed this question, I was informed (by a true science fiction aficionado) that a small percentage of dark matter, in the form of angels, would simply "find a way to shine."

That, in my opinion,[35] is like saying single-celled organisms "found a way to evolve." Or that, for some reason never to be discerned, the fabric of space "found a way to expand suddenly," and thus, the Big Bang.[36] It seems to me that science, in fact, implies belief, by saying "it" happened without having the ability to explain how. What Intelligence designed evolution? What unimaginable Power initiated the Big Bang? Why can't science and faith not only interact, but also strengthen each other? Why *can't* physics be "'done to the glory of God'" (*TAS* 393)?

Better minds than my own have considered these questions, and shared my views. In his book *Timaeus*, the Greek philosopher, Plato, writes about cosmology, physics, and the original Creation. He says the cosmos were created by a combination of necessity and intelligence, with intelligence at the helm, ". . . and in this way this universe was constructed from the beginning, through necessity yielding to intelligent persuasion" (quoted in Morrow).

Perhaps Pullman's Authority *was* a poser. Perhaps he coalesced from dark matter, arrived first, and convinced the world that he was the creator, when truly he was neither more nor less than any other angel of his hierarchy. But that does not negate the possibility of a true Creator, one who orchestrated the very roots of science. One whose light is the source of angelic radiance. One whom Pullman claims is dead. But I can see His handiwork, not only in the heavens, but in every living creature.

Then again, I believe.

ELLEN HOPKINS is an award-winning poet and author, with twenty published nonfiction books for children and three young adult novels-in-verse. *Crank* and *Impulse* are New York Times bestsellers. *Burned* was nominated for the 2006 National Book Award. Ellen's fourth novel, *Glass*, publishes August 2007.

---

[35] Which is probably not as humble as it should be.
[36] This one has bothered me for a very long time.

Ellen is the assistant regional advisor for the Sierra Nevada chapter of the Society of Children's Book Writers and Illustrators, and a member of Ash Canyon Poets. She is a Nevada Artist in Residence and a Nevada Arts Council Tumblewords artist.

REFERENCES

Bernthal, Craig. "*Spilt Religion: Philip Pullman's* His Dark Materials." 1 Aug. 2007. <http://www.kirkcenter.org/bookman/44-1-bernthal.html >

Milton, John. *Paradise Lost.* Indianapolis: Hackett Publishing, 2003.

Glenn Morrow, "Necessity and Persuasion in Plato's *Timaeus,*" *The Philosophical Review.* 59 (1950).

Philip Pullman interview. "Phillip Pullman." KidsReads.com. 16 July 2007. <http://www.kidsreads.com/authors/au-pullman-philip.asp>

In Pullman's world, many have presumably asked, "Where do dæmons come from?" In ours, the parallel question is, "Where does the soul live?" For centuries people have wondered if the soul has a physical home inside us—our blood, our hearts, our heads. Examining this question, Vaught takes us on a trip to the very center of the brain, and from there to a possible future in which we may one day literally face our own dæmons.

DÆMONS AND THE HUNT FOR THE HUMAN SOUL

SUSAN VAUGHT

Soul: the animating and vital principle in humans, credited with the faculties of thought, action, and emotion, and often conceived as an immaterial entity (*The American Heritage Dictionary of the English Language*).

Brain: the portion of the vertebrate central nervous system that is enclosed within the cranium, continuous with the spinal cord, and composed of gray matter and white matter. It is the primary center for the regulation and control of bodily activities, receiving and interpreting sensory impulses, and transmitting information to the muscles and body organs. It is also the seat of consciousness, thought, memory, and emotion (*The American Heritage Dictionary of the English Language*).

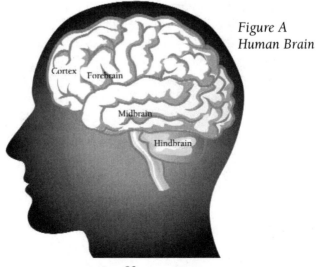

*Figure A
Human Brain*

"Meter means measure," said Pantalaimon. "Like thermometer."
— *THE GOLDEN COMPASS* (70)

Since mankind first postulated that humans possessed souls, one troubling question has captivated scientists and philosophers alike:

If humans do indeed have souls, where *are* they?

Do they have a meter? A measure, as Lyra's dæmon, Pan, defines the term in Philip Pullman's *The Golden Compass*? Can they be snipped and clipped and rearranged like livers, hearts, or elbows? What about sliced, frozen, or preserved? Can a soul be excised from its body, as Mrs. Coulter and the General Oblation Board believe?

If people have this mysterious bit of animating, vital principle, where in the complex human body does it reside?

Before the sixth century, philosophers and scientists such as Aristotle argued that the soul must be in the heart, the blood, or in bodily fluids such as phlegm or bile. To find the soul in this philosophical model, an adventurer into the human body would need to open a door to the chest, walk inside a few steps, and gaze at the starting point—that red beating mass responsible for blood flow and oxygen exchange, the heart.

If no soul became apparent, the explorer would need to examine the blood itself, check its patterns, color, and the force of its movements. Absent success through this method, the explorer would have to turn left or right and make close inspection of the sticky secretions made by the lungs, otherwise known as mucus or phlegm. If that, too, failed, the explorer would need to turn south, walk a few paces, and quantify the bile, or that yellow or green alkaline detergent created in the liver and stored or processed in the gall bladder and pancreas.

The philosopher Hippocrates—a man not unlike Farder Coram in his interests and pursuits—disagreed with these first hypotheses and instead believed reason and intelligence emanated from the brain. The work of British physician Thomas Willis in the 1700s confirmed this, indicating that the brain, not any other organ, ruled human bodies. So, intrepid adventurer, aim for that spot between the eyes, open a door through the skull, step inside, and survey the gelatinous mass of folds and wrinkles. To perform an intercision on a human being in our world, you might have to use the General Oblation Board's terrible silver knife on *this* organ.

In the 1800s, René Descartes, a scientist-philosopher like Lord Asriel, put forth the idea that human souls lie in the pineal gland, a tiny endocrine structure shaped like a pine cone and located in the forebrain near the brain's physical center. To find the pineal gland, open that door between the eyes and walk forward. Then walk forward more, to the middle of the area, and turn slightly downward. Modern science has proved Descartes wrong, however, as it seems this gland regulates melatonin production, not spiritual existence.

In contemporary philosophical thinking, the seat of reason has been shifted into the forebrain, into the cortex itself—that part of the brain closest to the skull, at the top and front of the head. Open that door between the eyes, walk in and step upward a few inches. Maybe even double back a step, and stop. Yes. Right there.

Scientists who study brain and behavior have learned that functions such as language, emotions, judgment, planning, and problem-solving can be directly traced to regions in the cortex. It is a short leap to assume that this area of the brain now lays claim to the soul in the minds of many neurobiological philosophers. After all, the part of human beings directly responsible for thinking and reasoning and talking *must* give rise to the soul—right?

If only the answer were so clear-cut.

The human brain weighs only about three pounds, or approximately 1/40 of the body weight of most people, but it is far more complex than Lyra's alethiometer. Scientists before and after Descartes began studying the brain by attempting to break it into physical regions by its structure. In 1907, German neurologist Korbinian Brodmann came up with fifty-two regions. Since then, brain science and brain imaging have evolved. Now there's Computerized Tomography (CT or CAT scan), Magnetic Resonance Imaging (MRI scan), Functional Magnetic Resonance Imaging (fMRI scan), Positron Emission Tomography (PET scan), Single Photon Emission Computerized Tomography (SPECT scan), Diffuse Optical Imaging (DOT scan), brain mapping, and other techniques.

Someday, scientists may map the human brain gene by gene—creating an infinite number of divisions, areas, and regions to be studied. In fact, the Allen Brain Atlas has already succeeded in offering such a map of the *mouse* brain; see www.brainatlas.org for a sample of how complex and detailed these regions can become—in a mouse brain!

Despite all this technology, entire areas of the human brain remain mysterious to scientists and researchers. To make matters even more complex, functions can vary slightly with respect to location from person to person, from nationality to nationality, between men and women, children and adults, and even right-handed and left-handed people. For example, a right-handed Chinese male might process language in a different location than a left-handed Chinese male. Most assuredly, both will process language in different areas from an American female, irrespective of hand dominance, because in China, people learn to read from right to left instead of from left to right, and that changes brain organization.

Thus, no matter how advanced science has become, no matter where thinkers may shift the seat of reason inside this complicated structure within the human cranium, the ancient debate continues.

Where, oh where, does the material aspect of the soul reside?

Enter Philip Pullman and the alternate-Earth humans showcased in His Dark Materials. In the creation of dæmons for his alternate-Earth humans, Mr. Pullman has entered this ancient philosophical debate and offered his own twist.

Lyra Belacqua and the professors of Jordan College in Oxford might give the answer to the question, "Where is your soul?" more simply and quickly than persons in Will Parry's world—our world.

Souls reside in dæmons, of course.

"Her dear soul, the daring companion of her heart . . ." (TGC 248). Lyra's description of Pantalaimon, rendered after she almost lost him to Mrs. Coulter and the General Oblation Board's dark experiments, makes that clear.

But do dæmons qualify as souls by the definitions used in this world? Yes.

Dæmons have names, shapes, and voices all their own, unique to each person when they "settle" on a shape in adulthood. As Lyra's friend, the able seaman, notes, "'There's plenty of folk as'd like to have a lion as a dæmon and they end up with a poodle'" (TGC 14). The final shape and form of each person's dæmon is based on his or her experience and personality, even his or her role in life. Servants in Lyra's world invariably manifest dog dæmons, for example, and the higher level the servant, the fancier the dog.

No one can travel far from their dæmon unless they happen to be a witch. "'It was such a strange tormenting feeling when your dæmon was pulling at the link between you,'" Lyra reflects, "'part physical pain deep in the chest, part intense sadness and love'" (*TGC* 170). When Pan makes a point by attempting to walk away from her and they ultimately reunite, Lyra notes that she would rather die than go through that again. "[I]t would send her mad with grief and terror" (*TGC* 171).

If a human's dæmon dies, the human is rendered less than whole, pathetic, to be pitied like the severed children. And ultimately, their body dies, the way little Tony Makarios's did when he was cut away from his dæmon, Ratter. Likewise, if a human's body dies, their dæmon winks out of existence. Certainly, then, dæmons are a vital and animating principal for the people of Lyra's world. Dæmons possess a portion of one's guiding thought, action, and emotion, and are inextricably linked with the humans to whom they are attached. As such, they appear to qualify as souls by the definition of this world.

But if Lyra and her friends and kin have their souls outside their bodies, and our souls are believed to reside inside the brain, does that mean their brains are fundamentally different from ours? Is Lyra's brain constructed in some alternate fashion, or seated differently in her skull?

No—or not necessarily.

Human brains in this world are quite capable of generating dæmons, just like the ones found attached to the people of Lyra's Oxford. Of course, the sensory reality of those dæmons to people who are not experiencing them might remain questionable. But human brains of this world *can* achieve dæmon production.

As early as 1922, humans in this world have had documented experiences with creatures very much like dæmons. The French neurologist Jean Lhermitte was the first to describe patients who reported experiencing unusual vivid, complex visual perceptions related to lesions in, or damage to, certain areas of the brain. More specifically, these people reported seeing formed, visual images of people, animals, plants, scenes, or geometric patterns, in full color. In fact, the first case Dr. Lhermitte described involved a patient who saw common animals such as chickens, in addition to people in costumes, or children at play. Later cases reported by other doctors involved patients who reported seeing animals such as dogs, lions, or pheasants.

A few years later, Belgian neuropathologist Ludo van Bogaert began to call this type of experience *peduncular hallucinosis*. Despite the fact that the phenomenon is called *hallucinosis*—hallucinations, or false, unreal visual perceptions usually caused by physical or mental illness—the fascinating thing is that these visual perceptions cannot be traced to central nervous system illness, psychiatric illness, or sensory illness (damage in areas important to visual functioning and visual processing).

More importantly, the visual images do not involve loss of contact with reality. In other words, the people seeing and experiencing these animals and other vivid visual perceptions do not appear to be insane, suffering from delusions, or having other problems with living in, or interacting with, the "real world." The images do not frighten patients, but instead interest them, comfort them, fascinate and capture them, or even amuse them, as Pan often does Lyra. In one memorable scene from *The Golden Compass*, Lyra reports standing "shivering in the fo'c'sle," but "laughed with delight as her beloved Pantalaimon, sleek and powerful, leaped from the water with half a dozen other swift gray shapes" (146). Lyra enjoys seeing what her dæmon might choose to do, just as the people in our world who experience peduncular hallucinations often enjoy the antics of what they see.

Some patients believe the objects (most frequently animals) they see are not real, while others believe they are not only real, but tangible, with color and texture. A few patients even interact with or hold conversations with the objects.

Because of all these factors, the argument has been made—and continues to be made—that this phenomenon does not represent classical hallucinations at all. Instead, peduncular hallucinosis appears to arise from damage to, or differences in, the actual brain itself.

Thus, the question becomes, given the science of this world, is it possible to locate that exact part of the human brain responsible for peduncular hallucinosis?

Yes.

Open that door between the eyes and walk forward. Keep going, plunging through the chosen region of modern philosophers, the cortex. There are lots of ridges and valleys to cross (called *sulci* and *gyri*; huge valleys, or very big gyri, are called fissures). Scale them all.

Proceed through the region of most fascination to Descartes, the pineal gland at the edge of the forebrain. Now go a step farther.

Enter the "older" and sometimes less understood region of the brain, and turn south for a few steps.

Welcome to the midbrain.

Above the midbrain hangs all that cortex and forebrain, like a big ceiling. Very little stretches out below it, however. There's hardly a floor, more like a thick beanstalk; it's called the hindbrain, and it's something that many animals and even reptiles and "lower life forms" possess. Refer back to the picture at the beginning of this essay to see how insulated and cushioned this region of the brain seems. Very protected. Hidden from view unless you do a lot of prodding and cutting.

The perfect place to hide a soul, perhaps?

Maybe. . . .

As case reports dating back almost ninety years suggest, people in Will Parry's world—our own world—generate dæmon-like perceptions when this area of the brain is damaged, stimulated, or affected in usual ways. Based on Pullman's exposition in the books that comprise His Dark Materials, the people in Lyra's world likely generate dæmons and hold that powerful connection with their external souls right here, in this special, shielded, centralized region of the brain.

Even the symptoms Lyra suffers when Pantalaimon walks away from her hint that the midbrain is the likely connecting point. When Lyra goes too far from Pan during her childish experiments, she experiences pain, anguish, longing, worry, and autonomic arousal such as shortness of breath or hyperventilation, a flushed face, and sweating. This separation syndrome is apparently common to most people in her world, and continues until the dæmon and human are once more united or in close enough proximity. Separation, in and of itself, does not produce lasting wounds if the connection between human and dæmon is not severed. Thus, this could be likened to "stimulation" of the connection as opposed to "damage" to it.

In this world, abnormal stimulation of a person's midbrain would result in shaking, drooping eyelids, abnormal eye movements, pupil dilation, hyperventilation, possible production of tears, possible autonomic arousal, and in some cases, even loss of consciousness. Thus, the effects are quite similar, if not identical, and reinforce the idea that dæmons and dæmon-like experiences are connected to the human midbrain.

But the witches in Lyra's world can travel far from their dæmons, or even send their dæmons to do tasks completely separate from the witch-es themselves. Do the abilities of the witches mean that dæmons are not truly connected to the human brain in Pullman's trilogy?

No.

The witches of Lyra's world have learned to overcome, or at least endure, the sensations typically generated by separation from dæmons. Can we find models for similar behavior in our world, where people learn to override basic brain functions to the point that their abilities seem like magic?

Yes.

Even small children in our world experiment with this, just as Lyra did when she distanced herself from Pan to see how much she could stand. Children (and adults) in our world conduct such tests by holding their fin-gers over flames, running as far as lungs and muscles allow, or even com-peting in body-challenging sports such as gymnastics, wrestling, power-lift-ing, or boxing. The question is the same: How much pain and challenge can the body—or more importantly, the mind—endure?

The witches in Lyra's world can be likened to persons who have taken this question to heart and pursued it as a lifestyle. In our world, yogis, mystics, magicians, fakirs, and swamis such as the renowned Himalayan masters can and do learn to exert voluntary control over functions such as heart rate, blood flow, flexibility, and breathing. They can control these functions, which are usually regulated automatically through aspects of the midbrain and even the more primitive hindbrain, just as witch queen Serafina Pekkala controls the sensations of separation when she sends her snow goose dæmon, Kaisa, far from her physical body. It stands to reason that, if swept into Lyra's world, our yogis, mystics, magicians, fakirs, and swamis might quickly seek out Serafina Pekkala and associate with her clan. The groups might have much to teach each other.

So, do Pullman's dæmons, with their midbrain qualities and our pow-erful reactions to them as readers, hint at the anatomical location of the material aspect of souls in this world? Might the physical correlate of our souls be located not in the cortex or forebrain, but in the midbrain?

Possibly.

Literature or creative arts frequently foreshadow science. History is rife with examples of literary creations becoming reality, or close to reality— of speculative fiction (science fiction and fantasy) either sparking or guiding scientific exploration, or imagining where that exploration will go a few (hundred) years before it occurs. Examples of this include, but certainly are not limited to, robotics (Isaac Asimov's *I, Robot*, published in 1950), genetic experiments (H. G. Wells's *The Island of Dr. Moreau*, published in 1896), and even helicopters (rudimentary sketches done by Da Vinci in the 1400s). It is possible, then, that from the well of creativity, truths float to the surface that humans otherwise cannot grasp, and cannot yet begin to prove.

With the advent and increasing use of neurotechnology such as Deep Brain Stimulation, which involves placing a small device called a brain pacemaker into the brain tissue in order to treat conditions such as Parkinson's disease, more possibilities arise. If we could locate the human soul in the brain, perhaps we could intermittently—or continuously—stimulate that area with electrical impulses.

If our souls do lie in the midbrain, stimulating the area with a device like the brain pacemaker could allow us to "see" our own souls. We could speak to them as Lyra and the people in her world do, converse with them and see what form or shape, whether it be animal, plant, or otherwise, they would assume. We could have them for constant companions, and learn from them as Lyra often learns from Pan. We could connect more closely with others by allowing our souls to touch on a literal, not just metaphysical, level. Additionally, genetic mapping of human brains might allow us to know the building blocks of different types of souls. Combining this knowledge with the stimulation technique described above, we might be able to intervene with evil-leaning souls, do direct "talk therapy," or other behavioral work to heal troubled souls, and perhaps work toward healing troubled aspects of the world as a whole.

By giving us dæmons with distinctly midbrain qualities, Mr. Pullman has tossed his hat into the ring in the pursuit of the soul's location, whether he intended to or not. In years to come, as gene-by-gene mapping of human brains progresses, we may discover whether he was visionary, or merely brilliantly creative and entertaining—already a given. As with all great and deep literature, His Dark Materials gives us ample food for speculation—and exploration.

SUSAN VAUGHT is the author of *Trigger*, which was called "A powerful cautionary tale" by *Publisher's Weekly* in a starred review, and *Stormwitch*, winner of the Carl Brandon Society Kindred Award. Both were named Best Books for Young Adults by the American Library Association. She is a practicing neuropsychologist and lives with her family and dozens of pets in rural Tennessee.

FASCINATING RESOURCES

Churchland, Patricia Smith. *Neurophilosophy: Toward a Unified Science of the Mind-Brain*. Cambridge, Massachusetts: MIT Press, 1989.

Damasio, António. *Looking for Spinoza: Joy, Sorrow, and the Feeling Brain*. New York: Harcourt, 2003.

Goldberg, Stephen. *Clinical Neuroanatomy Made Ridiculously Simple* (3rd Edition; Book & CD-ROM). Miami, Florida: Medmaster, 2007.

Grayling, Anthony Clifford. *Descartes: The Life and Times of a Genius*. New York: Walker, 2006.

But wait, perhaps we do have dæmons! With us every day, they grow and learn alongside us, storing images, songs and memories, slowly becoming extensions of our very souls. Until their hard drives crash, that is, and we find ourselves horribly severed, suddenly alone.

GHOST IN THE MACHINE

DIANA PETERFREUND

My first reading of *The Golden Compass* left quite an impression on me: I started having recurring nightmares about intercision. I began cautioning friends who had bought the novel for their seven-year-olds (fresh off reading Narnia) and recommending the book to folks who like to be scared. Forget Stephen King; I've got Philip Pullman. But where the master of horror capitalizes on the everyday object or circumstance (rabid dogs, killer automobiles) in order to inspire fear in his readership, Pullman evokes terror through a form of torture completely alien to our own experience.[1]

It is telling that, of all the pain inflicted on the characters throughout the trilogy—severed fingers, watching a loved one die and knowing you are the cause, being shot, nearly bleeding to death, realizing that you are a murderer, having your brains dashed out, losing a newfound love forever—not one is written with the same depth and visceral detail Pullman devotes to the physical and emotional anguish you have the potential to experience when your soul lives outside your body.

Dæmons are the most beloved and most commented-upon aspect of the books—an emblem of the series, more so than the Tolkienesque objects (alethiometer, knife, spyglass) that lend their names to each title. The story begins and ends with dæmons, and dæmons and their nature are crucial to every turning point in the trilogy.

---

[1] Though there is an argument to be made that hurting children—innocents—as the Oblation Board does is a universal outrage, even if we can't quite relate to the form the torture takes.

In *The Subtle Knife*, the supremacy of dæmon-related distress is made explicit when, in chapter two, Mrs. Coulter fails to get information out of a witch through standard methods of torture (breaking fingers), but in Cittàgazze in chapter fifteen, she overcomes all resistance in a matter of paragraphs with the simple, devastating formula of Specter + dæmon. The witch in question "could have resisted any torture but what was happening to her dæmon now" (*TSK* 277).

Yet you don't have to read to the end of the second book to realize this. Pullman's genius lies in the speed and subtlety with which he makes a world with dæmons seem not only acceptable, but natural. By the time we reach the nightmare-inducing scene in chapter twelve of *The Golden Compass*, where Lyra travels to the Arctic village and finds poor Tony Makarios and his pathetic scrap of dried fish, we share her gut-deep horror at the abomination of a severed child. The word "Ratter" is still enough to cause goose bumps to break out over my skin, and the scene in which Lyra carves the dæmon's name into a coin to place in the dead boy's mouth never fails to move me to tears.

I had no dæmon, but that didn't stop me from speculating upon what form my soul might take in Lyra's world. The childhood game of, "If you were an animal, what would you be?" turned into Lyra and her friends' very real contemplation as to what animal their dæmons would "settle" as. I remember anticipating Lyra's reaction when she comes across Will Parry in the second book. However, just as she can recognize, on sight, that Serafina Pekkala's far-ranging Kaisa is not a bird, but a dæmon, she is also able to discern that Will, despite the lack of animal familiar, is no severed child. His soul is simply inside of him. Lyra's periodic curiosity as to the shape of Will's invisible dæmon ("it would express a nature that was savage, and courteous, and unhappy" [*TSK* 24]) is a reminder that our dæmons exist, even if we can't see them.

Or recognize them for what they are.

Days after I first finished *The Golden Compass*, my computer died. Lancelot the Laptop (yes, I named it) had been a gift from my brother, and it's no exaggeration to call the machine my constant companion. It was the repository for every piece of writing I'd ever done, the bearer of memory in the form of more than a thousand photos of my journeys abroad, and the medium through which I accessed the world: e-mail, iTunes, blogs, news sites, even television shows.

I was bereft. I carried it to the Apple Store, mournfully clutching its case to my chest as a woman might cradle an ailing infant, and begged the repair staff (called "geniuses" in the company parlance) to help me save it. They took it, clucked their tongues sadly over its prospects, and told me to leave it with them for a few days.

This is when the trouble really started. When I wasn't haunting the Apple Store, hoping that making friends with the geniuses would encourage them to work harder to resuscitate Lancelot, I was at home, tapping away on my boyfriend's ancient Dell (named Red, if you're curious) and growing increasingly agitated. Red was not Lancelot. Nothing was Lancelot. What would I do without my laptop? I had nothing. Not my passwords or bookmarks, not my friends' e-mails, not my hard-earned work. (Yes, I know that I should have become acquainted with a little something called a back-up drive. Lesson learned.) Meanwhile, my beloved laptop was lying, cold and powered down, in some storeroom in the mall, and there was a big empty space next to my mouse. What were we without one another?

Finally, my boyfriend noticed my despair. "Are you okay? You're not acting like yourself."

"I'm not myself," I snapped. "I've been severed."

Initially, I was joking. I'd lost my computer; I hadn't been permanently—and fatally—relieved of my soul. But the more thought I gave to my retort, the more I realized that it made a lot of sense. My laptop did indeed fulfill many of the roles associated with dæmons in Lyra's world.

Like the soul-spirit-consciousness makeup of dæmons, my laptop was largely devoted to increasing both my wisdom and my experience. Pantalaimon revels in each of Lyra's adventures. As Lyra acclimates to life on a gyptian boat, Pan changes into a dolphin and relishes an aquatic existence. When Lyra climbs mountains, he becomes a gamboling mountain goat; when she envies the dragonfly mounts of her Gallivespian companions, he turns into a flitting insect. Similarly, my laptop stored sense-memories of all my own most precious experiences—photos that in a minute could take me from the volcanic cliff faces of New Zealand to the underwater vistas of the Great Barrier Reef. And, as Lyra often uses Pan to find out information she can't by talking to other people's dæmons, flying up and surveying the countryside from a vantage point she can't reach, or merely giving her the straight dope on things that don't "feel right," my computer can tell me virtually anything I need to know. What are the helpful "if you liked X, try Y" cookies on sites such as Amazon or Netflix if not the result of dæmon communication? My computer knew I'd like a movie before I did!

In other words, whenever I used it, I attracted a ton of Dust. (Perhaps that's why I needed to clean the screen so often.) We are told that Mrs. Coulter's dæmon-less zombis have no fear and no imagination. However, the dead, also sans-dæmon, seem to have both. Otherwise, they would not be able to tell those stories that the harpies require as the price of passage through the land of the dead, nor would they fear the harpies' Authority-given ability to torture them with their own sins. This seeming contradiction shows that Mrs. Coulter's experiments are for naught—dividing you from your dæmon will not free you from the "taint" of Dust.

In addition, when I was with my laptop, I was never subject to that most desolate of Pullmanian horrors: being alone. Both Lyra and Will constantly allude to being alone as their greatest fear and/or greatest burden. Lyra pities Will for his lack of external dæmon to keep him company in times of stress, and she asks the armored bear Iorek Byrnison if he is "lonely" without his. Will reflects upon his friendless life and the lack of support he has received from his parents. (One wonders why he never bothered getting online in his world.) With Lancelot's help, I had access to every single one of my friends over e-mail, not to mention dozens of blogs and other Internet communities that were, if anything, overactive.

Finally, and perhaps most effectively, a computer (and through it, an online persona) is not you, but a reflection of you. Like the hissing polecat Pantalaimon becomes whenever Lyra is on a particularly violent tear, it can be a distillation or amplification of some aspect of your personality. Or it can reveal a part of your nature to the Web that no one would ever suspect if they knew you "in real life." Upon their first meeting at the house of Sir Charles in *The Subtle Knife*, Will marvels that the lovely Mrs. Coulter and her evil monkey are "one being" (180). Mrs. Coulter, like Dorian Gray, manages to consign her soul's ugliness elsewhere—in this case, into the form of the deadly, golden dæmon. While she lounges in the cave, bored, at the opening of *The Amber Spyglass*, her soul's manifestation entertains itself by torturing small animals. How many computer users, through the utilization of snarky anonymous blogs, "trolling," or even far more disturbing means, indulge their malevolent sides online?

In the trilogy, there is great emphasis on what your dæmon's form says about you. Once you see your dæmon's adult shape, "'you'll know the sort of person you are,'" as the gyptian with the seagull dæmon explained to Lyra in the first book (*TGC* 147). Servants and other obedient followers become dogs; witches' far-ranging and fierce dæmons are always birds; and in one unlucky instance in *The Golden Compass* we learn of a man whose dæmon settled as a dolphin, forever limiting him to a life at sea. But if my dæmon were a computer—specifically a laptop—what would that say about me? That I'm a wordy know-it-all who likes to travel? How different is the soul of a laptop person who has a Mac versus one who carries a PC?[2]

Or maybe the computer itself is not the dæmon, but merely the object through which we can access it. Just as Dr. Mary Malone needs the Cave or the amber spyglass to view Dust, maybe we can't get to our dæmons without the machines. And perhaps it is through online avatars, with their multitude of shapes and ability to physically reflect the personality of their owners, that the people of our world come closest to possessing a dæmon.

There are different kinds of avatars. First there are the square-shaped icons that commonly appear next to postings on Internet forums, blogs, or instant message windows. Regular visitors to these sites (or regular IM partners) learn to recognize the writer of a posting by his or her icon as much as they do by his or her screen name—if not more—and great care is taken by users to choose the icon avatars that best represent them. In some cases, such as the blog platform LiveJournal, a user can choose from several icons, perhaps according to his or her mood or the topic under discussion. Presenting yourself as tough? Maybe an image of *Battlestar Galactica*'s Starbuck blowing smoke rings. Whimsical? Try a big-eyed manga waif surrounded by sparkles. Such usage is very similar to Pantalaimon in mood-ring mode.

However, just as the shifting dæmon is one that belongs to an undeveloped

---

[2] The current "I'm a Mac" advertising campaign takes this idea to the extreme, representing each computer with a human counterpart: a pudgy, be-suited middle-aged man for a PC, and an attractive young hipster in blue jeans for the Mac. The point is clear: if your computer has a soul, this is what it looks like.

child, so the two-dimensional Internet forum icons are a type of avatar that is not yet fully realized. To see the true potential of virtual avatars, one must look at their manifestation within the realm of online role-playing games: from the text-based MUDs (Multi-User Dimensions) of the last century—in which an avatar is nothing more than a few lines of description—to the more advanced and elaborate three-dimensional constructs of MMORPGs (Massive Multiplayer Online Role-Playing Games)—some of which give users the ability to make their avatars take any shape they'd like. For instance, in the game *Second Life*, an entire economy has arisen in which graphic artists earn real money designing clothes, skins, hairstyles, facial features, and more for the user who desires an avatar with a very specific appearance.

In *The Golden Compass*, a gyptian tells Lyra that there are plenty of people who want their dæmons to be lions instead of poodles. Of course, our avatars are much easier to hide behind than the soul-baring physical form of the dæmon. We can even subvert our "natural selves" entirely and become a different kind of person. Online, a person who is mostly poodle-y can indulge his or her desire to be more of a lion through a ferocious game avatar.

Other games, such as the enormously popular *World of Warcraft*, have more limited parameters when it comes to a user's choice of avatar. In *World of Warcraft*, a user can choose from a set of "races" (elf, human, troll, etc.) and classes (warrior, priest, hunter, etc.) before performing minor customization regarding such details as hair color or skin tone. And yet, even within these restrictions, users find a way to make these characters their own. Many players insist that there are "types." People who play priests, whose main concern is to stand back from the battles and heal, have a different personality than those who play warriors, who dive headlong into battle. When I play the game with my boyfriend, characters will often ask my character (as dæmons wheedle information from other dæmons) if the two avatars they see are a couple "in real life."

As with the dæmons of Lyra's world, it is common for gamers to create avatars of the opposite sex. The shaman John Parry is amazed to discover that "part of [his] nature was female, and bird formed, and beautiful" (*TSK* 189), and such a revelation is not unusual for those who choose to connect with their feminine or masculine sides through online avatars. In his 1999 book *My Tiny Life*, journalist Julian Dibbell devotes three months to playing a MUD, and discovers his niche once he creates a female avatar named Samantha: "For here was the second surprise about being Samantha: it felt delicious. It felt soft, and graceful, and sexually alluring . . . and several other ideally feminine things I thought myself too sophisticated to imagine" (Dibbell 127). In Samantha, Dibbell created his first "morph," or true alter-ego. Rather than playing a role, he slipped inside, and got in touch with his feminine side, a feat that the men of our world often find difficult to do unless, like John Parry, they blunder into Lyra's universe and meet their feminine-aspect dæmons face-to-face.

Naturally, an avatar is a personal construct, and playing with, or otherwise manipulating, someone else's is every bit as much a taboo as touching another person's dæmon is in Lyra's world. It is indeed a telling moment in *The Amber Spyglass* when Will and Lyra grab each other's identical dæmons and it hardly fazes them, whereas in the first book, at Bolvangar, dæmon-touching is portrayed in the same terms often used to describe molestation: "She *felt* those hands. . . . It wasn't *allowed*. . . . Not *supposed* to touch . . . Wrong . . ." (*TGC* 241). In fact, the main storyline in *My Tiny Life* deals with the aftermath of a virtual "rape"—a player who hacked into the system in such a way that he could force other players' avatars to appear to commit obscene acts. Now, more than a decade and a half later, similar (though less violent) programs are incorporated into games as a matter of course. *World of Warcraft* features "spells" that can make avatars flee in random directions or break into dance. However, it is still assumed that, in general, only one person plays any given avatar, and is responsible for that character's actions. Having their accounts hacked and their avatars utilized (or, more commonly, stripped of their hard-won possessions) is most players' greatest fear.

Still, despite these similarities, I felt uneasy making too many comparisons between the soul-manifestation of a dæmon and a bit of plastic that Steve Jobs & Co. were telling me was toast. After all, humans in Lyra's world don't create their own dæmons; they can't (much to the dismay of Iofur Raknison). Possession of a dæmon is clearly what makes a human *human* in *The Golden Compass*, but people aren't the only creatures in Lyra's world with consciousness.

Pullman avoids ever making a pronouncement on where the armored bears fall on the spectrum of creation. Gallivespians have (invisible) dæmons, since Tialys and the Lady Salmakia leave *something* on the shore of the land of the dead, and are inspired to help Lyra so that, when they die, they will not be trapped in that horrible netherworld. The wheeled *mulefa* are similarly Dust-covered "people," and Lyra also sees them in the land of the dead. But, throughout *The Golden Compass*, there is an emphasis on the fact that bears are *not* humans, and if they try to become so—as the usurper Iofur Raknison does with his gilt and his castle and his rag-doll "dæmon"—they not only fail, but they also lose that which makes them worthy as bears. Angels, who *are* Dust, are spirit and soul without the body. Are armored bears body and spirit without the soul? What would Mary Malone see were she to turn her spyglass upon Iorek?[3]

And yet Iorek, one of the most finely-drawn characters in the series, is much more like *people* than the Dust-free "grazers" Mary meets in the *mulefa's* world. He forms alliances, loves Lyra and Lee Scoresby, and, most noticeably, forges armor through the kind of craftsmanship that we know, from Mary's studies, creates/attracts Dust. If a scrawl on a bit of bone can be covered with Dust, Iorek's armor must be gilded with it!

It is this armor and Iorek's other ingenious bits of metalwork (reforging the subtle knife, making a prison for the spy fly) that lift him above the rank of animal. Without it, the bear is a wastrel, content to live his life performing meaningless service at a pub and drinking himself into oblivion to dull the pain of his loss. When he is exiled from the *panserbjørne*, his armor is taken away, and until he reforges it with "sky metal," he considers himself "incomplete." Upon hearing this, Lyra proclaims that "'bears can make their own souls'" (*TGC* 197).

The fact that a true bear's armor is made of "sky metal" is another indication of the presence of Dust, which also falls from the sky. By comparison, Iofur Raknison's weaker armor, which he does not view as soul-sufficient, is made from earth metal. It is Iofur's inability to recognize the nature of the bear-soul that leads to his downfall. Armor and the Dust-attracting workmanship of raw materials are not enough for him, and

---

[3] Despite Mary Malone's references to St. Paul's body/spirit/soul construct, the pieces (big surprise) do not line up exactly in His Dark Materials, since one would think that Dust, consciousness, "that which belongs to all of creation," would be the story's approximation to "spirit," and that the ghosts, which possess personality, are "souls." Yet dæmons are often likened to a "soul" in the text and have individual personality to boot. So for the purposes of this article, "soul" shall correlate to "dæmon," and "spirit" to the "ghost" that remains after death or intercision. Sorry, Paul.

thus he is made even less than what he was. He can be tricked and lied to, which is not natural for a bear, and in the end Iorek kills him in the most animalistic way possible—he tears off his jaw, rendering Iofur incapable of "human" speech.[4]

In this way, Iorek's armor serves a similar function to the wheels of the *mulefa*. The *mulefa*, despite being every bit as developed as humans, are not born with "dæmons" or the higher consciousness that marks them with Dust. It isn't until they become adults and learn to work the wheel and utilize the Dust-enhanced seed pod oil that they become complete, Dust-renewing people. Their story of the Fall paints a *positive* picture of the temptation of the serpent—for the gentle *mulefa*, the birth of wisdom and technology and the redemption of the soul are one and the same.[5]

So if the *mulefa* can cultivate the outward manifestation of their souls through agriculture and road trips, and the *panserbjørne* can forge theirs in meteorites and fire, then how come the humans of our world can't create their own as well? Why can't our dæmons be pixellated avatars, or the technology we have developed to learn and grow and communicate with others? For, according to Pullman, Dust-renewal depends on the work of people increasing wisdom in the universe: the more work, the more craft, the more Dust.[6]

A few days after I first turned over my computer to the geniuses at the Apple Store, they gave me the bad news. My computer was a goner. It was possible, they said, to retrieve some of the information on my hard drive, but as for most of my saved addresses, bookmarks, and other familiar interfaces, I would have to start over. And so, taking as my example Iorek Byrnison, who reforged his armor after his exile from Svalbard, I bought myself a new computer. Turning it on for the first time was a joyful revelation. It wasn't the same, just as Pan changes as a result of his long separation from Lyra in the land of the dead. And yet, like Lyra's new, witch-like dæmon, maybe I got an upgrade. My dear, white iBook G3 was no

[4] *Cf.* the Talking Beasts of Narnia, whose status as superior creatures depends totally upon their ability to speak.
[5] It is notable that the *mulefa*, of all the creatures in the trilogy, are the ones whose bodies (the "'best part,'" as the angels tell Will in *The Amber Spyglass* [392]) are most closely integrated with the workings of Dust. Perhaps this is the reason only they can see it with their naked eyes.
[6] With the exception of that supreme bit of human technology, the subtle knife, which upon application actually serves as both a Dust-drainer and a Dust-eater.

more. Lancelot, and all he entailed, was lost forever. But now I had a brand-new white iBook G4, with a bigger hard drive (and a back-up), a better operating system, and, best of all, the potential to reclaim all the knowledge, all the Dust, that I'd collected before.

I named him Pantalaimon.

DIANA PETERFREUND writes adult fiction for Bantam Dell, and young adult fantasy for Harper Collins. She was raised in Florida and graduated from Yale University in 2001 with degrees in geology and literature. A former food critic and an avid traveler, she now resides in Washington D.C. Her first book, *Secret Society Girl*, was named to the New York Public Library's Books For the Teen Age list. When she's not writing, Diana volunteers at the National Zoo monitoring beautiful golden monkeys and spends entirely too much time online. Her Web site is dianapeterfreund.com.

REFERENCES

Dibbell, Julian. *My Tiny Life: Crime and Passion in a Virtual World*. New York: Henry Holt and Company, 1998.

"I want a dæmon! Why don't I have a dæmon?" wonders many a reader of His Dark Materials. Constant companion, faithful confidant, best friend forever of your dreams . . . what's not to love about dæmons? But Caletti asks if perhaps there are some very sound reasons why our souls are hidden on the inside.

WHERE YOU LEAD, I WILL FOLLOW
The Joys and Perils of Dæmon Ownership

DEB CALETTI

The concept of dæmons has been called Philip Pullman's most masterful idea — "a coup," according to Michael Chabon. Pullman snitched the notion from Socrates, and then made it his own. Socrates' *daimon* was his own sense of a divine presence within — an early warning detection system, something like your own inner smoke alarm, except you never have to get on a chair and change the batteries. Pullman's dæmons, on the other hand, aren't wispy inside entities, but take a real, physical shape — your dæmon is your creature companion that represents who you most are; your walking, talking soul in animal form. (And for all you who've already decided that the guy next to you has a donkey for a dæmon, knock that off). Mrs. Coulter in *The Golden Compass* is cool and calculating, sleek and crafty, and her dæmon is a golden monkey. The commanding Lord Asriel's dæmon is a snow leopard. Servants generally have dogs; warriors have wolves. A person's dæmon becomes fixed at puberty (a better prize, it seems, than a first bra or a squeaky, breaking voice), so our child heroine, Lyra, who is sometimes bratty and spoiled, plucky and brave, adventurous and restless, has a dæmon, Pantalaimon, who shifts from moth to mouse to ermine to wildcat.

But Pullman's concept is more than simply great invention — the idea of a dæmon, a dæmon of your own, is *enticing*, the kind of enticing that requires your mind to roll this proposal around and around like a hard butterscotch candy in your mouth. *What dæmon would I have?* If you can read *The Golden Compass* and not ask the question. . . . Well, you can't

103

read *The Golden Compass* and not ask the question. It's irresistible. The same way that those quizzes in magazines are irresistible: *What Does Your Favorite Color Say about You? What's Your Love Style? Who Are You—Chocolate Brownie, Strawberry Cheesecake, or Apple Pie?* The same way that quickie zodiac signs are irresistible: *Capricorns are even-tempered and have an eye for beauty. . . . You're a flirt, Gemini, and are the last to leave a party!* Here is where the idea veers from whimsy to genius—the dæmon-thought flicks at the deepest, darkest, hungriest places of our humanity: our desire to know ourselves. Our sometimes/often fear of being alone. The need to see ourselves as unique and separate, coupled with the contrary need to unite with and take comfort in "other." Pullman pokes at those vulnerabilities of ours, then lures us with a tempting, comfy solution that our weakest parts feel good swimming around in for awhile. Permanent self-knowledge. An ever-constant companion. A dæmon.

Would you really want it?

Let's review the rules. In addition to reflecting your true spirit, your dæmon is usually of the opposite sex. Pullman felt that this would give a wholeness to the pair, a sort of yin/yang completion. A perfect life companion—minus the in-laws, having to share your closet, and that annoying something's-stuck-in-the-garbage-disposal sound he makes when he brushes his teeth. Just you and mini-you, in perfect harmony. It goes everywhere you go, which means that if it needs water to live, you must be near the water always. In fact, your dæmon cannot be separated from you without great physical pain. When you die, it dissolves; if it is harmed, you will be, too.

Oh, and one small but important detail: You don't get to choose. You are who you are (darn it), just like in real life. So while it's fun to figure out if you'd want your dæmon to be something cheery and helpful like a ladybug, or elegant and fast like a gazelle, or cozy and friendly like a Labrador (in spite of the lowered social status of servant), this isn't about how you'd like to be. This isn't about how you'd like to have others see you. This is about who you are at your ugliest or most ravishing core.

Kind of wipes out the puppies and kitties, doesn't it, then, if we're being honest? Opens the doors to crows and snakes and ostriches that spit. I know a few people who'd have shark dæmons and other animals that eat their young, and a handful of others who'd possess something plodding but well-intentioned, like a draught horse, maybe. Definitely there are peacocks. Alpha male gorillas and prima donna birds playing songstress on a tree branch. So, what's your dæmon? Are you, at your soul, a chimpanzee? An ant that will carry a bread crumb twenty times its own size on its back for the good of others? A smart, playful, communicative dolphin (which, in a completely irrelevant side note, or maybe not, is one of the few other creatures besides humans to fool around for the fun of it and not just for mating purposes)? It helps to know your animal facts for this game.

In a 2002 BBC interview, Philip Pullman was asked what his own dæmon would be. He said that of course you can't choose your dæmon, but if he could choose, he might select something attractive and beautiful and photogenic, things he felt he wasn't. What he really would be, he guessed, was a bird—a Jackdaw or a Magpie, nothing beautiful to look at, but a creature that collected shiny things like diamond rings and aluminum foil. "That is what storytellers do," he said. "We look for bright, shiny interesting bits of gossip or bits of news or bits of information that reveal a character or something. And we collect them all and take them back to our nest; so that is what I think my dæmon probably would be, but I can't choose and I don't know."

I love that last line, the way he settles the angst of the just-right answer: "I can't choose, and I don't know." Reflecting on the question, my own reply would be similar—to plead the Fifth, on the grounds that the answer might incriminate me. Which brings up the first problem in the enticing idea of a dæmon companion. We want to be seen, sure. We want to be known and to know ourselves. But would we really want to be completely revealed? To wear our soul on our sleeve? All the time? We, who love our Cover Girl and beef-me-up power drinks, clothes that hide and reconfigure, the white lie: *Yes, I floss. I'm a flexible self-starter. Spontaneous, adventurous HWP female seeks same.*

I wonder if this idea is even wise. To confess your Labrador nature to the golden monkey is a bit like exposing your zebra throat to the lion. Nature encourages hiding for self-protection; we have built-in subterfuge for our survival. A piece of coral is not a piece of coral, but a fish. That twig is really an insect. We don't give our relationship history and credit card number to some guy we just met. You guard those deep pieces because they should not be shared with golden monkeys and lions and opportunists. But with a dæmon—you can run but you can't hide. Your soul walks or flies or swims beside you, advertising to all what you most are.

That your dæmon settles at puberty and becomes your fixed identity is something that bothers me, too, as it does Lyra. She discusses this with a seaman on board the ship bound for Trollesund with John Faa, Farder Coram, and the others, as she stands on deck and watches Pantalaimon play joyfully in the sea. She asks the seaman why the dæmons have to settle, and he tells her that they've always settled and always will—that it's part of growing up. He tells her that at some point she'll want a settled form for Pantalaimon, but Lyra doesn't believe him. She will never want that, she insists, and I'm rather inclined to believe her. Still, the seaman assures her that she'll want to grow up like the other girls, and that there are compensations for a settled form, compensations that include knowing yourself and what kind of person you are. The seaman describes his own dæmon, Belisaria, a seagull. He understands the choice—she's not grand or splendid, but she's strong and a survivor, and she can find food and company anywhere. That's who the seaman is, and he's content with this knowledge. But Lyra is still not so sure. When she asks again, her question even seems a bit pleading:

> "But suppose your dæmon settles in a shape you don't like?"
> "Well, then, you're discontented, en't you?" (*TGC* 147).

This is tough news for late bloomers, those of us who are still trying to get it right well into adulthood. The thought of settling down into a relationship with the me I was at twelve or thirteen makes me want to eat an entire box of Pop-Tarts in alarm. The prospect of change is a cherished one, an essential root of hope. I feel sad for the discontented people the seaman describes. No new beginnings, no insight, no therapy or altered view to move them forward; no fresh vision long-earned or suddenly realized, no doors opening to bigger places. Getting stuck with a dæmon that disappoints you would be akin to getting stuck with a job dunking French fries into grease at Burger King for the rest of your life. Change, as lousy as it is a great deal of the time, is essential. If we stayed the way we were at a given point in time, we'd have a whole lot of people walking around wearing Barney backpacks, and for that reason alone, a fixed state is a frightening idea.

And moving on from the dæmon as a reflection of your soul, what about the concept of an ever-present relationship with another creature? Imagine—a perfect, balanced mutuality. Someone who knows your every thought and looks out for you. A constant, loving companion. With a dæmon, that's what you get. The idea is alluring. It hits hard, smack at our lonely spots and cravings, at that desire to be joined in man/woman wholeness. It hits at that base, primitive longing not to be the single, small person in a big and dark foresty world. It sounds so comforting, not to be alone. We love the dæmon relationship in *The Golden Compass* in good part, I believe, because the idea of that bond is just so soothing. We relish the lovely scenes of intimacy and connection between Pantalaimon and Lyra. When the pair investigates the alethiometer together, it feels positively cozy, with Pantalaimon crouched beside Lyra in the form of a cat, sharing "a glimpse of meaning that felt as if a shaft of sunlight had struck through clouds to light up a majestic line of great hills in the distance—something far beyond, and never suspected" (*TGC* 117–118).

And, too, after visiting the armor-less bear, Iorek Byrnison, Lyra thinks sadly about his lonely, savage self, living a solitary existence in his dirty lean-to. She thinks of him, and is grateful to be human so that she can have a dæmon to always talk to. To underscore the drowsy contentment of Lyra and Pantalaimon in comparison to the poor, friendless Iorek, Pullman then has Lyra fall asleep to the rhythmic creak of the ship, with Pantalaimon sleeping on her pillow beside her.

Ah, bliss. Sign me up.

The following passage, though less lovely and connected and a bit more on the side of Dæmons Who Love Too Much, also pokes at our fear of being solitary and abandoned, as Lyra and Pantalaimon demonstrate the kind of undying devotion that our smallest, most vulnerable pieces might latch on and cling to in envy. Farder Coram has just told the group on the ship about seeing the young woman who had no dæmon:

> It was as if he'd said, "She had no head." The very thought was repugnant. The men shuddered, their dæmons bristled or shook themselves or cawed harshly, and the men

soothed them. Pantalaimon crept into Lyra's arms, their hearts beating together (*TGC* 144).

It's a bit like the couple on their couch in each other's arms, watching reruns of *Sex and the City* and thanking God they're not single. Pullman gives us a weird, vicarious comfort with the concept of dæmons, and with the thought that there's a world and a place where you're never alone. Ever.

But what would that look like, in reality? Never alone? *Never?* The mere thought gives me a rush of panic to the degree that I'm wondering right now where I've stashed my passport. Because while we *need* to connect and bond with another (need, yes, it's how nature's got it crafted), we are also independent entities, self-sufficient singular systems, symbiotic when we want to be, fine when we're not. At least, that's the healthy model. Attachment at the level of the dæmon is of the sort that usually requires an eventual restraining order. So while Pullman plucks at our small, base fears, and demonstrates all the good, fine things about connection with another, there's a squirming, suffocating feeling that descends when you think about the realities of the constant presence of another. Pantalaimon, while the embodiment of Lyra's soul, is still a separate entity, one who NEVER LEAVES.

Think of it: Honey, I'm going for a drive. *I'll come, too!* Hey, I'm going to have dinner with friends tonight. *I'll come, too!* Do you mind stopping at the next gas station? I have to use the bathroom. *I'll come, too!* You get the idea. It's way worse than that bizarre girl who used to follow you around at recess in the third grade. She didn't come home with you and sleep on your pillow.

The mere thought of it—I need air. I need a FAST CAR. My life with a dæmon would become a Die Hard movie, with attempted escapes and fiery explosions.

Some of the most powerful and heart-wrenching passages in the book, though, are the ones that describe what separation would mean for Lyra and Pantalaimon. The feelings are what any severely lovelorn soul is familiar with—a torment that feels physical, a pain in the chest that is one part terrible sadness and another part intense love. And Pantalaimon tests this separation, the same as many lovers do, seeing how far is too far. He goes far enough away that the pain becomes unbearable, until Lyra sobs with longing. Finally, when the pain is too great for them both, Pantalaimon turns into a wildcat and leaps into Lyra's arms and they cling together tightly as they cry and clutch in the intensity of almost losing each other. Lyra says she would rather die than face that sadness again.

It's painful to read. There again, I believe, Pullman shows his genius by tugging at our tender places, the ones where we know what it's like to lose someone, to get our hearts broken, to fear the possibility of that loss. And then he brings the pair back together, so that we can, for a moment, feel the dreamy, lulling sense of never-aloneness, the relief of never-loss.

And yet, loss of independence is a high, high price to pay for never-aloneness. Independence—the chance to singularly decide, to singularly act—is more than just accumulated moments of feel-good freedom. It's how we come, and it's our innate pattern of development. We come with one heart, one brain, dependent initially on others to survive. The pattern, repeated in nature again and again, is to move toward singularity, to grow toward self-sufficiency and autonomy. It's what we are *supposed* to do. We are one, and we are able to choose two. To partner or not to partner. To be physically bonded is unnatural. To be emotionally bonded is unhealthy. Love, the good kind, needs space and sky, as well as water and tending.

So while Pullman's idea of dæmons is tempting, enticing, and irresistible to play with, I would choose to pass. Yes, a dæmon promises permanent self-knowledge and devoted, endless companionship. But we real humans need room. We need room to be alone and room to choose with whom we will trust our real selves. We need room to grow and to modify, to screw things up and start again. Our souls are sometimes restless and ever-forming, and it is often a very good thing that they are. And sure, the thought of having a dæmon of our own might soothe those deepest, dark-soul fears of ours—fears of confusion and abandonment. But the soul's real adventures lay in making peace with those fears. The most important and thrilling quests are on the joyful and perilous route to independence and to attachment, and there, too, on the ocean voyages and snowy, arduous trips through change and self-discovery.

DEB CALETTI is the award-winning author of *The Queen of Everything*, *Honey, Baby, Sweetheart*, *Wild Roses*, and *The Nature of Jade*. In addition to being a National Book Award finalist, Deb's work has gained other distinguished recognition, including the PNBA Best Book Award, the Washington State Book Award, and School Library Journal's Best Book award, and finalist citations for the California Young Reader Medal and the PEN USA Literary Award. Her fifth book with Simon & Schuster, *The Fortunes of Indigo Skye*, will be released April 2008.

REFERENCES

Chabon, Michael. "Dust and Dæmons." *The New York Review of Books*, 25 Mar. 2004.

Pullman, Philip. Interview by fans. "Hotseat: Philip Pullman." *Newsround*, BBC, 23 Jan. 2002. <http://news.bbc.co.uk/cbbcnews/hi/chat/hotseat/newsid_1777000/1777895.stm>

His Dark Materials abounds with Christian motifs—souls in peril, a war among angels, a real and physical hell—and yet it was written by an avowed atheist. Perhaps these images echo an older tradition than Christianity. Marillier explores the trilogy's metaphysics, and makes an unexpected comparison between Pullman's dark materials and the ancient wisdom of the Druids.

DEAR SOUL
The Nature of Dæmons: A Druid's Viewpoint

JULIET MARILLIER

> Her dear soul, the daring companion of her heart. . . .
> —*THE GOLDEN COMPASS* (248)

I am a Druid. People who learn this before they meet me can be disappointed to encounter not a Gandalf-like figure with robes and a staff, but an ordinary-looking woman who could be—and, in fact, is—someone's mother or grandmother. So what does it mean to be a Druid in the twenty-first century?

Modern Druidry is based on ancient ideas, but it is entirely apt for our times. It's not so much a religion as a philosophy to live by. In his book *Druid Mysteries*, Philip Carr-Gomm describes it as "a philosophy which emphasizes the sacredness of all life, and our part in the great web of creation. . . . It does not separate spirit and matter—it offers a sensuous spirituality that celebrates physical life" (Carr-Gomm 12).

Like Wiccans, Druids recognize the divine or spiritual in all things, including human beings, other animals, and the plant and mineral realms. That means we love and honor the divine within ourselves as well as in all other parts of the natural world. Storytelling is central to Druid practice. We believe that stories are a way of passing on wisdom from generation to generation, and that they have a capacity to teach and to heal. Druids celebrate the beauty and magic of life, and take responsibility for the preservation and protection of the planet. Druidry has no dogma and is always evolving—we see our path as one of constant learning. The term *soul* is not used very much in Druidry. It is more common to refer to spirit, meaning the shared divinity that is present in all things.

In our daily lives, we try to put into practice all aspects of Druid philosophy. Druids are generally involved with their local communities in conservation work, and often champion environmental causes or issues of social justice. We love storytelling, music, dancing, and all other forms of creative activity, as they are a means of celebrating the gift of life. We tend to be organic gardeners and enjoy cooking, especially when the result can be shared with family and friends. We honor the wisdom of our elders, both those who are still with us and those departed. Some of us believe in reincarnation. Within Druidry there are various interpretations of this concept.

When I read Philip Pullman's His Dark Materials, I was surprised to find many ideas that ran closely parallel with the philosophies of Druidry. This was especially true of dæmons, the companion creatures that take the place of souls in the world of Pullman's main protagonist, Lyra. Dæmons are central to Pullman's trilogy, and the bond between human and dæmon is described in powerful, emotive language. Reading the human/dæmon scenes, I began to suspect there was a touch of the Druid in the man who had written them. How could this be? Druidry is based on a recognition of the divine in all things, whereas an atheist—what Philip Pullman professes to be—does not believe in the existence of a god or gods. What was it about dæmons that struck such a Druidic note for me?

We know Pullman intended dæmons to represent souls, as we are told this both directly and indirectly in the trilogy. Lyra calls Pantalaimon her soul in the intercision scene of The Golden Compass, and in The Subtle Knife she explains to Will that this is what dæmons are, and that in his world (our world) people carry their dæmons inside them. Just what Pullman means by souls, we find out as the story unfolds.

1. *Humans and their dæmons can't move far apart without physical and emotional pain.*
2. *When the human dies, the dæmon vanishes.*

In Lyra's world, humans and their dæmons are two parts of the same entity. Physical separation by more than a short distance causes human and dæmon acute pain, both physical and mental, as when Pan leaves

Lyra in an attempt to reach the fearsome armored bear, whose help they need. To do this, Pan must change his physical form to that of a badger, so he can use his claws to pull himself away from her.

In the same scene, Lyra muses that if she were to die, she and Pan would still be together, like the Scholars whose skulls she has seen in the crypt at Jordan College, each containing a memento of the departed person's dæmon. But in fact, when we reach the third book of His Dark Materials we discover that humans (as ghosts) travel to the land of the dead *without* their dæmons. When humans die their dæmons are instantly snuffed out. In a battle scene we observe a Tartar warrior falling to an enemy arrow—his wolf dæmon vanishes the instant the man is hit. When Lyra embarks on her mission to the world of the dead she discovers that she must leave Pan behind. Here, it is made clear that human and dæmon are two parts of the same entity, divisible only by death.

There's an interesting exception to the separation rule. We are shown in the story that a witch or shaman can learn to separate physically from his or her dæmon. The equivalent in our world is a shaman journey or astral travel, perhaps experienced during meditative trance, when the spirit moves away from the physical body. Whether this is something the author actually believes or merely a useful story element there is no telling. Pullman writes about witches, shamans, and magic with more respect than he does about God and the church. The element of the books that deals with shaman healing indicates an openness to earth-based ideas of spirituality. And John Parry, an explorer from our world, acquires shamanic powers—and an osprey dæmon—after a long, unintended exile in worlds other than his own. Initially seen as a disheveled wild man, he is revealed as brave, honorable, and wise.

Dæmons do not conform to the Christian belief that a soul is capable of damnation or redemption in the afterlife depending on its human's behavior in this life, since dæmons do not travel on after death with their humans. Besides, in Lyra's world it's not only the humans who have souls. Lyra is told by Iorek Byrnison, the armored bear, that his armor is his soul. As Iorek constructs his armor himself, it seems that bears can manufacture their own souls. If this sits a little oddly with the rest of the story, never mind—it's a great fantasy concept and Iorek himself is one of the most compelling characters in the series.

Pan often seems more rational and logical than Lyra, holding her back from precipitate action. This is evident from the first chapter of *The Golden Compass*, when Pan cautions Lyra against remaining in hiding in the Retiring Room. When Lyra tells him they could prevent a murder, Pan points out that Lyra is incapable of keeping still for four hours in a poky wardrobe. Throughout the scene Pan is alert to danger while Lyra becomes engrossed by the unfolding drama. Here, Lyra seems to represent the emotional, impulsive part of their dual nature and Pan the coolly rational. There are similar scenes elsewhere in the books. So, although it's been said that the soul is the seat of human emotions, this does not seem completely true of dæmons.

As an atheist, Philip Pullman is more likely to apply principles of philosophy than those of religious faith to his invented world, whose angels and spirits don't exist to uphold tenets of religious belief but to challenge them. In fact, Pullman has said he got the idea for dæmons from the Greek philosopher Socrates, who used the word *daimon* for an inner voice that provides guidance in times of confusion. If Socrates was about to make an error of judgment, his *daimon* would speak up and put him on the right track. Philosophers and psychologists in later times have debated whether the *daimon* is separate from the self—a kind of divine adviser—or a driving, instinctive power that determines the actions of a person without his or her conscious choice.

While dæmons seem to be the most inspired element of His Dark Materials, Pullman has said that he devised the concept for an entirely practical reason. He needed a window into Lyra's mind so he would not have to keep explaining what she was thinking, and Pan provided it. Dæmons may have started simply as a structural device in the novels but they appear to have developed into far more as Pullman progressed through the story. Let's note a few more significant points.

3. Humans love their dæmons deeply.

This applies across the board, from Lord Asriel to poor Tony Makarios. One of the saddest scenes in the trilogy is the one in which Lyra finds Tony, the "severed child"—a boy who has been cut apart from his dæmon by the appalling intercision machine. In Lyra's world, a person without a dæmon is as shocking to behold as a person without a head— an abomination, something that cannot be. The boy is alive but not a whole person anymore. He clutches a scrap of frozen fish, the only thing he can find to approximate the part of himself that he has lost, and the only words he speaks are pathetic requests for his dæmon, Ratter. Lyra is physically sickened by the sight of him, yet filled with compassion; we begin to see her true strength in this scene. Pan longs to comfort the boy with an embrace, but the taboo on touch (a person does not touch another person's dæmon) forbids this.

In the third book Lyra and Will visit the land of the dead, where there are no dæmons. Lyra is accompanied by the Gallivespians, tiny people who ride on dragonflies, and the dead cluster around eagerly:

> The ghost children looked up with a passionate longing, and Lyra knew at once why: they thought the dragonflies were dæmons; they were wishing with all their hearts that they could hold their own dæmons again (*TAS* 264–265).

4. *Dæmons show many of the same characteristics as their humans. While the human is a child, the dæmon will often change form, sometimes as a means of escaping harm, sometimes mirroring the changing emotional state of its human.*

Pan often reflects Socrates' idea of the *daimon*—he is a wise adviser to Lyra, holding her back from impulsive action. He can also mirror her moods in his physical form, giving weight to the idea that the soul is the fluid, emotive element of the human. Twice Pan abruptly turns pure white when Lyra receives a shock. When Lyra is frightened or distressed Pan sometimes moves through a series of quick changes:

> "I'm nearly there!" [Lyra] gasped. "Nearly there, Roger!"
> Pantalaimon was changing rapidly in his agitation: lion, ermine, eagle, wildcat, hare, salamander, owl, leopard, every form he'd ever taken, a kaleidoscope of forms . . . (*TGC* 344).

These changes are also helpful when Pan needs to get himself out of trouble, as in the scene in *The Amber Spyglass* where Lyra is emerging from her drugged sleep and Mrs. Coulter is trying to prevent Pan from warning her of danger. Pan flicks from shape to shape to evade the grip of Mrs. Coulter's monkey dæmon.

Because dæmons stop changing once their humans reach puberty, it seems they represent a part of us that becomes less flexible as we become adults. I would be deeply depressed if I believed I had become fixed in my temperament at the age of twelve, but this seems to be what Pullman is telling us. Certainly, in both Lyra and Will we can see qualities that are likely to be keys to their adult selves—Lyra's courage, compassion, and dogged determination, Will's formidable strength of mind and fierce drive to protect his own. If dæmons can't change form after puberty, does that mean a soul is incapable of further development after that age? As a Druid I find that unthinkable. I believe the whole of life is a journey of learning and that we can always grow wiser and better in spirit. Perhaps what Pullman means is that the most critical elements of the human soul are in place by this age and that the years of childhood are those in which we "try on" our soul in various guises before finding the one that fits us best—the one we can love and be comfortable with for the rest of our lives.

Some of Pullman's observations about dæmons seem to be more in the nature of fantasy world-building than a reflection of his concept of souls. Certain interesting points are made once or twice but never developed. For instance, we learn that it is rare, but not unknown, for a dæmon to be of the same sex as its human. Some commentators have interpreted a same-sex dæmon as an indication of homosexuality, but Pullman does not elaborate on the idea. Servants' dæmons, the author mentions casually, are almost always dogs. This uniformity appears again in a regiment of Tartar warriors—they all have wolf dæmons. Does the author believe that by puberty a person has already developed a tendency toward subservience or aggression? If the dæmon is fixed in form by the age of twelve or so, we must assume the individual human gains his wolf before deciding to become a warrior. Do children with a natural "wolf-temperament" tend to become warriors, or does the dæmon's settling in wolf form determine which career option its human should choose? This uniformity is more plausible with servants than with soldiers. In Lyra's Oxford the children of servants are probably in service themselves before the age at which their dæmons settle into dog form. This seems to imply that the nature of one's soul can be determined, in part at least, by social expectations.

5. As well as representing emotions, dæmons embody the sensual/sexual impulses of the human.

We see this demonstrated in an unsettling scene between Lord Asriel and Mrs. Coulter near the end of *The Golden Compass*, and in another scene from *The Subtle Knife*, where Mrs. Coulter's monkey dæmon fondles Carlo's snake dæmon as she tries to get information from him. In the intercision scene from *The Golden Compass*, the language Pullman uses to describe Lyra's response when her captors touch Pan suggests their action is like a sexual assault.

When Will and Lyra first break the human/dæmon touching taboo they do so by accident—both dæmons have taken the form of cats, and the humans mistakenly pick up each other's dæmon. Later, when the two young people have discovered the nature of their feelings for each other, they stroke each other's dæmon lovingly and experience not shame and revulsion, but delight. We learn here that their dæmons will never change now because they have felt a lover's hands on them. This is the moment of maturing from child to adult—the getting of wisdom.

6. After death, dæmons vanish. Humans, as ghosts, go to the land of the dead, as determined by the Authority (God). If released they dissipate joyfully into their component atoms, to return to the great web of life.

This is a form of reincarnation, and is shown by Pullman as a blissful release from a dreary existence in the land of the dead. In the words of a ghost: "'We'll be alive again in a thousand blades of grass, and a million leaves; we'll be falling in the raindrops and blowing in the fresh breeze; we'll be glittering in the dew under the stars and the moon'" (*TAS* 287).

It even seems that, despite the disappearance of a dæmon upon its human's death, the two may be reunited in the end. One of the most powerful sections of the trilogy is the depiction of Lee Scoresby's last stand. In a later passage the remnant of Lee rises to the stars, "where the atoms of his beloved, Hester, were waiting for him" (*TAS* 373).

I can't read that beautifully written passage about Lee and Hester without sensing something spiritual in the author's view of death. At the very least, it is clear he understands the beauty and value of life in all its

	HIS DARK MATERIALS	DRUID PHILOSOPHIES
1	Deep and passionate bond of love between human and dæmon (two parts of the same being).	Recognition of the divine in all things, including oneself—therefore, love of oneself.
2	Respect for/love of natural world shown in loving descriptions of animal-formed dæmons.	Recognition of the divine in all things—respect and love for all parts of the natural world.
3	Dæmons contain the sensual/sexual impulse.	Celebration of physical life.
4	On release from the world of the dead, human disperses to atoms and returns to the web of life—may be reunited with atoms of dæmon.	Influence of past lives is significant in Druid lore—wisdom is accumulated through the "spirit of the journey."

many forms—this is plainly demonstrated in the loving physical descriptions of animals that abound in these books.

This is only one of several ways in which Pullman's philosophies, as expressed in His Dark Materials, come surprisingly close to those of Druid teaching.

There are some further parallels to be drawn as well, not discussed previously because they don't relate specifically to dæmons. I mentioned that storytelling is central to Druid philosophy—we see it as a means of passing on wisdom from one generation to the next. There are two very important references to the value of storytelling in His Dark Materials. In *The Amber Spyglass* the harpies are persuaded to take on the job of guiding ghosts through the land of the dead and out again to their final release. The Gallivespian Salmakia tells them the payment will be in stories—the ghosts will tell the harpies their stories as they pass through. These stories will be proof that each individual has lived life to the full and learned something to tell. Those who have not done so will not be guided out of the land of the dead. In Pullman's world, the key to immortality—not in a Christian heaven, but as part of an endless recycling in the web of nature—is how fully a person has lived his or her Earthly life.

This is further clarified at the end of *The Amber Spyglass*, when Lyra explains to Pan that they shouldn't live as if what comes after death is

	His Dark Materials	Druid Philosophies
5	Storytelling reflects wisdom gained through Earthly experience—each of us should live and learn well enough to have a story to tell.	Storytelling enables us to pass down wisdom from generation to generation; it is a powerful tool for teaching and healing.
6	The most important thing is how well we live this life. If each of us takes individual responsibility we can make the world a better place ("the Republic of Heaven").	Individuals have responsibility for the preservation and protection of the environment, self-development, intellectual and spiritual growth. Druidry does not separate spirit and matter.

more important than Earthly life. Instead, they must use their lives in their own world to build "the Republic of Heaven."

There's one element present in the right-hand column and not in the left: references specifically to the divine or spiritual. This is a fundamental difference between the philosophy presented in His Dark Materials and that of present-day Druidry. Despite this, I suspect that Lyra's future in building her better world might be not so very different from that of an individual doing his or her best to follow the Druid path, with its love for and commitment to the health of all parts of the web of life, ourselves included.

The key lies in our very first point of similarity: love. Without the love of self, which Druids recognize as love of the divine within, how can we reach out to others, to teach, heal, and journey together? It is the passionate and tender bond between Lyra and Pan, the love between human and soul, that provides them with the strength to step forward bravely and help make the world a better place. Perhaps it does not matter so much whether we view a soul as something divine and spiritual or as an essential and beloved part of our physical self. It's more important that we recognize it, love it, and let it illuminate our path in life. And in this, His Dark Materials has a lesson for all of us, whatever our personal beliefs.

JULIET MARILLIER is the author of eight critically acclaimed historical fantasy novels for adult readers. She recently branched out into young adult fiction with *Wildwood Dancing* and the forthcoming *Cybele's Secret.* Juliet was born in New Zealand and now lives in a hundred-year-old cottage by the Swan River in Western Australia. She is a member of the Druid order OBOD (The Order of Bards, Ovates, and Druids). Her dæmon is an owl.

REFERENCES

Cahn, Steven M. *Exploring Philosophy: An Introductory Anthology.* New York: Oxford University Press, 2000.

Carr-Gomm, Philip. *Druid Mysteries.* London: Rider, 2002.

Lenz, Millicent. *His Dark Materials Illuminated: Critical Essays on Philip Pullman's Trilogy.* Edited by Carole Scott. Detroit: Wayne State University Press, 2005.

From their home lives to their religious conversions to their vocations as Oxford scholars, the lives of C. S. Lewis, J. R. R. Tolkien, and Philip Pullman show astonishing parallels. Perhaps it's unsurprising that their works bear the marks of that common life experience and education. Melling examines the characters, conflicts, and invented cosmologies of Narnia, Middle-Earth, and His Dark Materials, illustrating how the authors' common backgrounds shape the connections among three enduring works of children's literature.

TEMPEST IN A BRITISH TEA CUP
Philip Pullman vs. C. S. Lewis and J. R. R. Tolkien

O.R. MELLING

There's no need to pull any punches. Philip Pullman has been quite clear about what he thinks of C. S. Lewis and J. R. R. Tolkien. You can find his comments online and in interviews and newspaper articles, but here are two quick quotes to paint the picture. Pullman has called the Chronicles of Narnia cycle "one of the most ugly and poisonous things I have ever read" (1998), accusing C. S. Lewis of misogyny, racism, and gratuitous violence. Of the Lord of the Rings he has commented, "There's nothing truthful in it about human nature, or society, or men and women. Nothing true in it at all. It's all superficial adventure" (2006).

Them's fighting words, indeed, and they have caused much confusion, dismay, and even outrage among readers. But this is just a tempest in a British tea cup, for what may appear to be all-out war is really nothing more than a family squabble. Look closely and you will see that there are more things similar than dissimilar in the lives and works of these three Englishmen. When all is said and done, His Dark Materials is cut from the same shining cloth as Narnia and Middle-Earth.

No one will argue with the idea that an author's life experience and, in particular, his childhood can exert a powerful influence on his work, and a quick survey of the lives of Lewis, Tolkien, and Pullman shows some astonishing parallels. All three suffered the deep wound of parental loss at a very young age: Lewis lost his mother at age ten; Tolkien his father at age three and then his mother at age twelve; and Pullman his father at age seven. Each was left with one brother, though Pullman did gain more siblings when his mother remarried.

Around the time of these terrible deaths, the three boys also experienced the upheaval of leaving home and country. C. S. Lewis was sent from Belfast, Northern Ireland, to school in England the same year his mother died. Tolkien was on a visit to England from South Africa (where he was born) when his father died and thus the visit became permanent. Pullman, though born in England, lived for a time and was schooled in Rhodesia (now Zimbabwe), where his airman father was stationed. When Pullman's mother remarried, he was moved to Australia. Later, he was educated in Wales and also England, where he lived with his grandparents. Being essentially private men, the three authors say little about the trauma of these events or the suffering that such loss and disruption in their home life must have caused them. Still, it's no surprise that they could imagine sweeping epics that cross countries and worlds and, more tellingly, that many of their main characters are orphans, like Frodo and Lyra, or temporarily orphaned, like the Pevensie children. (In the latter case, many of these "war orphans" who were sent into the countryside during the bombing of London did lose their families and never returned home.) And their main characters not only show great courage, tenacity, and sense of adventure in the face of hardship, but also a strong desire to help and even save the adults around them: Frodo's support of Bilbo, Lyra wanting to free her father and help him in his work, and Digory hoping to cure his mother.

Despite their connections with other countries, all three writers were clearly shaped by a classical British education. Even though Pullman is much younger than the other two, photographs of the three in their youth show typical English school boys in gray short pants, jackets, white shirts, and ties. All attended Oxford and went on to teach. Lewis and Tolkien became dons of their alma mater. Pullman began as a middle-school teacher and then became, continuing into the present, a lecturer at—yes—Oxford. These almost identical academic paths play out in the three men's works, which are distinguished by intellectual vigor, didactic overtones, and moral, philosophical, and religious scholarship.

The latter is no coincidence, as each of the men also comes from a strong religious background and each can be said to have undergone a conversion experience. Though C. S. Lewis's maternal grandfather was a Church of Ireland minister, Lewis lost his faith at age thirteen and then converted back to Anglicanism at age thirty-one. When Tolkien was eight years old, his mother converted to Roman Catholicism and was disowned by her Baptist family. This caused great hardship to the widow and her sons. The fact that Tolkien always viewed his mother's death in her thirties as a kind of martyrdom underscores the emotional impact of the religious change, to which he remained loyal throughout his life. (Note: As he was only twelve when she died, Tolkien came under the guardianship of a Catholic priest until he was twenty-one.) Like C. S. Lewis, Philip Pullman's maternal grandfather was an Anglican minister, but though Pullman clearly loved and admired his grandfather, with whom he lived for a time, Pullman lost his own faith as a teenager. Nevertheless, he is not simply an agnostic, but a vocal and dedicated proponent of humanistic atheism, which is a belief system in itself. The passion with which Pullman denounces religion, and in particular Christianity, is unquestionably that of a zealous convert. Thus each of the three authors underwent a powerful conversion experience that can be seen in the content of their work, for all three deal with religious and spiritual themes.

Before we consider these themes, however, let's have a quick look at various characters, scenes, and motifs from *The Golden Compass* that mirror counterparts in the Chronicles of Narnia and the Lord of the Rings trilogy.

Pullman's twelve-year-old heroine, Lyra, begins her adventure hiding in a wardrobe, even as Lucy begins hers in *The Lion, the Witch, and the Wardrobe*. Though wild and short-tempered, Lyra is not only good at heart but noble, loyal, and heroic, ready to brave the worst perils to save her friend, Roger. Would she be out of place in Narnia or Middle-Earth? She is very like Jill of *The Silver Chair*, who is also short-tempered and stubborn but a true heroine in the end. Lyra is also a girl who has big dreams. Along with saving Roger, she plans to free her father from imprisonment and help him build a bridge to cross the worlds. This side of her character is very like that of the young heroine of *The Horse and His Boy*, Aravis, who bravely sets out with only Hwin, the Talking Horse, to seek freedom and a new life in Narnia, even though she has no guarantee that she will be accepted, being Calormene.

There are parallels in the authors' villains as well as their heroines. Mrs. Coulter is a true sister to C. S. Lewis's evil females—the White Witch, Jadis, and the Green Witch. These women are cold, beautiful, cruel, and powerful. They stand alone, with no male authority over them. All have no qualms about using and abusing children. All fit the classic fairy tale archetype of the "anti-mother," or evil stepmother. Both Mrs. Coulter and the Green Witch are described as having light, musical voices. In *The Silver Chair*, the Green Witch is happy to sacrifice Jill and Eustace to the cannibalistic giants of Harfang, even as Mrs. Coulter blithely sacrifices the stolen children to the Church's experiments. The White Witch ensnares Edmund with Turkish Delight; Mrs. Coulter lures her prey with chocolatl. Both women appear gracious, sweet, and kind, praising and cajoling their unsuspecting victims. When angry, Mrs. Coulter is described as giving off a hot metallic smell, calling to mind a sulfurous demon or witch. She can be as sadistic and murderous as Jadis of *The Magician's Nephew*. Jadis coolly destroys her world with the Deplorable Word; Mrs. Coulter coolly plays the worldly game of Church politics and likes to watch as children and dæmons are pulled apart.

One could also view Mrs. Coulter as a foil or direct opposite of the Lady Galadriel. Both women stand alone in their power, with lesser men in their shadows—Mrs. Coulter, her cuckolded dead husband, and Galadriel, the weaker Celeborn, who does not have a Ring of Power. Both women appear golden and shining: Mrs. Coulter through her monkey dæmon's lustrous fur and the Lady Galadriel of the Golden Wood with her hair of deep gold. It's understood that Tolkien had in mind Mary, the Mother of God—called by Roman Catholics "Our Lady"—when he wrote his Galadriel. It's also known that C. S. Lewis based Jadis and the two witches on Lilith, Adam's first non-human wife in Talmudic literature and the first witch in medieval demonology. But whom did Pullman have in mind when he wrote Mrs. Coulter? Perhaps the creations of the other two men.

All three authors depict male-dominated worlds in which a few strong female characters, chiefly evil ones, stand out against a backdrop of women as secondary citizens. While Pullman's witches are independent and autonomous, even as C. S. Lewis's dryads are, this female race does not rule beyond its own territory, and they have male consuls to represent them in the wider world. As a woman of power, Mrs. Coulter is seen as an exception, even as Galadriel and Eowyn are exceptions in their worlds. Pullman shows through Lyra that female Scholars in the alternative Oxford are regarded with disdain, paraphrasing Samuel Johnson's infamous misogynistic remark about female preachers: "they could never be taken more seriously than animals dressed up and acting a play" (*TGC* 59). No explanation is given for this statement, and one is reminded of C. S. Lewis's offhand remarks against vegetarians, non-smokers, teetotalers, and people who let their children call them by their first names. In addition, Pullman's depiction of masculine power reflects that of Lewis and Tolkien. Of John Faa, lord of the western gyptians, he writes: "[T]here was nothing to mark him out but the air of strength and authority he had. Lyra recognized it: Uncle Asriel had it, and so did the Master of Jordan" (*TGC* 102). The gyptian women are also like Lewis's and Tolkien's female characters: though strong and motherly and free to speak up at the Roping, they are not equal to their men and are excluded from the expedition despite asking to join. It's evident that the gyptians do not like to put women in dangerous or violent situations, even as Aslan tells Lucy that women shouldn't go to war and the Rohirrim shelter their women in caves while the men go out to fight.

There are also scenes in *The Golden Compass* that reflect scenes in the works of the two older authors. When Lyra is woken before dawn to meet secretly with the Master of Jordan College and given the alethiometer (of which there are only six in existence, like Tolkien's seven Seeing Stones) we are reminded of Dr. Cornelius waking the young Prince Caspian in the middle of the night before sending him off to meet his destiny. When Lyra is saved from Turk traders by Tony Costa, she thinks, "A gyptian! A real Oxford gyptian!" (*TGC* 92). These words are almost identical to Prince Rilian's in *The Silver Chair* when he is rescued by Puddleglum and the two children: "Do I see before me a Marshwiggle—a real, live, honest Narnian Marshwiggle?" (Lewis 626). In both cases, the speakers are referring to something safe and wholesome that belongs to "home."

There is one particular moment in *The Golden Compass* that sent a shiver of recognition through me. Serafina Pekkala says to Lee Scoresby, "'We are all subject to the fates. But we must all act as if we are not . . . or die of despair'" (*TGC* 271). This is an exquisite echo of Puddleglum's declaration to the Green Witch in *The Silver Chair* that "'[he's] going to live as like a Narnian as [he] can even if there isn't any Narnia'" (Lewis 633).

In the area of recurring motifs, all three authors share the prejudice against wolves found in European fairy tales, as opposed to, for example, Native American tales in which the animal is a hero. In *The Lion, the*

Witch, and the Wardrobe, wolves guard the castle of the White Witch as her secret police, and by killing their leader, Maugrim, Peter proves himself a man fit to be High King. Tolkien's wargs are evil wolfish creatures named after the wargs of Norse mythology, which included the great wolf Fenrir, son of Loki. In *The Golden Compass*, wolves are the dæmons of the Tartars, who guard the evil experimental station. It can be noted here, also, that all three men have similar "enemy" races. Despite Pullman's charges of racism against C. S. Lewis and Tolkien, his own Turk traders and Tartar guards recall Lewis's Calormenes and Tolkien's "swarthy" men of the East who follow Sauron.

Similarity of character, scene, and motif aside, it is at the core of their work, the central themes, that we find the true connection among these men. Though they all use various mythologies as well as their own imaginative inventions to enhance their tales, the chief belief system underlying each man's work is Christianity. Now, there may be Christians who would like to burn Pullman's books—and, if we were in darker ages still, the author himself—but there's no doubt that Pullman owes a huge debt to his former religion. Quite simply put, without Christianity there would be no His Dark Materials.

The series's title itself comes from Milton's *Paradise Lost* (a verse of which is quoted at the beginning of *The Golden Compass*), an epic poem dealing with Satan's rebellion against Heaven, the great war amongst the angels, and the fall of Adam and Eve. Though Pullman is re-telling this story from an anti-religious, anti-Church perspective, nonetheless, the narrative is still firmly entrenched in the Christian world view. As a humanistic atheist, Pullman is not attacking religion through the mythos of Islam or Hinduism or Buddhism. Like Lewis and Tolkien, he writes through the filter, the mentality, of the religion in which he was reared, the religion that inevitably played a major part in forming his character and thought. His work itself begs the question: Would one attack so fervently something one was indifferent to? Something that had no influence or effect? Indeed, His Dark Materials could not have been written by someone who *wasn't* steeped in Christian belief and theology, as Christianity is the driving thematic force behind the plot.

Firstly, we have the great war of which Serafina speaks with Lee Scoresby: "'[A]ll of us, humans, witches, bears, are engaged in a war already, although not all of us know it'" (*TGC* 270). Here, Pullman, though a committed atheist, is utterly invested in the central Judeo-Christian myth of the ancient war between good and evil, light and darkness, which, of course, both Tolkien and Lewis also present. This dualistic vision of the essential nature of reality—what C. S. Lewis called "the great divorce" in opposition to William Blake's "marriage of Heaven and Hell"—is a grand theme found at the heart of most world religions. Oddly enough, though Pullman claims to belong to Blake's party, his story largely follows both C. S. Lewis's and Tolkien's line in terms of simple demarcations between good and evil. The Church and all its servants are irredeemably bad, while its victims—innocent children and their dæmons, Lyra, the gyptians, the captured witch, and so on—are clearly good. True, the rebellious Lord Asriel is a dubious and conflicted hero, but for the most part it is as easy to identify "the good guys" and "the bad guys" in Pullman's world as it is in Narnia or Middle-Earth.

There is also the major motif of dæmons as the outward manifestation of an individual's "soul" (Pullman himself uses the term when he has Lyra comment that Iorek Byrnison's armor is his soul). This is a deeply spiritual concept, no doubt the reason why dæmons appeal to so many of us; their roots are in the oldest and most universal of religions, shamanism, which sees everyone with animal spirit guides.

And then there is Pullman's most beautiful, enchanting, and heart-breaking creation—the witches. Elemental beings, preternaturally wild and long-living, singing like the Aurora itself, they are linked to earth and sky through their cloud-pine sticks. As mentioned above, it is Serafina Pekkala, clan queen, who underscores the great war between good and evil. And contrary to Pullman's own predilections, his witches clearly have a religion. From the scene in which the witch is tortured by the Church aboard ship, we understand that witches live with the certain knowledge that Yambe-Akka, their mother-goddess, will come to them at the moment of death.

It is interesting that one of Pullman's complaints about the Chronicles of Narnia is that Lewis foists his religious views upon unsuspecting children. Yet Pullman presents his own humanistic, atheistic, and anti-religious opinions quite aggressively in His Dark Materials through his depiction of the Church as thoroughly evil and, most specifically, through Dr. Malone's arguments in the last volume of the trilogy. But this is where I must make a personal confession: though I was reared an Irish

Roman Catholic, I have to admit that when I first read all three of these authors, I did *not* recognize the influence of any religious or irreligious beliefs in their work.

I read the Chronicles of Narnia as a nine-year-old and did not catch even a glimpse of the allusions to Christianity—not even when Aslan died and was resurrected!—until the very end of *The Voyage of the Dawn Treader*, when the Lamb turned into Aslan. Even then, I remember being quite confused by the juxtaposition and so, like all children faced with an intrusion into a wonderful story, I ignored it. Truth is, the Christian element of the Chronicles of Narnia held no interest for me as a Christian child. I loved Aslan because I loved Aslan, not because he even remotely resembled anything in my religion.

A few years later, at twelve years of age, I read the Lord of the Rings trilogy and found Tolkien's world strangely devoid of religion and in fact quite godless. Much later, as a university student, I was shocked to discover that the good professor was, in fact, a staunch Roman Catholic, for I found not the slightest trace of Catholicism in his work. Indeed, I had assumed that he was typically English, with a tepid attitude toward religion—so different from the fervent Irish!—and I had guessed him to be a tolerant secularist.

As for Pullman's work, I'm sure he would shudder to discover that this adult reader entirely missed the fact that his work was a diatribe against religion in general and Christianity and Roman Catholicism in particular. Honest to God, until I was a long way through the final book, I was under the impression that "the Church" was a metaphor for the modern-day scientific establishment! After all, Pullman's Church is interested in elementary particles, discusses theology in scientific terms, and conducts experiments on children in the same cold-blooded and clinical manner that our scientists carry out tests on animals. When I did eventually come across the religious debates concerning His Dark Materials and Pullman's own comments against Christianity, my reaction was: "Oh."

When I began this paper, I assumed that, like many readers, I enjoyed these men's works regardless of or despite their personal beliefs. Indeed, I have always considered those passages where overt ideology intrudes to be weak points in the narrative drive—when Lucy mentions the Stable, or Faramir questions the hobbits about grace before meals, or Dr. Malone makes bald statements against the Church. Certainly lesser authors lose readers by preaching—except, of course, when they are preaching to the converted. But these men are bestsellers and widely read and loved, even by those who disagree with their beliefs. That's when it occurred to me. Perhaps the very reason they are so appealing—and with every kind of reader—is precisely because their books resonate with their beliefs.

The works of Pullman, Lewis, and Tolkien are not simply action-packed fantasy adventures with cardboard characters and shallow, if exciting, plots. These works are deeper, richer, and infinitely superior to the average genre fiction set in other worlds. It is the strength and passion of belief—regardless of what that belief may be—that brings *spirit* to a book, and it is that very spirit that calls out to readers. The truth is, these three authors take us on journeys that traverse the latitudes and longitudes of our souls. Yes, their books have epic plots, compelling characters, breathtaking scenes, and ingenious inventions of the imagination, but more than that, they are infused with a fire that some might call "divine."

O.R. MELLING was born in Ireland and grew up in Canada with her seven sisters and two brothers. She has a B.A. in Celtic Studies and an M.A. in Mediaeval Irish History. Her Chronicles of Faerie series—*The Hunter's Moon, The Summer King, The Light-Bearer's Daughter,* and *The Book of Dreams*—has been translated into many languages and is being published in America by Harry N. Abrams, NY. Melling lives in a small town by the Irish Sea with her teenage daughter, Findabhair, and her cat, Emma. Visit her at www.ormelling.com.

REFERENCES

Lewis, C. S. The Chronicles of Narnia compendium edition. New York: HarperCollins, 2004.

Pullman, Philip. "The Dark Side of Narnia." *The Guardian*, 1 Oct. 1998.

Pullman, Philip. *The Wand in the Word: Conversation with Writers of Fantasy.* Edited by Leonard S. Marcus. Cambridge, Massachusetts: Candlewick Press, 2006.

His Dark Materials wears its influences on its sleeve, especially the poets who were Pullman's muses. Their words appear overtly, in epigraphs and in the series's title, and also echo subtly throughout the language of the books. Croggon examines how Rainer Rilke gave HDM its angels, how John Milton provided the central conflict, and how William Blake inspired its passion and fire.

PULLMAN'S DARK MATERIALS

Alison Croggon

All writing, if it is any good, generates a lot of its energy from contradiction. Writers are usually quite shameless about this. (As the French poet Baudelaire said famously: "I contradict myself? Well, then, I contradict myself!") And there is a deep contradiction in Philip Pullman's His Dark Materials. Itself a most unpoetical work, it draws a great deal of its intellectual and emotional depth from poetry.

This may sound like a strange thing to say. How can a book of such imaginative richness as His Dark Materials be described as unpoetical? And how can I say such a thing, given that there is no satisfactory definition of poetry? Perhaps I should first explain what I think poetry is, and why I think it is different from what Philip Pullman is seeking to do.

Poets have been arguing about what poetry is for thousands of years, and no one has ever come up with a definition that satisfies everybody. Worse still, people have been long trying to work out what the difference is between poetry and prose, and they still have no good answers. There *is* a difference, and it's a difference that usually you know at once, as soon as you begin to read, but it's very difficult to describe.

You might suggest, for example, that poetry rhymes and prose doesn't; but there are lots of poems that don't rhyme. Or you might say that prose has lines that run all the way across the page, while poetry doesn't, but that's not true, either: I have read novels that look like poems, and poems that look like novels. The difference lies a little deeper, in the very DNA of the writing; perhaps it is the first glimmerings in a writer's mind that determine whether a work will be a poem or something else. But that, as you might imagine, is very difficult to define, let alone to discuss.

Writing prose is very often a struggle to control the multiple meanings of language that poets, on the other hand, are always attempting to make deeper and more complex. Poetry is often clear, but it is never unambiguous: it shimmers with many meanings, which shift and coalesce like the images and meanings of Lyra's alethiometer. Sometimes you might see one meaning through a poem, and sometimes you might see another that is completely different, even opposite, and neither of these meanings will be untrue.

(This is why writing essays for school about "What is the poet trying to say?" is such a bad idea—the poet isn't trying to say *anything*, the poet is simply saying. This is quite a different activity. And it is also why it is very unfortunate that most people first encounter poetry at school, because unless you are very lucky and have a gifted teacher, you will be taught that a poem has a "proper" meaning that is the correct one and on which you can be marked, and that other meanings are incorrect. But that is, in fact, a deep misunderstanding of poetry, and destroys what is most meaningful and exciting about it. This doesn't mean that to look carefully at a poem is to destroy it: it means the reverse. If you look carefully at any great poem, you will find that no single meaning covers everything it touches: it is only careless readers who maintain that a poem has a "correct" and "proper" reading. The same point can be made, of course, about novels, which is why you get into such trouble when you start talking about the differences between poetry and prose, but I do think it's easier to be wrong about a novel than it is to be wrong about a poem.

But I fear I am wandering off the point. This is, of course, a hallowed tradition of essays: the word "essay" comes from the French word "essayer," which means "to attempt," to make a speculation, to wander, and I am sure that many great essayists would have been marked down badly at school for excessive wandering. But I had better wander back to Philip Pullman before this essay, being prose, takes charge and becomes something other than I intended. . . .)

These different ways of thinking about meaning are, I think, the main reason why when I rewrite a poem, it always ends up shorter, while when I rewrite a novel, it always ends up fifty pages longer. In both cases, I am seeking greater accuracy—but a poem has one particular kind of accuracy, and a novel has another kind. This might be clearer if you think of language like a coiled spring. A poet will always be seeking to make the coil tighter and tighter, so that when you read it, it releases in your mind with a sudden explosion of energy; the novelist is trying to stretch the spring out, so that each individual coil winds out into a shining, enchantingly beautiful spiral.

Phillip Pullman is very much this second kind of writer. But one of the reasons why His Dark Materials is so interesting is that he takes many of his ideas—including the very title of the trilogy—from poetry. Pullman himself is very clear on this. In his acknowledgments, he thanks three writers in particular: Heinrich von Kleist, who is not a poet but a fine short story writer, playwright, and essayist who lived in Germany in the early 1800s, and two poets, John Milton and William Blake.

Because this essay is about poets, I won't talk about Kleist. It's very obvious, if you read the famous essay that Pullman cites, how Pullman welded Kleist's ideas to William Blake's metaphysics and John Milton's poem *Paradise Lost* in order to create the startlingly original premise of his own trilogy. But it's worth noting that Kleist has connections to other poets who turn up in the book; for example, his ideas turn up in a poem by Rainer Maria Rilke, whom Pullman quotes at the beginning of *The Amber Spyglass*.

Tracing the ways in which writers take their ideas from other writers is a fascinating process that creates a shimmering, chaotic, and rich web of connections. This is not mere copying, or being "unoriginal," or plagiarism, or any of the other contemporary sins that seem to be regularly leveled at hapless writers. It is in fact how writers write: literature comes as much from other writing as it does from a writer's individual imagination and life experience. The first rule for any writer is to read as widely and deeply as possible: writers want to write because, in the first place, they read books that excited and inspired them so much that they wanted to do the same thing themselves.

In fact, writers are exactly like bower birds. Bower birds are Australian birds with a fascinating courtship ritual: The male birds clear a circle of earth and make a construction out of sticks and leaves, which can be shaped like a hut or a maypole or a walkway. They decorate these structures, or bowers, with all sorts of colorful objects that they collect—shells, leaves, flowers, stones, bits of glass or plastic. They even steal especially lovely objects from other birds. Every bower is different, according to the individual taste of the bird. Once the bird has made his bower, he dances within it to attract his mate, who goes from bower to bower, looking for the best dancer with the most beautiful construction. Like these birds, writers dance within bowers they have built out of their own imaginations, hoping to attract readers—but they adorn these bowers with shining fragments that they scavenge from everything they have ever read or seen or experienced.

So all literature is studded with allusions to and quotations from other books. Writers make these references and quotations on purpose, often for their own pleasure: they like to nod gracefully to other writers they admire. And those allusions are in fact part of the generosity involved in slipping into the wide stream of human culture that is there for all of us to share. It's how writers remain alive and always new, no matter how long they have been dead, which is why it's a generous act. And Philip Pullman is exemplary in both his thievery and his generosity.

If you are familiar with their work, the poets who have most influenced Pullman are very easy to find in His Dark Materials, even without looking at the acknowledgments. Sometimes they are directly quoted, but most often Pullman slips in allusions that anyone who has read those poets will recognize. They are woven into the story in such a way that you aren't confused if you haven't read them, but if you have, you will find a deeper pleasure in the books. And perhaps Pullman is also suggesting that, if you enjoyed his books, you might also enjoy the poets who have inspired him.

The epigraphs at the front of The Amber Spyglass are all from poets. The quotes are about angels, although the poet who wrote most famously about angels—the German lyric poet Rainer Maria Rilke—is speaking instead about love (which is also an important idea in the books). But here Pullman is also subtly alerting us to an inspiration behind his own angels. The poem from which he quotes is Rilke's The Duino Elegies, a series of ten poems that contains the most famous angels in modern literature. Pullman's angels are drawn as much from Rilke's imagination as his own. Rilke's angels move easily between worlds—they "often don't know if they pass / over or under the living or the dead." And although Pullman's angels are much more human than Rilke's strange and terrifying forces, they, too, envy the physical world of human beings. As Rilke says in the *Elegies*, it's the ordinary things that astonish angels:

> Praise the world to the angel, not the unsayable, to him
> you can't brag of magnificent beatitude: in the world
> where he so feelingly feels, you are a novice. So show
> him the simple, formed from generation to generation,
> which lives as a part of ourselves near the hand and in looking.
> Tell him the Things. He will stand astonished, as you stood
> beside the roper in Rome or by the Egyptian potter.

Like Rilke—and practically every poet he names—Pullman believes that the most fascinating, interesting, and amazing things are also those that are considered the most ordinary. But to say why properly would take another essay.

Another poet who turns up throughout the books is the English Romantic poet John Keats. Pullman quotes him directly in describing the state of mind that Lyra must find to read the alethiometer, or Will to use the subtle knife. It's from a very famous letter in which Keats describes a capacity he calls "negative capability"—"that is," says Keats, "when man is capable of being in uncertainties, Mysteries, doubts without any irritable reaching after fact & reason." It's a very important idea that Pullman links to understanding the truth, which is complex and always shifting, and never only one thing—like poetry itself. It is a knowledge that rests on doubt itself. Pullman says that Lyra's negative capability when she reads the alethiometer is a kind of "grace": a gift that is lost when innocence vanishes with the coming of self-knowledge. But at the end of the book, he also says that, with patience and hard work, this grace can be relearned.

The two most important poets to the book, without any argument, are John Milton and William Blake—and perhaps Blake is the most important of all. Milton wrote the poem *Paradise Lost*, from which Pullman takes the title of his trilogy and the idea of the rebel angels who make war on God. I didn't read *Paradise Lost* until a few years ago: it rather intimidated me, and it sat on my bookshelf for a long time as a good intention, something that I felt I ought to read if I was to call myself a literate person. But when at last I picked it up and began to read it, I found myself totally swept away. For a start, the language is breathtakingly beautiful. As Pullman himself says in his introduction to a recent edition of *Paradise Lost*, poetry is enchantment, and Milton is a master of this kind of magic:

> It has the form it does because that very form casts a spell; and when [people] thought they were being bothered and bewildered, they were in fact being bewitched . . . the poetry, its incantatory quality, is what makes [*Paradise Lost*] the great work of art it is. I found, in that classroom so long ago, that it had the power to stir a physical response: my heart beat faster, the hair on my head stirred, my skin bristled.

What I didn't expect when I picked up the poem was that it would also be a page-turner. I couldn't put it down. Milton's Satan—the angel who was once Lucifer, the most beautiful of all of them, who in his pride rebels against God and is thrown out of Heaven—is one of the most charismatic villains in all literature. He is no simple bad guy: while he is complex, proud, ambitious, and selfish, he is also capable of compassion, and admirably refuses self-pity. (I have sometimes wondered whether he's partly a self-portrait of Milton himself.) When Satan says, "Better to reign in Hell, than serve in Heaven," we can't but feel our hearts quicken in sympathy at his proud defiance. He is, in fact, the model for Lord Asriel; and the gloomy grandeur of Milton's Hell, where Satan prepares to make war against God, has its exact counterpart in Lord Asriel's massive castle, where he prepares to make war against the Authority.

Milton was a Puritan; as far as he was concerned, Satan was the bad guy. However, as with all poets, it's a little complicated: in the seventeenth century, the Puritans were also rebels, who led a revolution against the King, and Milton was punished by Charles II after the Restoration of the English monarchy for supporting the view that the public had the right to depose and punish tyrants. So even when he wrote it, Milton's story about the angelic rebellion was perhaps a little ambiguous and more subversive than, at first glance, it might seem. It took another poet, writing two hundred years later, to point out the basic contradiction at work in *Paradise Lost*. William Blake noticed that in Milton's poem, Satan is a much more fascinating character than God, who is rather dull and portentous. As Blake said in a famous poem of his own, *The Marriage of Heaven and Hell*:

> The reason Milton wrote in fetters when he wrote of Angels & God, and at liberty when of Devils & Hell, is because he was a true Poet, and of the Devil's Party without knowing it.

Blake was far from being an atheist as Pullman is—in fact, Blake died joyously singing hymns of praise, and he regularly had visions of angels—although the eighteenth century was a revolutionary time, and quite a few of Blake's contemporaries were as militantly atheistic as Pullman is today. But it's from William Blake that His Dark Materials gets the flavor and poetry of its atheism. Blake's radical metaphysical fantasies become the materials for Pullman's attack on the party of Heaven.

Blake is most famous for two books of poetry: *The Marriage of Heaven and Hell* and *Songs of Innocence and Experience*. The words "innocence and experience" must strike a chord with every reader of His Dark Materials: they haunt the books, and are at the heart of one of its most important themes. The loss of innocence is the beginning of consciousness, which is embodied in the idea of Dust. Every time Pullman uses the phrase "innocence and experience"—and he uses it very often—he is paying a little tribute to William Blake.

However, Blake's influence goes much deeper than that. Between them, Blake's two books explain the entire metaphysics of His Dark Materials, which is not drawn from Milton's world view at all, no matter how deeply Pullman pillaged Milton's imagination. Milton is Puritanical and also, I fear, rather misogynistic, and His Dark Materials is neither of these things. For inspiration for his own rewriting of the story of the Fall, Pullman turned instead to Blake. Blake was a true rebel angel and, unlike Milton, he knew it.

Pullman is very clear about his sympathies. All through the books, he places the fear and loathing of sexuality represented by the Church against the wisdom and pleasure and sorrow of the life of the body. The churches seek complete control over a subservient population, and the Authority—ultimately a frail, demented, pitiable old man under the thumb of his evil Regent, Metraton—cheats every conscious being of his or her life with its specious promises of a non-existent Heaven. As a ghost says to Will and Lyra when they visit the land of the dead:

> "When we were alive, they told us that when we died we'd go to Heaven. And they said that Heaven was a place of joy and glory . . . [a]nd that's what led some of us to give our lives, and others to spend years in solitary prayer, while all the joy of life was going to waste around us. . . . Because the land of the dead isn't a place of reward or a place of punishment. It's a place of nothing.
>
> "But now this child has come offering us a way out and I'm going to follow her. Even if it means oblivion, friends, I'll welcome it, because it won't be nothing. We'll be alive again . . . we'll be glittering in the dew under the stars and the moon out there in the physical world, which is our true home and always was" (*TAS* 286–287).

Pullman's view of the Church is probably best shown in the character of Father Gomez, "pale and trembling with zealotry" (*TAS* 62), who is pardoned in advance by the Magisterium for his task of murdering Lyra before she re-enacts the Fall of Eve. He is pitiless and fanatical, and nothing shakes his life-hating vision, because he is certain that he is right. As Father Gomez looks through the telescopic sights of his rifle, preparing to shoot Lyra in the head, he is momentarily bewildered when he sees the expression on her face, because she is falling in love with Will. He cannot understand "how anyone so steeped in evil could look so radiant with hope and happiness" (*TAS* 490).[1] Although the evidence that Lyra is not evil is right in front of his eyes, he never questions his beliefs.

Pullman's ideas about the Magisterium didn't come from nowhere; he's cobbled them together from many sources. Blake is, however, central. It is probably worth quoting the whole of a verse from Blake's poem *The Marriage of Heaven and Hell*:

---

[1] In the 2001 Scholastic Point UK edition.

All Bibles or sacred codes have been the causes of the following Errors:
1. That Man has two real existing principles: Viz: a Body & a Soul.
2. That Energy, call'd Evil, is alone from the Body, & that Reason, call'd Good, is alone from the Soul.
3. That God will torment Man in Eternity for following his Energies.
But the following Contraries to these are true:
1. Man has no Body distinct from his Soul: for that call'd Body is a portion of Soul discern'd by the five Senses, the chief inlet of Soul in this age.
2. Energy is the only life and is from the Body and Reason is the bound or outward circumference of Energy.
3. Energy is Eternal Delight.

In these lines, Blake reverses the usual picture propounded by the Church. Good is the natural joy of the sensual body, and evil is the "reason" that seeks to contain it. It's an idea that turns up in all Blake's poetry, as does his hatred of the priests who seek to destroy pleasure and love. His poem "The Garden of Love," from *Songs of Innocence and Experience*, shows this clearly:

> I went to the Garden of Love
> And saw what I never had seen:
> A Chapel was built in the midst
> Where I used to play on the green.
>
> And the gates of this Chapel were shut,
> And Thou shalt not. writ over the door;
> So I turn'd to the Garden of Love,
> That so many sweet flowers bore.
>
> And I saw it was filled with graves,
> And tombstones where flowers should be:
> And Priests in black gowns, were walking their rounds
> And binding with briars, my joys & desires.

It's not hard to see Pullman's Magisterium in that poem. But Pullman's

Church suppresses intellectual knowledge as well as the pleasures of love: for example, it names the idea of parallel universes as a heresy, even though it knows that it is true. The "intellectual fruit" with which Satan tempts Eve in *Paradise Lost* is the right to self-knowledge, and Pullman and Blake both rebel against this ban. At the end of *The Amber Spyglass*, the witch Serafina Pekkala tells Dr. Mary Malone what the angel Xaphania has told her:

> "[A]ll the history of human life has been a struggle between wisdom and stupidity. She and the rebel angels, the followers of wisdom, have always tried to open minds; the Authority and his churches have always tried to keep them closed" (*TAS* 429).

In fighting for the Republic of Heaven, Lord Asriel and his allies are fighting for the revolutionary Liberty that Blake summons in the final verses of *The Marriage of Heaven and Hell*. Asriel is Pullman's version of Blake's "son of fire," who "spurning the clouds written with curses, stamps the stony law to dust, loosing the eternal horses from the den of night, crying: Empire is no more! and now the lion & wolf shall cease."

But in the end, I think the single most important informing idea behind His Dark Materials is in the line that rings out like a clarion trumpet at the end of Blake's poem, for me one of the most beautiful lines written by this most beautiful of poets. And it is perhaps what you might most fruitfully take as the "meaning" of these books:

For every thing that lives is Holy.

———————

ALISON CROGGON is a prize-winning poet, playwright, critic, and novelist who lives in Melbourne, Australia. She is the author of the fantasy quartet, the Books of Pellinor, published by Candlewick Press.

REFERENCES

Blake, William. *The Marriage of Heaven and Hell*. Oxford: Oxford University Press, 1975.

____. *The Complete Poetry and Prose of William Blake*. New York: Doubleday, 1998.

Keats, John. *John Keats: Selected Poetry and Letters*. San Francisco: Rinehart Editions, 1969

Milton, John. *Paradise Lost*. New York: Oxford University Press, 2005. Introduction by Philip Pullman.

Rilke, Rainer Maria. *The Duino Elegies*. Translated by Alison Croggon.

His Dark Materials was conceived as a kind of anti-Narnia, an atheist parable to counter C. S. Lewis's biblical allegory. Certainly, the Authority is no Aslan. But as Vizzini compares the tropes and techniques of the two works, he wonders if they aren't more alike than their warring ideologies would suggest.

GOD IS IN THE STORIES
His Dark Materials vs. Narnia

NED VIZZINI

I remember where I was when, as a child, I decided that there wasn't any God: in church. I wasn't in the pews, though; I was upstairs, in a sort of well-furnished attic, sitting quietly as the service went on below me. I wasn't a disorderly child, so I'm not sure why I was up there, unsupervised. Now it would have been grounds for a lawsuit.

In any case, I spent a few moments looking out the window, counted a few cars (this was in New York, by the tram that leads to Roosevelt Island), and decided, in that quick, breezy way that children sometimes do, that God didn't exist and it was all a sham.

From then on, when I went to church and said the Lord's Prayer, I always left off the last word of each line:

> Our Father, who art in
> Hallowed be thy
> Thy kingdom
> Thy will be. . . .

———

Clive Staples Lewis had a similar start. His had a more intoxicating pre-amble—the headmaster of his first school was removed and placed in a mental institution—but then he settled into atheism under the guidance of a private tutor of the rigid, intellectual persuasion. Things stayed that way until he entered Oxford, where he began to take a look at Christian

143

texts in his studies of medieval and Renaissance literature. He found that he quite respected the writing (Jones).

It might seem silly to convert because of good work, but Lewis had some prodding from his colleague at Oxford, a young upstanding Christian gentleman named John Ronald Reuel Tolkien.[1] After befriending each other, the two founded a club, the Inklings, in order to drink and challenge one another in literary matters. The first two works they produced were science fiction epics; the second two were the Lord of the Rings trilogy and the Chronicles of Narnia (Jones, Miller).

The authors went about their Christianity in different ways. Tolkien shrouded his in the darkness of Middle-Earth and in relatively subtle connections (Frodo carries the ring up Mount Doom; Christ carries the cross up to Golgotha). Lewis made his bold and explicit.

The Lion, the Witch, and the Wardrobe may be the most effective introduction to the Gospels since the Bible. Since its publication in 1950, it has presented a barely concealed Christ story to 100 million young readers, much to the dismay of those who wish for children to avoid overpowering religious indoctrination. What's more, the Jesus of Narnia is not the pleasant, compassionate carpenter who encourages his followers to turn the other cheek, but an oversized warrior lion capable of commanding a frightening army of beasts. This version of Christ is a direct reflection of Lewis's own views of Jesus as a muscular, athletic, militant figure. And it is to this image that Philip Pullman responds with the His Dark Materials trilogy (Lurie).

HDM goes after a pretty big fish: a God-free Narnia, a lasting story for children and open-minded adults that isn't founded on Christian ideals, Greek mythology, or even folklore, but on the ideas of the Enlightenment and the dense imagery of *Paradise Lost*. It makes its atheism every bit as explicit as Lewis's Christianity and, outside the narrative, Pullman has attacked Christianity for its perpetual violence and the Narnia books in particular for being propaganda and religious claptrap (Miller, O'Brien).

If Lewis were alive, we might have a fascinating English Oxfordian dogfight on our hands. But in many ways, Narnia and HDM both reflect a submission of religion to something more powerful and primal: story.

---

[1] RE: "upstanding"—at the behest of the girl's father, J. R. R. Tolkien refrained from seeing his high school girlfriend for three years (Doughan).

By age ten I *really* didn't care about God. Mostly I liked to make fun of the hymns. I still did the "Our Father" mangling but sometimes I forgot since I was so focused on guessing what rhymes would end each line of each hymn.

There are a limited number of choices, really. Every time you see "giv'n" you know you're getting a "heav'n." If you see "love," as in "God's love," you're going to get "move," as in "in me doth move." If you see anything with "ah," "Hallelujah!" is coming up!

But as my opinion of God diminished, my opinion of church much improved. I had friends there now, and with the friends came some great times. In particular, there was a fellow named M. who was a complete pyromaniac. When we went on church retreats, he set about producing fires that could likely be seen by planes. The adult supervision didn't like what he was doing, but what could they do? If they turned their backs for a few seconds, another fire would spring up.

I had a job with the fires, too. I collected the wood. There was something so simple and satisfying about it: you left the campfire, went fifty feet in any direction, and picked up different classes of fuel, judging as you went along. *Oooh, this stick would be a nice bottom support for a log cabin. This would be perfect kindling for the next fire. This would complete a teepee formation that would create a column of flame.* Between M. and me, we had a great thing going with the fires, and once they were roaring we would sit around and talk about what the animals must think, how far away they had to scurry from our man-made marvels. Then we talked about video games.

On trips home, we'd have tall tales for our families and friends. We didn't just make the fires, we told them. We jumped them; we coaxed them into burning again the next day. We were fire masters. We would have made good cavemen. Never mind that all I did was collect wood. I was important, a co-hero in our little tales.

The Chronicles of Narnia stretches far and wide for stories (like my proud fire tale) that support its Christian message, utilizing Greek and

Irish sources as well as the Bible. *The Voyage of the Dawn Treader*, for instance, is based on the Irish legend of St. Brendan and his journey to the Land of Delight. Tumnus the double-crossing fawn bears a passing resemblance to Judas Iscariot (Jones, Grattan, Flood, and Hartig).

Pullman eschews these influences. He creates his story himself, stating in interviews that from the outset he intended to make HDM an epic of Miltonian scope but not explicitly based on any prior works. His cribbing from *Paradise Lost* is largely limited to the theme of the Fall of Man and the Milton quotes he uses in his title and in the chapter headings for much of *The Amber Spyglass*.[2] In lieu of the Greek menagerie of centaurs and satyrs, Pullman populates HDM largely with real people: explorers, priests, and scientists (Miller).

Therefore, aside from some cheeky references to Narnia (eight pages into *The Golden Compass*, Lyra is hiding in a wardrobe; at the start of *The Subtle Knife*, Will encounters an entrance to another world beneath a streetlight), Pullman and Lewis appear to have little in common in terms of their submission to story over religion. However, their works intersect in unexpected places. Both rely on a plot device that does *Alice in Wonderland* one better: the multiverse.

In Narnia it's done via a forest filled with pools. In HDM it's done with the subtle knife. But the multiverse is a powerful idea in epic children's fantasy that ups the ante on our natural desire to lose ourselves in another world. In these books there isn't merely a fantasy *elsewhere* for us to explore, there are multiple worlds and the implication of an infinite number of them.

The existence of a multiverse cleanly shears HDM and Narnia from traditional folktales as well from LOTR. The first two feature strange occurrences in this world (laced with morality), and drive home practical lessons. LOTR is detailed and thrilling, but you can never get to Middle-Earth, and this lack of possibility prevents the series from being true *children's* literature. Older children and many, many teenagers and adults are capable of appreciating the books' fantastically detailed worldbuilding, but LOTR never has a chance to connect with young readers the way that Narnia and HDM do. Pullman, in the *New Yorker*, speaks to this effect: without the possibility of the reader entering its world, LOTR

---

[2] Chapters 5–7, 16, 22, and 30.

is an exercise in charts and language rather than a story—inferior, even, to Narnia (Miller).

I didn't just tell people stories about church. At age twelve, I began telling stories *in* church, which played in exclusive engagements in my own head, about women in pornographic films. These stories made me tuck myself into the top of my pants to avoid setting off any alarms with my mother and came courtesy of my friend J., a story in and of himself: an El Salvadorian adopted by Jews, with a yen for violence and art.

J. had cable television. I had it, too, but not in my room. Channel 63 on cable was the Spice Channel; the porno channel, which I discovered later featured not hardcore porn but strategic camera angles and looped shots of faces that blocked out all the good stuff. The channel was off-limits to us without a credit card, but J., enterprising and warped, found a way around it.

If you selected channel 63 by pressing the keypad on top of the cable box, you would see about a half-second of the channel before the blocked blue screen—"To activate Spice, call 718/358-0900"—appeared and spoiled your fun. This meant that you got a chance to glimpse what could be an elbow or a woman's nether region for one garbled moment. But if you pressed 63 again, you'd get another garbled moment. And another. And another. Until you could almost make out a scene.

So J. and I would sit in his room watching scrambled, vague porno, building fantasies for ourselves to focus on later in the evening or the next day. I got to be excellent at alternating my fingers to get the best picture possible, and although it warped certain perceptions of mine (I got very confused about how a few sex acts were conducted, with the constant wavy bars blocking things), I loved it.

When I brought the images into church in my brain, I had a good story for God: *It was J.'s fault. He figured out the technique; I was only enacting it. And besides, God, the way I worked my fingers taught me how to play bass guitar in your name.* (I did some church songs once.)

The similarities between the self-contained churches of Narnia and HDM don't stop with a dependence on multiple worlds. They also work with a shared cultural heritage that runs deeper than either series's didactic ambitions. After all, can it be a coincidence that both Narnia and HDM feature orphan children and talking animals? These archetypes tell us more about storytelling techniques, childhood psychology, and Western thought than they do God or His lack. To wit, here are a few methods that both series employ:

1. *The orphan child and the villainous adult.*

The heroes of children's epics have to be children—specifically, they have to be child orphans. In Narnia the heroes are war orphans, victims of the inscrutable world of adult conflict. In HDM they are orphans in name only: Lyra, who is ignorant of her parents' identities, and Will, whose mother is an invalid and whose father is missing.

Why is this a necessary setup? There are a few reasons. The first has to do with scope: a child knows how to be a child, not an adult. Therefore, even if the adult world is fascinating, a young reader cannot put himself in the place of an adult protagonist, and so the protagonists of children's books have to be children.

Since the hero of a children's story must be a child, and no story is a story without a villain, who can the villain be? Another child?

That idea is instinctually unpleasant, a horror-film scenario that works better as social commentary than sweeping epic (see *Lord of the Flies*, *Battle Royale*). It disrupts our adult sensibilities because we don't like to think of children as fighting the way adults do—we still like to ascribe *some* innocence to them. It displeases children for a more practical reason: children fight all the time. A young reader has enough problems with playground wrestling and sartorial ostracization; he or she doesn't want to go home and occupy him- or herself reading about children battling one another.

Similarly, a large theme (fate, the "self") cannot serve as an antagonist in children's literature. Besides being difficult for even an adult to understand, studies in cognitive development tell us that children live in a state of egocentrism that literally prevents them from concerning themselves with such things (Nye and Carslon).

Can animals be antagonists? Good try. Unfortunately, any animal that can serve as an adversary in children's literature is an anthropomorphized one: a human in disguise.

With all other options expended, we are left with adults to be the enemy. This is immensely satisfying for children, since they are programmed to rebel against adult instruction. This also explains why it is best that the hero be an orphan. To create a sense of drama and danger, a child cannot battle an adult with the help of his or her parents. The child—the hero—must take on the adult alone, and become an adult by defeating the adult. The parents might be discovered along the way, but as the child-as-hero leaves home—especially if this step is the beginning of a three- or seven-part book series—there must not be a home to go back to.

2. Orphans: a footnote.

Not to mention, we just *like* orphans; we're immediately on their side. Who's not going to root for an orphan?

3. Talking animals.

The most memorable of Philip Pullman's inventions is the dæmon—a talking animal, each intimately tied to a person. In Narnia, talking animals are not tied to people but are their own burbling entities: beavers, deer, Marsh-wiggles, and the like.

These animals (in Narnia, the "talking beasts," which are separate from the beasts who serve as game) serve many purposes for the young reader. They provide relief from what would otherwise instantly become a boring hodgepodge of characters. In Narnia, Tumnus the fawn as a grotty little man and Iorek Byrinson the armored bear as a burly Norseman are infinitely more interesting than a grotty little man and a Norseman. In HDM the talking animals serve as tags, identifying and revealing the traits of the characters they are tied to.

But anthropomorphized animals have a stronger purpose: they tap directly into childhood notions of the fantastical, the make-believe, the elsewhere that exists in other universes. One of the first rules that children learn is that people can talk and animals cannot. When this rule is broken, other possibilities become immediately available and believable. It is no mistake that Lucy's encounter with Tumnus and Will's look at Lyra's dæmon are the first times that each character truly realizes that he or she is in another world.

The talking animal additionally offers our heroes wisdom, guidance, mystical knowledge, and history. Human veneration for animals runs much deeper than our present disrespect for them; animals are still worshipped by shamans and attendees at the Westminster Kennel Club Dog Show. They are assumed to have a knowledge of and connection to the spirit world that we do not.

Finally, what child hasn't wished that his or her pet might open up and say a few words? This is a particular cruelty of youth: someone with whom a child shares mutual love and respect can't communicate properly. In retaliation against this injustice, many people *do* talk to their pets, despite not getting any answer.

At church, the actual women came next, and M. and I liked them better than fire. One in particular, a female J., blossomed when I was thirteen into an olive-skinned walking statue capable of stopping not just my heart but ancillary organs as well.

I talked with J. downstairs after every service, about anything I could get my head around: sports, music, tests, other people, future plans. She seemed to reciprocate—I didn't know the signs as well back then, the comfortable flipping of hair and hands—but I didn't get a chance to do anything until one Tuesday afternoon when I went to her house in an entirely non-church, non-God situation.

First we played cards downstairs with a third party—a guy who I wanted to see disappear into one of the HDM or Narnia universes. When he left—some sort of blessed extracurricular obligation—she brought me up into her room and played the first Violent Femmes record for me. She wore mango perfume, and ever since then I've had a problem with it. She sat three feet from me, then walked around as if she didn't know her own near-religious power, but I couldn't do anything. I was scared, convinced of my own incompetence; I resigned myself to sulking in rejection later on.

Only after I left and requested that God make things possible for me next time—make there *be* a next time—did I realize that I might soon be convinced of His existence. J. had some grand intelligence working through her, I was sure of it.

HDM argues against the thirteen-year-old me with the vigor of a running politician. Narnia congratulates me for my conversion. But do both works lose something as they deviate into pedagogy?

Narnia, when explicitly Christian, falls into sappy, obvious imagery: tear-shedding and aggrandized speeches on the part of Aslan, whose death on the stone table is exaggerated to the point of treacle. Meanwhile, Pullman has a difficult job with HDM as he has no godlike figure to lead him through his didacticism. Instead he must make his statements of purpose blatant, risking breaks in the action that can bludgeon the reader—there are only so many times that characters in *The Amber Spyglass* can declare that there is no God and Christianity is a mistake.

Story, then, becomes the best way to evaluate both series. Story is dependent on both plot and writing, and Lewis and Pullman match up equally in the former and differ in the latter. Narnia's plot is unsatisfying in its lack of ambition—couldn't the seven tales be woven together?—but partly redeemed by the simplicity and narrative satisfaction of each installment. Pullman has a solid plot that runs through all three books, but many of his twists and turns make little sense, such as the sudden switch on Mrs. Coulter's part from enemy to loving mother, and the discovery by Mary Malone of a portal between two worlds placed, with no explanation, by the elderly couple in Cittàgazze.

This brings us to the writing. In comparing it, we have a remarkably fair playing field. Narnia weighs in at 1696 pages with pictures,[3] HDM at 1243 pages without.[4] Both are written in third-person omniscient point of view. Both have the similarities discussed above. How do they compare?

Lewis's lyricism can sometimes annoy: events occur in threes, and overly polite English phrases end paragraphs that can only be described

---

[3] Totaled from illustrated recent editions on Amazon.
[4] In the U.S. paperback 2000 editions.

as posh. However, the action moves along with the right amount of sparse imagery for our imagination to fill in the rest. There is also a sense of pacing: Lucy is in the wardrobe by page five noticing that something besides mothballs is underneath her feet.

Pullman, on the other hand, takes 140 pages to get to Lyra's decision to go North to rescue her friend Roger in *The Golden Compass*. The economy of his prose suffers from the fact that characters are constantly repeating themselves, having adventures and then relating them to other characters. The world-building is impressive, especially Mary Malone's travels to the land of the *mulefa*, but the prose itself is full of excerpts such as this one from *The Amber Spyglass*:

> Will considered what to do. When you choose one way out of many, all the ways you don't take are snuffed out like candles, as if they'd never existed. At the moment all Will's choices existed at once. But to keep them all in existence meant doing nothing (*TAS* 12).

The repetition of three "exists" sets the tone for much of the series, which could benefit from some editing.

I became convinced that God was real when I was in my early twenties, and not because of church, friends, or even women. I decided that he (or He, doesn't matter to me) was real because of stories. Like Pullman, who talks about the power of story in his speeches and rails against the corruption of story by religious fundamentalists to promote violence, I have a respect for and fascination with narrative.

Think about it: it's everywhere.

We're born, we live, we die. One, two, three, like Lewis's prose. Three fates. Three Norns at the bottom of the tree of the world. Three books in HDM. All around, stories with beginnings, middles, and ends.

And the people who made the stories before Narnia listened to the stories of their ancestors. The people who look back on us will see only our stories. It's a little bit like atoms, or like Dust—atoms with knowledge of themselves—the foundation of story. An atom that knows itself has a tale to tell. The molecule that owns that atom has a longer one. The part of my arm that owns the molecule has a longer story. I've got stories you wouldn't believe. I'm part of this insane American story that we're involved with right now. This Earth has a pretty crazy story going on. So if it scales up like that, narrative upon narrative, doesn't it make sense that there's one big narrative way up top? That it has a beginning, middle, and an end, too, but the beginning is infinitely long ago and the end is infinitely far away, just like the atom is infinitely small and the universe is infinitely large?

That's what I call God. It could also be called science. In this way, both Narnia and HDM admit to something larger than themselves.

NED VIZZINI is the author of *It's Kind of a Funny Story*, *Be More Chill*, and *Teen Angst? Naaah.* . . . He has written for the *New York Times Book Review*, the *New York Sun*, Bookslut, Huffington Post, Dogmatika, 3:AM, and Underground Voices. His work has been translated into six languages. He lives in Brooklyn, NY.

REFERENCES

Jones, Leslie Ellen. "Author Biographies for Young Adults: C. S. Lewis." EBSCO Publishing, 2003.
<http://www.epnet.com/thisTopic.php?topicID=16&marketID=6>
Miller, Laura. "Far From Narnia: Philip Pullman's Secular Fantasy for Children." *The New Yorker*, December 2005.
Lurie, Alison. "His Dark Materials." *The Guardian*, 3 Dec. 2005.
O'Brien, Breda. "Narnia Critics Risk Secular Fundamentalism." *The Irish Times*, 24 Dec. 2005.
The Catholic Encyclopedia, s.v. "St. Bredan."
Nye, W. Chad and Jerry S. Carlson. "The Development of the Concept of God in Children." *Journal of Genetic Psychology* 145, no. 1 (1984): 137.
Paglia, Camille. *Sexual Personae: Art and Decadence from Nefertiti to Emily Dickinson*. New Haven, Connecticut: Yale University Press, 1990.
Doughan, David. "J. R. R. Tolkien: A Biographical Sketch." *The Tolkien Society*.
<http://www.tolkiensociety.org/tolkien/biog_frame.html#1years>

His Dark Materials teases the boundaries of fantasy and science fiction. Within its covers both witches and physicists assert the many-worlds theory, and angels are made of dark matter—or is it Dust? To put it bluntly: How many children's books feature both quantum mechanics and talking bears? Owen questions the logic of Pullman's cosmology, and examines how he and other storytellers have fused the elements of science and fantasy into metaphors, magic, and meaning.

DANCING WITH THE DUST
A Mote from the Periphery

JAMES A. OWEN

And I will show you something different from either
Your shadow at morning striding behind you
Or your shadow at evening rising to meet you;
I will show you fear in a handful of dust.

—FROM "THE BURIAL OF THE DEAD,"
THE FIRST SECTION OF T. S. ELIOT'S *THE WASTE LAND*

There is an old storytelling trope (which was originally voiced by noted author and visionary Arthur C. Clarke) often used in certain kinds of fantastical fiction, that says science, if sufficiently advanced, is indistinguishable from magic. This is usually invoked for one of two reasons: 1) the writer is just being imprecise, lazy, or sloppy, and doesn't want to go to the effort of mapping out the mechanics of whatever wondrous device/event/theory it is that is integral to the plot but still unimportant enough to fully work out; or 2) the writer realizes from the onset that the functional underpinning of the device/event/theory isn't in and of itself all that important—but the metaphoric bridge it provides *is*.

The only problem with this is that readers of such stories (or rather, critics and/or academics) often mistake the latter case for the former, and then immediately proceed to chop the metaphor into smaller and smaller digestible, logical, rational chunks, the better to explain, prove, or disprove what they think the author meant while completely overlooking the *actual* impression the metaphor was intended to convey.

Invented worlds and events need enough detail to look, feel, and taste real, so to speak—but not so much that questioning the logic of the presented facts takes precedence over the flow of the story itself.

Perhaps Apollo did carry the sun in a chariot across the sky; perhaps he didn't. But during the thousands of years before we knew why it moved across the sky, the story helped us to believe that we understood. Perhaps the world was once covered in a great cataclysmic flood, which was survived only by Gilgamesh, or Deucalion, or Noah, or all three, or none of them. The story remains, regardless of the details. The details would almost lessen its power, because if the details were more precisely known and explained, then the story would actually feel less true to more people.

Works of fantasy rarely include elements of science fiction; it makes it an awful lot easier to credit (or blame) the progression of the story on a magic cloak, or mystical atlas, or what have you. Actual science never needs to come into fantasy to make it work. But sometimes science fiction skirts dangerously close to incorporating fantasy. Go far enough, and not only is the advanced "science" indistinguishable from magic, it's also sometimes the only way that the writer can make the leap from point A to point B—by constructing a bridge, not of invoked specificity, but of implied metaphor.

Marion Zimmer Bradley frequently mixed the two genres in her Darkover novels. They were science fiction standards that included fantasy elements—but she was more or less just having a good time mixing the two, rather than using the combination to express a particular viewpoint or concept. Roger Zelazny did the same thing much more deliberately with his Amber novels, and along with the combined scientific/magical elements added a third factor: the idea that *Will* could drive everything else.

The one author who combined science fiction/scientific inquiry and fantasy in seamless metaphor was Madeleine L'Engle, in her Time Quartet about the Murry family and their prodigy child Charles Wallace. The book *A Wrinkle in Time* introduced millions of children to the concept of a *tesseract* (a folding of spacetime, which allows instantaneous travel), and implied that there was a scientific basis (read as: *rational* basis) for everything that took place in the story. But not once did L'Engle attempt to explain any of it *scientifically*. Because, as she well knew, it was unimportant to do so. It was enough that she'd established that the Murrys were scientists, and that all forms of scientific inquiry, both macro and micro, would come together *somewhere*.

To L'Engle, these books were neither science fiction nor fantasy; they were *all* metaphor. This meant she could address any scenario in any way she chose: time travel; intergalactic travel; the existence of angels and dragons alongside supernovas and sentient stars and mitochondria. All these worked in her stories because explaining them was less important than the fact that they served a purpose in being there.

In the book that followed *A Wrinkle in Time*, called *A Wind in the Door*, Charles Wallace becomes ill because of the destruction of his *farandolae*: minute, sentient creatures that live inside his mitochondria (which are a functional part of every cell of a person's body).

The answer to curing Charles Wallace comes from realizing that those near-invisible sentient particles are connected to the larger world—on a galactic scale. Thus does the microcosmic affect the macrocosmic.

In the latter novels of his Ender cycle, Orson Scott Card took this idea one step further: elementary particles of Will itself comprise the underpinning substance of reality. What made this potentially dangerous was that he actually started to spell out how that worked. Building upon an idea/concept originated by Ursula K. LeGuin (that of the ansible, a superluminal communications device), Card postulated the existence of *philotes*: particles so small that the only properties they possess are location and duration.

Every chunk of matter, every molecule, every atom, has a philote of its own, and each is interconnected to other philotes via the twining of their connections—a process that can be augmented by Will alone, which, according to Card, is itself found in an intelligent "conscious" philote called an *aiùa*. It is the Will of the aiùa that brings together the countless philotes (and associated particles) to form an individual (and, well, anything else).

Thus, our essence, our identity, our very selves and souls, are a result of the Will found in a single particle of dust.

The fact that Card spells out its function so specifically does not make the concept of the aiùa less powerful for the reader; in fact, he does it so well that it's nearly as compelling viewed as speculative science as it is as fiction. But in doing so, Card treats these elements of his story more as metaphysics than metaphor. It's as I said at the beginning: science, sufficiently advanced, is indistinguishable from magic—or at least requires a metaphysical structure that, for all intents and purposes, might as well be magic. And that's where the footing becomes very precarious—because a metaphysical structure can be very easily mistaken for a metaphor, and vice versa. Even, sometimes, by the writer himself.

Which brings us to Dust.

In Philip Pullman's first book in the trilogy His Dark Materials, *The Golden Compass*, he introduces a lot of intriguing inventions. Some are as fanciful as talking bears and shape-shifting dæmons, while others appear to be more rooted in science, like machines that trace DNA and explorations of particle physics. Pullman is always walking a tightrope on this border between science and magic, making us question how real or not real we are supposed to see his world(s) as being. Foremost among his inventions is the concept of Dust, an elementary particle that (much like Card's aiùa) possesses consciousness. The presence of Dust implies sentience and intelligence—conferred by what is basically an invisible particle. Dust, and the examination of its properties, is one of the fulcrum points of Pullman's story, and it may be the first metaphor of the trilogy that it is introduced as something to be examined scientifically. Logically. And that just doesn't work out very well for the characters doing the inquiry.

Pullman makes a transition from describing the particles scientifically (as Rusakov Particles, after their discoverer in Lyra's world) to describing them as the more metaphoric Shadows (as they are described in our world). Interestingly, this switch also relates to a shift in the inquiry itself: the first approach is focused more on what the particles *are*, while the second is concerned more with what they *do*.

This is what made the concept of the aiùa work in Card's stories, and the farandolae in L'Engle's: once it was established that they existed, the emphasis changed from how they worked to what their effect was on the protagonists. (Which, oddly, may make an examination of the particles more valid—L'Engle described farandolae so convincingly, and in virtually the same breath as tesseracts and mitochondria, that many readers still are unaware she made them up out of whole cloth.)

Ironically, the bridge to making concepts like Dust work as metaphor may be his inclusion of metaphysical elements. The fact that the alethiometer—the titular golden compass—works by virtue of the Dust, as does the I-Ching system of divination, takes us a good stretch past Lord Asriel's scientific observations into metaphysics (which we as readers are asked to simply accept). The Intention Craft airship runs on, well, the pilot's intentions: a pilot must have a dæmon to fly, but the craft is driven by faith—or Will, if you, ah, will.

There's also the fact that in His Dark Materials, the Church (as Pullman portrays it) sees Dust as a physical manifestation of Original Sin, which makes for an interesting metaphor all by itself: it is a manifestation of sin that confers significance, wisdom, intelligence, and meaning. And sin is something that requires a deliberate human act, because angels, in Pullman's tale, are comprised entirely of Dust, but are less free, willful (or Willful), and capable than humans. The fact another name for Dust is Shadow may refer to this as well.

There are echoes of Peter Pan, and his missing shadow, here. Peter Pan's shadow was largely independent of him (much like the dæmons in *The Golden Compass*), but he is lessened without it. To be without one's dæmon brings tragic results in Pullman's stories (as seen through a series of experiments); and for a universe to be without Dust seems to imply the same, but on an immense scale. It also brings to mind Pullman's Specters, which resemble shadows but which are drawn from the Abyss between worlds whenever the boundaries are torn.

There's another interesting parallel to be made with Card's philotes: in Card's stories there is an insect-like race called the Formics that are comprised of a hive-queen and many worker drones (the Formics are the source of the humans' knowledge of philotes and ansible technology). The drones all have many philotes, but only the queen possesses an aiùa. Her aiùa is twined with the philotes of the workers, making them extensions of herself. A drone is capable of independent action (to a very limited degree), but the only real intelligence is in the queen. A drone severed from its queen has no Will. So perhaps Pullman's Specters are akin to collections of philotes seeking an aiùa: beings driven by purpose, but unguided by intelligence. However, the fact that Pullman has already so thoroughly explained—or overexplained—Dust takes the reader in unplanned directions, asking questions Pullman may not have intended us to ask:

1. If the angels are made entirely of Dust (philotes), but are not able to function at the same high level as humans who are not made of Dust but instead draw it to them, is it possible that Pullman, on a metaphysical level, was postulating the same organization in his Heaven that Card had with his Formics? (The Formics are able to see aiùas, just as Pullman's *mulefa* are able to see Dust unaided by any device.)

2. Are angels merely collections of philotes, controlled otherwise by an unseen aiùa?

3. And are humans, through an exercise of Will, able to build their own Heaven simply because they realize they can, as the First Angel built his Heaven for others to fight over?

All good questions for an essay, but not so much when they come up while reading the work itself, especially if you get lost in the process of asking. Adding too many scientific details to a metaphor risks sending readers off on tangents as they try to understand how all the rules fit together logically rather than how they make the story flow.

In *The Golden Compass*, Lord Asriel shows Lyra a passage in the Bible that states we are all made from the dust, and shall all return to the dust, and many other readers have speculated as to whether the Dust itself is, in fact, God. That is a question that I don't plan to answer. And not because I don't *have* one, but because I think my answer is *irrelevant*. And so is everyone else's, except to themselves.

What is significant here is the line of inquiry itself: the recognition that the metaphors are there for us to find in pursuit of our own answers.

Metaphors are powerful tools in large part because the interpretations can differ with every reader and, in fact, with every reading.

Describing the actual function of the tesseract would have made Charles Wallace's journeys a lot less interesting; similarly, delving too deeply into why quantum entanglement makes Pullman's lodestone resonator work would end up boring readers long before they became entranced with talking polar bears.

I think the reason Dust works so well as a metaphoric device (and why it evokes so many questions on so many levels) is because it taps into something humans have done for the whole of our history: tell stories to try to make sense of our world. The details of everyone's stories are different, but the core is always the same. This is where I always became nervous in reading the latter books in Card's Ender cycle, and where I simply came off the rails with regards to *The Golden Compass* and its sequels: the writers tried too hard to add details to what was otherwise a perfectly functional metaphor.

Card holds it together. Pullman does also—but only if you realize what he's trying to do, and gently, diplomatically, set it aside in favor of what he's actually *done*.

Dust, as it exists in the world of Lyra's Oxford and the parallel universes beyond, serves the exact same purpose as L'Engle's farandolae and Card's aiùas/philotes: to illustrate that everything is connected, from the smallest particle to the greatest expanse of universes, and that what connects everything is Will and intelligence. The fact that, ultimately, Dust is what recreates the universes, and the only way to preserve it throughout the multiverse is for two children to make a profoundly wise and moral decision, is telling as to what Pullman may have had in mind.

A lot has been made of Pullman's positions on Christianity (while, strangely, Jesus is nowhere to be found in the books themselves), which is exactly what I was getting at with regards to specificity: readers are focusing on the trees, and missing the forest. Indeed, Pullman himself may have drawn that focus, with his implied and outright stated positions on orthodox religion, Christianity in general, and the nature of God and Heaven. And I think the truest view of all his viewpoints is in what he already stated, quoting the Bible: "In the sweat of thy face shalt thou eat bread, till thou return unto the ground; for out of it wast thou taken: for dust thou art, and unto dust shalt thou return" (Genesis 3:19, *King James Bible*).

It's all about Dust, literally.

Dust is an elementary particle, which is drawn to intelligence but also confers wisdom, and may be the physical manifestation of love itself. Dust is also drawn to the loss of innocence (a theme mirrored in Card's books, with his precocious child-warriors, and in L'Engle's Charles Wallace), and Lyra and Will must utilize the wisdom they have attained in preserving the Dust. They choose the harder path for the greater good—and in doing so must deliberately pull apart their twining. Another act of conscious effort, or perhaps of faith. It's implied that Dust may even have played a part in the development of intelligent life—which, if true, underscores a slight difference in what Dust is perceived to be: it is not *an* elementary particle; it is *the* elementary particle. And that's as far as I think I can go into exploring the nature of Dust.

With regards to the author's use of it as a literary device, I'd like to note that Pullman once commented that he believed ". . . what's important is what you do and not what you think." Similarly, what Dust does is far more important than what Dust is.

In Card's stories, philotes are everywhere, in everything, but an aiùa must be "called," summoned from "outspace." The arrival of an aiùa organizes uncountable numbers of philotes into sentience. In Pullman's stories, Dust is used as if it were comprised of nothing but aiùas, bestowing a degree of consciousness wherever it is drawn. But Pullman also positions Dust as a universal resource, renewable but also in danger of being exhausted (according to the tenets of the story).

It's his MacGuffin, his prime mover, the fulcrum on which the story turns. And it's a metaphor, which is why it is so powerful.

The attention, or perhaps love, of intelligent beings creates Dust—which is drawn to intelligence, and brings with it even more positive attributes—and Dust in turn, is what connects everything. All else aside, all controversy discarded, is this what Pullman was trying to focus in his morality tale that crosses the boundaries, makes science indistinguishable from magic and magic indistinguishable from metaphysics, all wrapped in a single metaphor?

I think so. I believe so.

I think some of Pullman's intentions with creating Dust were obscured by the controversies created in over-explaining aspects of his stories. But I think the story itself is strong enough to overcome. Then again, I could be entirely wrong. That's the trouble with a good metaphor—when all is said and done, it may still not work. But as Pullman himself said:

> . . . when you write for an audience that largely consists of children, you have got to put the story at the centre of what you're doing, and when you do that, you cannot be self-conscious and postmodern and tricksy and self-referential and all that sort of stuff that the literary types like. But that

is actually a great advantage to you as an artist, because stories can say things more wisely and more profoundly and more directly than any commentary on stories can (Spanner).

In other words, "Never trust the teller, trust the tale." And—dare I say it? I trust, in Dust.

JAMES A. OWEN has been working professionally as an illustrator and storyteller for more than two decades, which is notable mostly because he's still comfortably in his thirties. To date, in addition to numerous illustration and design projects, James has written and illustrated two dozen Starchild comics and books, a series of prose novels titled Mythworld, and *Here, There Be Dragons*, the first in the Chronicles of the Imaginarium Geographica, which is published by Simon & Schuster. James works at the Coppervale Studio, a 14,000-square-foot, century-old restored church in Northeastern Arizona. For more information, visit coppervaleinternational.com.

REFERENCES

Spanner, Huw. "Heat and Dust." *Third Way*. 16 Jul. 2007. <http://www.thirdway.org.uk/past/showpage.asp?page=3949>

In a world in which the box office revenues of Lord of the Rings, Narnia, *and* Harry Potter *exceed the wealth of small nations, a movie series based on* His Dark Materials *would seem a no-brainer. But Pullman's outspoken atheism stirs the sort of controversy that Hollywood prefers to avoid. Holder looks at the marketing of the screen version of* The Golden Compass, *and examines the stories we tell ourselves about the stories we tell our children.*

LOSING MY RELIGION
Good Faith, Bad Faith, and the Box Office God

NANCY HOLDER

Your children are not your children.
They are the sons and daughters of Life's longing for itself . . .
. . . You may give them your love but not your thoughts,
For they have their own thoughts.

—KAHLIL GIBRAN, *ON CHILDREN*

After the tragedy at Columbine, adults see us as the Devil.

—AUDRA ADAM, 15 (PATNAICK AND SHINSEKI)

Opening scene: My father is attending a Sunday service at the Unitarian church here in San Diego, shortly after the minister married him to my stepmother, who is a congregant. I am near Lyra's age, with my brand-new stepsisters in Sunday school, and we are discussing our class's upcoming project: to build a Pygmy hut in the canyon behind the church so we can study other cultures. Parallel dimensions? Maybe not, but when you're eleven, a Pygmy hut is awfully darn close.

Meanwhile, back at the service, the minister steps up to the lectern to deliver his message. While doing so, he makes the casual aside that, of course, as Unitarians, neither he nor his audience ascribes any particular supernatural divinity to Jesus—that "we" are all sons and daughters of God, but that Jesus did not die on the cross to save us from anything.

MY FATHER
(in disbelief and horror)
WHAT?

MY BRAND-NEW STEPMOTHER
(somewhat patronizingly)
Oh, come on, Paul.
Surely you don't believe all that nonsense.

MY FATHER
(very uncomfortable)
Well, no.
(beat)
But I don't want my kids thinking like this!

Adios, Pygmy hut. We never went back to the Unitarian church again.
Let us move on to many years later, when I am a new parent, and a
friend of mine and I sit down at a Christmas party to discuss his philosophy of childrearing. His son is about Lyra's age, and my sweet little
baby girl is asleep in my arms, cooing like a dove.

THE FATHER
As far as he's going to know, I never did *any* drugs. No
marijuana. No acid. No Thai sticks. No mushrooms.

NANCY
(stunned)
Nothing? You were a pretty serious doper.

THE FATHER
He will never know that. All he's going to hear from
school, TV—everywhere—is that drugs ruin your life.
And if my life isn't ruined, he's not going to believe it.
And drugs are stronger now. They *can* ruin your life.

NANCY
So why not tell him that?
Because if he finds out that you're lying to him. . . .

THE FATHER
He won't figure it out until he's old enough to know
what he's doing.

NANCY
But—

THE FATHER
Listen, don't even open that door. Lie to your kid if
you have to, but keep her safe.

In their book, *The Manipulative Child: How to Regain Control and Raise Resilient, Resourceful, and Independent Kids*, authors E. W. Swihart, Jr., and Patrick Cotter have this to say about the current state of parenting:

> Parents today approach childrearing with fear and trepidation rather than with the joy and high hopes of yesteryear. Many parents seem to regard their children as time bombs, sure that some unwitting parental transgression will start the clock ticking—with good reason; the facts aren't very heartening (2).

Back when my daughter was an infant, I was shocked by my friend's attitude, but ten years later, I get it. I try not to lie to my daughter, who is Lyra's age, but I catch myself thinking through what I tell her in case it starts that bomb ticking. She is a very brave, spunky kid who will push the envelope on the truth herself, sometimes just for the hell of it and sometimes to achieve a desired result—permission, evasion, or material gain.

So here comes the film version of *The Golden Compass*, based on the book of the same name (at least in the United States), featuring a brave, spunky liar named Lyra who, because she wants to rescue her best friend from having his soul cut out of his body, ends up learning how to open doors into parallel worlds. Lyra is so dangerous to the evil theocracy in which she lives that a priest-assassin is sent off to murder her. The author of the novel is an avowed atheist and no friend to organized religion, but has explored the notions of faith with such mindfulness and depth that, on the one hand, fundamentalist Christian film critics such as Peter Chattaway are already urging boycotts of the film while, on the other, the

Archbishop of Canterbury thinks the His Dark Materials trilogy should be required reading in Anglican religious formation education.

At the Cannes Film Festival, where the stars and the director are presenting some footage of the upcoming film, Charlotte Higgins of *The Guardian* reports:

> Referring to the Magisterium—the all-powerful religious body that wields total political power in the world of Lyra, the heroine—[screenwriter-director Chris Weitz] said: "In the books the Magisterium is a version of the Catholic church gone wildly astray from its roots. If that's what you want in the film, you'll be disappointed. We have expanded the range of meanings that the Magisterium represents."[1]

And my initial, knee-jerk reaction is that I, a Pullman fan, am getting the "I never did drugs" song-and-dance. That this is going to be Pullman-Lite and Pullman himself is colluding a bit, because, despite having taken the high road repeatedly when defending his written work, he wants the movie to be a success.

I'm trying to be fair; I won't be able to see the movie before this essay sees print. And I know that Pullman's work can be generalized as taking on "all authoritarian systems of thought, religious or otherwise, that set out to enslave their followers under the guise of caring for them" (Tucker). But Pullman's entire trilogy pays homage to Milton's *Paradise Lost*, which explores Satan's part in the Fall of Adam and Eve and their expulsion from the Garden of Eden. Likewise, the battle lines are drawn in His Dark Materials between the forces of the Authority (God) and, ultimately, the protectors of Lyra, referred to as "the new Eve," who ultimately sacrifices her happiness to save a multitude of worlds. It's there, in practically every line of text, and I'm with the camp that argues that by glossing over it or taking it out altogether, *The Golden Compass* would be gutted.

Here's the strange thing: I'm willing to defend this choice, even

---

[1] On the Web site Bookshelves of Doom, in reaction to New Line's lack of backlash containment, Leila Roy says: "Too bad. I'd love to see that ad campaign. How would they even go about it? 'The Golden Compass, new and improved! Now without that pesky anti-church vibe!'"

though it saddens me, because I also want the film to be a success. As an author and something of a free thinker, I deeply admire Pullman. I'm pulling for Pullman. So I'm cutting him some slack that I might not otherwise give an author who seemed to be doing a bit of spin on behalf of the Hollywood hit-makers.

Meanwhile . . .

> [Director Chris Weitz] added that there would be no specific marketing to neutralize any potential religious backlash in the U.S. "We're going to let the film talk for itself," he said (Higgins).

That initially appeases me somewhat, as if it's some ballsy move on the part of New Line not to bother with all that nonsense. But as I mull it over, I think New Line knows there is absolutely no way they can take on the religious fundamentalists who loathe Pullman and come out the winner.

Ralph Waldo Emerson said, "Who you are speaks so loudly I can't hear what you're saying." When Christian film critics such as Chattaway talk about *The Golden Compass*, they invariably quote Pullman's discourses on the wrongness of monotheistic religions and the cruelties Christians have inflicted on nonbelievers. They point to the following paragraph (spoken by Dr. Mary Malone in *The Amber Spyglass*) as proof positive that Pullman's books are the work of the Devil, and that no matter how much New Line might like to spin *The Golden Compass* for the sake of the box office, there can be no redemption (and no tickets sold to these literalist fundamentalists) because Pullman is an unrepentant heretic:

> "I used to be a nun, you see. I thought physics could be done to the glory of God, till I saw there wasn't any God at all and that physics was more interesting anyway. The Christian religion is a very powerful and convincing mistake, that's all" (*TAS* 393).

Despite assurances from New Line that the specifically anti-religious theme has been jettisoned, Pullman is simply too tainted for literalist fundamentalists to go see it in theaters. Or else they think New Line is actually lying to them.

For example, Chattaway points to the inclusion of the word "dogma" on the Web site's description of the Magisterium as New Line's secret code for "Christian beliefs." Godless Hollywood, it implies, is putting new wine in old skins, and Pullman's anti-Christian rhetoric will permeate every close-up, middle shot, long shot, and CGI effect.

This prejudice against the film is coupled with precisely the same "cruel to be kind" authoritarianism Pullman takes issue with. Here is a quote from an article in *Christian Today* that discusses FOX's creation of a new Christian content entertainment division:

> "The groundswell that happened with a film like the *Passion* [*of the Christ*] was really illuminating to Hollywood, that there were people willing to come out to the theatre who had previously eschewed Hollywood films because of the violence and questionable material," Ms. Neutzling said (Mackay).

The Passion of the Christ received an R rating specifically because of its graphic violence, which included flaying Jesus so violently that the left side of his rib cage became exposed. This means that a lot of people reading this essay wouldn't have been able to even see the film in a theater (unless their pastor rented it and held a special showing, which did happen). And despite cutting five minutes of the most graphic violence, Mel Gibson still could not obtain the PG-13 rating he sought upon the movie's re-release.

It boggles my mind that Ms. Neutzling can say this with a straight face. Violence and intolerance must be okay if Christians/Jesus are involved, because it might help bring people to the Lord.[2]

From a Pullman-convert standpoint, I see code words of a different sort. Here's what the author has to say about the film version of his book:

> There will be no betrayal of any kind. I would not have sold the rights to New Line if I thought they were incapable of making an honest film from the story I wrote. Every conversation I have had with them, every draft of every screenplay I have seen, reinforces my belief in the integrity and the good faith of the film-makers (Pullman).

---

[2] And don't get me started on the video game, *Left Behind: Eternal Forces*. Please go to http://www.talk2action.org/story/2006/5/29/195855/959 and I do believe your jaw will drop.

I have a friend who used to own a bicycle shop in Reno. One day a kid wandered in and asked him what would happen if he bought a bike there and then it subsequently broke.

"We stand behind everything we sell," my friend said.

The kid looked at him for a minute. "That's just TV talk," he said.

I am suspicious that Pullman's quote contains some TV talk. He also posits on his Web site that New Line knows *The Golden Compass* isn't about cavorting off to exciting new worlds or CGI effects, IT'S ABOUT LYRA (in capital letters.) And he also says:

> Anyone who read a piece I published in *The Guardian* on 6 November . . . the subject of theocracy and reading, will have seen very clearly that my main quarrel has always been with the literalist, fundamentalist nature of absolute power, whether it's manifested in the religious police state of Saudi Arabia or the atheist police state of Soviet Russia. The difference between those powers on the one hand, and the democratic powers of the human imagination on the other, are at the very heart of His Dark Materials—and to understand this, you need exactly the sort of intelligence that can grasp the nature of imagery (Pullman).

So basically, Pullman himself is working at containing religious backlash (else, why bother saying all this? Methinks he doth protest too much). Reassuring the literalists that he is speaking metaphorically encourages us faithful to be even more flexible: to look beyond his brilliantly conceived thematic notion of recasting the Fall of Mankind, to envision his movie as a kid's daring escape from a repressive organization of bad guys—the by-now Hero's Journey chestnut that describes everything from *Oliver Twist* to The Lord of the Rings.

Okay, *The Golden Compass*/HDM is a Hero's Journey and it is about Lyra. Additionally, it takes place in many fantastical worlds that will look great in CGI. And not everyone who is a fantasy film fan or even a Pullman fan is all bunched up about the religion stuff, and many may even think the fans who are worried about that are nitpicking literalists themselves. Genre theorists talk about "the construction of an audience," and there are a lot of other elements in the HDM "verse" that can draw viewers, particularly the varied creatures such as the Gallivespians, the *mulefa*, the armored bears, the witches, the Specters, and of course, the dæmons. And New Line is playing those marketing cards beautifully.

Their ace is the audience who helped make their Lord of the Rings trilogy a smash hit. The trailer for *The Golden Compass* opens with the words, "In 2001 New Line Cinema opened the door to Middle-Earth. This December they take you on another epic journey." The shining LOTR ring slowly spins, becoming Lyra's alethiometer. Some fans have complained that this makes *The Golden Compass* look like *The Lord of the Rings IV*, but those who complain are already won: they are clearly Pullman fans who want to make sure they're getting a real Pullman experience. Then the viewer is treated to several shots of Lyra's Oxford, the main characters, Svalbord (I assume), and how the dæmons (and their morphing) will be handled. Those shots serve the purpose of reassuring first-gen fans that the places (and dæmons) they love are still in the movie and informing people who are unfamiliar with Pullman and/or *The Golden Compass* that New Line has a cool new fantasy film on the way. And New Line is blatantly asking the LOTR fans who would welcome a fourth movie to give *The Golden Compass* a shot.

The official movie Web site has already been praised in marketing venues such as www.imediaconnection.com as a state-of-the-art marvel, especially when it comes to sound design and interactivity. It features downloadable wallpapers, hidden downloads of production art/concepts within the alethiometer, and, perhaps most effective of all, a questionnaire that, when answered, reveals your own dæmon. You can send your dæmon to your friends, who can change it, and once it has settled you can save it and upload it into MySpace and personal Web sites and blogs.[3] Visitors can also sign up to receive e-mailed updates on the film, keeping them engaged.

Also to be courted are online "Influentials," those who have taken ownership of carrying the torch for Pullman in what Chris Anderson, author of *The Long Tail*, calls "the reputation economy." These are fans who find value in their devotion to Pullman, and have built communities, both e- and virtual, serving as clearinghouses and peer reporters of all things

---

[3] It's addictive: columns have been devoted to selecting dæmons for celebs (including Nicole Kidman) in *New York Magazine*; for the editor of Pop Goes the Library (www.popgoesthelibrary.com/labels/deamons.html) and even for the righteous Peter Chattaway, although he rather regretted succumbing to temptation.

Pullman. New Line streams content—footage, stills, and news—to fan sites such as www.bridgetothestars.net and HisDarkMaterials.org (which are, in themselves, beautiful Web sites), interacting with its loyal core of influential fans. New Line is on the grid and paying attention, and so are Pullman's fans. My visit to the bridgetothestars.com site today featured a link to an Italian fan site, with an interview of an Italian technician talking about the film's "technical aspects." This allows loyal fans ("Sraffies," a term for HDM fans created from the *mulefa* word for Dust) to interact with fellow fans all over the world.

More locally, I sat down with Maile McKeon, the librarian at Miramar Ranch Elementary School and the former manager of the children's department at the Carmel Mountain Barnes & Noble in San Diego, to discuss the marketing efforts of *The Golden Compass*. She told me that His Dark Materials was the only set of books she could think of that was shelved in the children's, teen, and adult sections of the bookstore (although she wasn't sure about Lord of the Rings.) Harry Potter was definitely not located in the adult section, and kids sought out the Potter books on their own. Adults who wanted HP went to the children's section, too.

But, she said, in the case of HDM, parents sought out the books first, and showed them to their kids, saying, "You should read this. You'd like it." This makes sense, as *The Amber Spyglass* was the first children's book to win the prestigious Whitbread prize (in all other cases won by an "adult" novel) in England. Also, for a trilogy whose first book came out twelve years ago, HDM lacks both the "legs" of Harry Potter and the iconic stature of Tolkien's Lord of the Rings.

"I had to read *The Hobbit* in high school," Maile recalls. We agreed that, generally speaking, everyone *had* to read Tolkien but a lot of people (more than one hundred million) *wanted* to read Harry Potter. Where did that leave HDM, I wanted to know?

So we watched the trailer together. She declared that it was "brilliant" because it reproduced the same buying pattern that she had seen in the bookstore. She noted that Lyra was present in the majority of the shots, which clearly sent a message to kids that this was a kid's movie. (An aside: Dakota Blue Richards, the actress who plays Lyra, was selected from thousands of hopefuls, and this is her first acting role. An ordinary child entering a magical world indeed—shades of Harry himself.) But,

Maile pointed out, the adult roles were not filled by "warm, fuzzy actors who usually star in kid's movies." They were filled by actors who adults like—Nicole Kidman, Sam Elliot—and actors who teens and adults like—Daniel Craig, Eva Green. She especially thought the casting choice of Daniel Craig as Lord Asriel was genius.

> My twenty-seven-year-old male roommate had heard me talking about the books, but he didn't really have any interest in seeing the movie until he heard that the new James Bond is in it. Now he can't wait—and to fill the time until the movie comes out, he's reading the books.

So, despite the fact that *The Golden Compass* is being presented as a movie about a young girl, inclusion of A-list adult stars indicates that it is aggressively going after an adult audience that is not specifically LOTR-friendly and not even particularly SF/F-friendly. In other words, New Line is mainstreaming *The Golden Compass* for grown-ups, despite its kid-flick fantasy trappings.

About the fantasy aspect: Sraffies have expressed concern about the potential for misuse/overuse of CGI, and a contingent reported from Cannes:

> Chris Weitz spoke again of his belief that audiences were becoming tired of flashy special effects and reiterated that his vision for the film is a more personal one and he tries not to let the CGI take over the movie (Bridgetothestars.net).

Again, I believe that New Line is directly "shouting out" to its fan-peer reporters. They also streamed first peeks of ancillary merchandise—toys and games—to bridgetothestars.net.

So New Line has put in a lot of person hours, serious thought, and skilled effort into packaging and marketing *The Golden Compass* in hopes of appeasing the box office god. It has defused religious debate either by ignoring it or leaving it to Philip Pullman to discuss. It has assured HDM loyalists that it has Pullman's seal of approval. It has engaged net-users with beautiful interactive sites, special downloads, e-mail updates, and the ability to create your own dæmon. It cast A-list, non SF/F actors to play key roles. It feeds special information to fan sites.

And last but so very much not least, I'm not sure if New Line knows this, but it has timed the release of *The Golden Compass* perfectly. Behold:

A week ago, I attended a book club barbecue with six other mothers of almost-eleven-year-old girls. Our daughters are nearing middle school, and they are changeable, moody, and confusing. Their dæmons have clearly not settled. The moms were discussing Jody Picoult's *The Tenth Circle* (which I, regrettably, have not read) and were critical of her characterization of a fourteen-year-old girl who has been taking drugs and having sex.

> DISBELIEVING BOOK CLUB MOM
> (moaning and rolling her eyes)
> Come *on*, what fourteen-year-old does that?

> NANCY
> (in the same condescending tone as my sophisticated,
> non-believing stepmother)
> Oh, come on, surely you don't believe that!

Here I am in the land of *The Manipulative Child*: I see at once that, just like me, these moms are scared to death that they are going to screw up their daughters. That something we do might transform our sweet little girls into Columbine Devils. So when the Oblation Board talks about intercision to keep kids from sinning, when Lyra acts like a brat and Lord Asriel just wants to throttle her, when Lyra runs away from Mrs. Coulter—I think these things will resonate deeply with moms like us.

Or maybe, like me, these other moms will be bemused that, while worrying about Pullman's approach to Christianity, conservative parents don't seem to put up much of a fuss about how Lyra's own mother, the evil and ambitious Mrs. Coulter, mutilates children with the Church's full backing, or that, in his bid to throw off the yoke of religious oppression and explore the universe, her father kills the boy Lyra spends the entire novel trying to rescue.

In fact, as I ponder this, I, with my ticking-clock kid, find that I am so anxious about watching Nicole Kidman and Daniel Craig play Lyra's lying parents (neither of whom are redeemed by the end of the novel version of *The Golden Compass*) that I'm not sure that, given the deeply unpleasant subject matter, I'll even be able to *watch* the movie. Which would be the final irony, as far as I'm concerned: no matter how hard they try, no matter which one of the audiences I may be in, New Line might not be able to sell me, a Pullman believer, a ticket to see their movie.

> And if you would know God be not therefore a solver of riddles.
> Rather look about you and you shall see Him playing with your children.
>
> —KAHLIL GIBRAN, *ON RELIGION*

NANCY HOLDER is the author of approximately eighty novels and 200 short stories, essays, and articles. Three of her books have appeared on the New York Public Library's Books for the Teen Age, including *Pretty Little Devils*. Her most recent young adult novel, *The Rose Bride*, is on shelves now. She and her dæmon, Boreallus, a snow leopard, live in San Diego with her daughter, Belle, and Belle's dæmon, Tarquin, who has not yet settled.

REFERENCES

Anderson, Chris. *The Long Tail: Why the Future of Business Is Selling Less of More*. New York: Hyperion, 2006.

Chattaway, Peter. "These Are the Dæmons in Your Neighborhood." *Filmchat*. 12 May 2007. <http://filmchatblog.blogspot.com/2007_05_01_archive.html>

Higgins, Charlotte. "Newcomer Shines in Pullman's Golden Compass." *The Guardian*, 22 May 2007, <http://bookshelvesofdoom.blogs.com/book-shelves_of_doom/2007/05/golden_compass_.html>

Mackay, Maria. "Fox Brings Christ to Hollywood." *Christian Today*. 20 Sept. 2006. <http://www.christiantoday.com/article/fox.brings.christ.to.hollywood.with.new.christian.division/7681.htm>

Patnaik, Gayatri and Michelle T. Shinseki. *The Secret Life of Teens: Young People Speak Out About Their Lives*. New York: HarperSanFrancisco, 2000.

Pullman, Philip. "Chris Weitz, New Line, 'The Times,' and How to Read." *Philip Pullman's Official Web site*.
<http://www.philip-pullman.com/pages/content/index.asp?PageID=118>

Roy, Leila. *Bookshelves of Doom*. < http://bookshelvesofdoom.blogs.com/>

Swihart Jr., E.W, and Patrick Cotter. *The Manipulative Child: How to Regain Control and Raise Resilient, Resourceful, and Independent Kids*. New York: Bantam Books, 1997.

Tucker, Nicholas. *Darkness Visible: Inside the World of Phillip Pullman*. London: Wizard Books, 2003.

Will. "Latest News: Press Conference Report & Images." *Bridgetothestars.net*. 22 May 2007. <http://www.bridgetothestars.net/news/press-conference-report-images/>

No book is pure fiction: something must be shared between a novel's reality and our own, or we wouldn't begin to recognize what was going on. Pullman's Oxford may be full of zeppelin stations and anbaric lights, but it's closer to the real Oxford than you might think. Comparing the two, Wein shows how connections between truth and fiction make both more interesting, as if a measure of Dust were leaking between this pair of real and imaginary cities.

UNREAL CITY
A Visit to the Oxford of His Dark Materials

ELIZABETH E. WEIN

I'd like to be a tourist in Lyra Belacqua's Oxford. I've got a couple of unreliable maps and the dubious authority of having once circumnavigated the city in a punt[1]—twenty-two miles up the Isis, then the Oxford Canal, and finally down the River Cherwell. Lyra's Oxford seems familiar. I recognize the waterways, the street plan, and many of the buildings. But Lyra's city also contains unexplored territory for me. Where are the Claybeds that are her battlefield? How come I can't find the real Jordan College? What's real in this city, and what isn't? By comparing Philip Pullman's visions of Oxford in His Dark Materials with each other, and with the real Oxford in our own world, you can see how cunningly a fiction writer makes an imaginary world convincing. You, the reader, are teased into thinking that you recognize it. And because you recognize it, you believe in it.

I have two maps spread open in front of me as I plan my tour. One is a map of the "real" Oxford, called *A Souvenir Map and Guide to Oxford* and published by Postermaps; the other is a map of Lyra's Oxford, called *Oxford by Train, River, and Zeppelin* and "published" by Globetrotter. You could hang them on the wall and they'd make pretty posters. Each shows colorful, two-dimensional artistic drawings of stylized landmarks, rather than a straightforward grid plan. Both are decorated with areas of woodland, with

---

[1] A punt is a flat-bottomed boat like a small scow that you steer with a pole. Punting is a popular student and tourist activity in Oxford; you can rent punts by the hour from three different public boathouses, and many Oxford colleges and homes own private punts.

detailed boats and trains representing river and railroad traffic. The Postermap doesn't stretch as far as Oxpens Road, where the Zeppelin Station is supposed to be according to the Globetrotter. But if it did, the existing Oxpens Ice Rink *does* look a bit like a zeppelin station.

To my mind, neither map shows the *real* Oxford. That's because the Postermap was published no later than 1990, based on information gathered between 1984 and 1987. This map is nearly twenty years old. Of the sponsors printed on the back of the Postermap, many advertise shops that are now closed down. Every single telephone number listed on the map was made obsolete by a systematic change in the mid-1990s. The train and bus companies have changed and roads have been bypassed. The Oxford of twenty years ago resembles the "real" Oxford the way the Oxford of Lyra's universe resembles Will Parry's Oxford— they're alike, but they're not identical. You can't navigate accurately with either of these maps, but they look so much like the real thing that we believe they are reliable. In Pullman's world, Will's universe is meant to be the same as ours and should contain the "real" Oxford—only, of course, Will's Oxford isn't real, either. It's fictional, part of Pullman's imaginary landscape. Will's Oxford contains a gateway into an alternative world, a 33,254-year-old skull that projects traces of intelligence, a knight who knows what an alethiometer is, and a scholar who studies dark matter. It's not our world at all, but we are fooled into thinking it's like our world—that makes it seem real.

Jordan College is a good place to start our city tour of Lyra's Oxford. In an essay called "From Exeter to Jordan," Pullman explains how the opening of *The Golden Compass* sets up his imaginary world by drawing parallels to the world as we know it:

> I prefer to ease my readers in without startling them too much, so the fellows of Jordan College, in my imaginary Oxford, eat dinner in Hall and then retire elsewhere to drink coffee, almost as if it were real life; and that is the point at which the story begins (Pullman 2002).

On the Globetrotter map, Jordan occupies the spot where Exeter College stands in our world, "though rather more of it," as Pullman says (Pullman 2002). Exeter College is where Pullman himself was a student, and in writing the *The Golden Compass* he "didn't see why [he] should-n't make [his] college the biggest of them all" (Pullman 2002). That's a fine example of the author playing God, playfully creating a world as he'd like it to be! But, though Pullman makes a literary joke in placing Jordan where Exeter stands and though Lyra may think of Jordan as a kind of glorified playground, Jordan College is a serious place where great things happen. From what Pullman shows us of Jordan, we know that the university of Lyra's Oxford is traditionally formal. The Scholars wear robes, they prefer soft lighting; they live, die, and are buried in the medieval warren of buildings where they study. Jordan College supports scholarly research, which some people consider blasphemous, and the college Master is not beyond attempting murder to keep his beloved Lyra from danger.

Pullman uses the real geography of Oxford to highlight important aspects of Lyra's imagined life, her personality, and her world. The city outside Jordan College influences Lyra as profoundly as the secrets with-in Jordan's medieval walls. Beyond these walls lies an inland city bound by the Oxford Canal, the River Cherwell, and the River Isis.[2] In our own world, these waterways were once important transportation routes. They're mostly used for recreation now, but it seems natural for the gypt-ian community of Pullman's Brytain to count them as part of their watery highway system. It also makes sense that the fictitious Horse Fair is held in Jericho, at the point where the canal and the river meet, as this is an important junction even in our world. Pullman describes the real Jericho as "a watery, raffish, amiable, trickster-like world of boat dwellers and horse dealers and alchemists" (Pullman 2004). In *The Golden Compass*, he uses the colorful life of Jericho as a contrast to the stiff formality of Jordan College.

This contrast is closely related to "town and gown" rivalry. Lyra's Oxford, like the real Oxford, is a city where industry and scholarship are uneasy neighbors. In fiction and in reality, the university library is just around the corner from the city market. As Pullman suggests in his description of Jericho, even without clambering between universes you

---

[2] The River Isis is actually the River Thames. For obscure reasons it is called the Isis only as it runs through Oxford, even in this world.

can find several different "worlds" in a single city. Lyra, as university ward and unsupervised orphan (more or less), leaps sure-footedly between these worlds. She thinks of herself as "university," but even university society is divided into strict levels of class and rank, which Lyra conveniently ignores most of the time. Sometimes she's called upon to wear a dress and mingle with important visitors, but her best friend is Jordan College's kitchen boy, Roger, her companion in the scullery and on the street. Lyra is tutored by the university Scholars when they remember to do it, but what she likes best is organizing gang wars with gyptians and the detested children of the Claybeds. Lyra's tremendous ability to win loyalties, so important to her destiny, is demonstrated early on through her encounters with the Oxford city children and the university Scholars.

Lyra's Oxford also gives her the basis for her idea of womanhood. Even Marisa Coulter has an Oxford affiliation, and is a member of the women's college of St. Sophia's. Until Mrs. Coulter's appearance, however, the only women in Lyra's life come from the strikingly different social groups of her city, and she considers all women to be somewhat "below" her in rank; she is, after all (or thinks she is), the daughter of a count. These women include gyptian mothers, servants, and the occasional "female Scholar," whom she despises. Ma Costa is not a bad role model for a heroine, but Lyra doesn't think of her as a role model until perhaps later in the book. She is Lyra and she is a child, and until she meets Mrs. Coulter it doesn't occur to her that she could ever possibly turn into one of these grown-up female creatures—any of them.

So the city of Oxford acts as the frame for Lyra's entire world: its geography, its society, its politics, its intellect, its religion. It's important for Pullman to give us a convincing, intriguing sense of place in Oxford, because the opening chapters of The Golden Compass set the tone for Pullman's entire His Dark Materials trilogy. If you were to describe the Europe of Lyra's world, you would find much of its mechanics described first in Lyra's Oxford: the use of anbaric energy and naptha fuel for lighting and power, the wine and poison in vogue, the modes of transport, from zeppelin to gyptian barge. The politics, politicians, and religion of Lyra's universe are all first presented to us through Lyra's Oxford existence. Lyra's Oxford is by no means the largest or most complex location in His Dark Materials, but it is the most intimately detailed. It's the only location for which there is a published map (although this isn't included in the trilogy).

This one city in Lyra's world sets up a convincing picture of what the rest of the world will be like. Lyra's London is sketchier (and mostly seen from the inside of grand buildings). In *The Golden Compass*, the world of the Fens where the gyptians gather, and the world of the icebound northern wastes are as believable as Oxford, but Pullman never uses as much specific detail to describe them. He doesn't need to. He sets up our expectations back in Oxford, in the first few chapters of the series. We know what the gyptians are like because Lyra hijacks Ma Costa's barge. Our expectations for the Arctic voyage are set up during Lord Asriel's presentation to the Jordan Scholars. Oxford gives us a miniature glimpse into the entire universe of His Dark Materials. It shows us what to expect, and it is familiar enough that we are drawn into this strange universe without questioning its substance.

Let's climb from one world into another and visit some sites in a third Oxford: Will's Oxford.

In *The Subtle Knife*, Lyra is transported from her own universe to the in-between universe containing Cittàgazze, where she meets Will. Eventually she and Will climb through a window, cut into the fabric of that universe, and Lyra finds herself in an Oxford that is recognizably similar to ours. Pullman makes our own familiar world seem menacingly, uncomfortably alien by allowing us to view it through Lyra's eyes; this should be the city we know, but because we're visiting it with Lyra, it's confusing and upsetting. She thinks of it as a "mock-Oxford," in contrast to her own "real Oxford" (*TSK* 66), and finds it to be a "city that was both hers and not hers, [where] danger could look friendly, and treachery smiled and smelled sweet" (*TSK* 141). Even without evildoers in the picture, Will's Oxford is intimidating to Lyra. Traffic is faster and more frequent, there's a larger population, there are bigger (and to Lyra's eyes, uglier) buildings; there are mysterious inventions such as traffic lights and chewing gum. Lyra's foundation, Jordan College, does not exist. She is homeless here.

As a visitor to this other Oxford, the neo-Gothic Victorian architecture of one of the buildings attracts Lyra because it's a style she's comfortable with, and even though it's a place that doesn't exist in her own world, she goes inside. It turns out to be the Pitt Rivers Museum. While here, Lyra examines Arctic equipment and a case full of trepanned skulls. The real Pitt Rivers is a quirky, eclectic anthropological collection accessed through the back of the larger Oxford University Museum of Natural History. In its limited quarters the Pitt Rivers contains so many wondrous objects that Pullman has called it "a dream machine" (Pullman 2004). The Pitt Rivers is not as well known as its big sister the University Museum, and when I first read *The Subtle Knife* I was so excited to discover this twist in the story that I wrote to the Pitt Rivers to tell them about it. Felicity Wood, who edited the *Friends of the Pitt Rivers Newsletter*, reported back to me: "In the medical case there is only one skull. It has a hole near the back/base but the label only says it is Peruvian and [gives the] date of accession . . . 1906. The writing is on the skull itself and not on a card" (Wood 1998). She noted that various other objects "were not quite as described," and added later, "which of course is very reasonable if you are a novelist" (Wood 2007). The real world brings you up from the imaginary with a shock. I first wrote to Wood hoping that the objects would match up, and she first examined the cases with the expectation that they would.

Why, as readers, do we want the imaginary city to line up with the real city? Why do we want to stand beneath the hornbeam trees on Sunderland Avenue? Why do we want the imaginary objects of the story to exactly mirror the real ones in the museum? I think it's a case of what Sir James George Frazer calls "sympathetic magic," where "things act on each other at a distance through a secret sympathy." If the object exists, and you can see it or touch it, the story that includes it must be true. Finding the real thing—seeing the real row of hornbeam trees on Sunderland Avenue where the gateway from world to world is supposed to exist, looking up at the tower of the church of St. Barnabas and recognizing it as St. Barnabas the Chymist in Lyra's world, photographing the startling architecture of the science building where Mary Malone is supposed to work—makes *Lyra* more real. If we can point to a sled, skull, or sealskin coat and say, "That's the one," it makes the fictitious story suddenly come true for us. The fascination is not that Philip Pullman identified the skull, but that his heroine Lyra identified it.

Pullman makes little inside jokes in placing things around his imaginary city. The brickworks are set on a site that may have actually housed a brickworks (Pullman 2002), the existing green and distant woods of

Wytham and Shotover become White Ham and Château-Vert, the Eagle Ironworks—known familiarly to Oxford residents as "the Lucy" after its nineteenth-century owner William Lucy—takes its name in Lyra's world from the dæmon of the long-dead alchemist Randolph Lucy (Pullman 2003). How wonderful it is for the lucky reader who "gets" these jokes, who can feel that he or she shares an insider's view of the city with the author, or better yet, with Lyra herself!

We never do find out why the objects Lyra sees in the Pitt Rivers Museum *exactly* match the objects she uses on her journey to Bolvangar in her own world. Maybe there is no "why." The objects are an example, for Lyra as well as for the reader, of the intricate connection between the many universes of His Dark Materials in general, and between Will's and Lyra's universes in specific. The kinship Lyra feels with these museum objects in a world strange to her must help to convince Lyra of her importance and her role as the center of the universe (which, in many remarkable ways, she *is*). The rope she finds in the museum isn't just any familiar object; it is—or is twin to—a rope that she was once *bound* with. Lyra has a personal connection to these museum objects, which eventually helps to convince Mary Malone first to believe Lyra, and then to set out on her own remarkable journey.

Pullman calls the Pitt Rivers Museum a "time machine" as well as a "dream machine" (Pullman 2004). Here's another way he manages to convince us that his imaginary Oxford is as intricately and intimately connected to our Oxford as the museum's display objects are to Lyra: he makes Lyra's Oxford appear to be set in another time. Lyra's fictional world is similar to ours, but in a masterstroke on Pullman's part, it seems to be set in what's recognizably the *past* relative to our world. Our own past is also another world for us, which we know a bit about but can't ever visit or fully understand. Lyra's world shows us a different past, a foreign and ultimately imaginary past; but our own past is foreign enough that we recognize Lyra's Oxford in the same way we recognize the Oxford of twenty years ago, or of eighty years ago—as a place that doesn't exist except in the maps of our mind. The Oxford of eighty years ago *did* exist, but as we read Pullman's books, we suspend disbelief and imagine that Lyra's Oxford may have existed alongside it.

In one way Lyra's Oxford is the more immediate of the two; for the reader immersed in the books, it exists here and now. So you could say that the twenty-years-past Oxford of my Postermap is *less* real than Lyra's Oxford. Lyra's Oxford exists out of time; it exists as you read and it doesn't age. The catalogues and books advertised on the Globetrotter map are always relevant in the context of Lyra's fictional world, unlike the closed shops and obsolete phone numbers on my real map. "Mary Malone lives here," says the fictitious handwritten note on the edge of the Globetrotter map.[3] In Pullman's fictional universe Mary Malone still lives there; she will always live there. Our world changes and grows older; the fictional world always exists in its own present.

My favorite (real) object in the Pitt Rivers museum is a Chinese orb consisting of interlocking balls, one inside another like a series of Russian dolls, carved from a single piece of ivory. You can turn the smaller balls inside the larger ones, but you can't remove them. That's just the way the different Oxfords work—the fictional, the historical, and the actual. They all exist together, even though you can't see them all at the same time—the real Oxford of laborers, and scholars, and council workers, and tourists, and the imaginary Oxfords of Lyra and Will and many others.[4] They overlap and interlock. The only one you see properly is the outer layer; you get glimpses of the first few inner layers, but you have to take it on faith that the rest of them are really there.

And so our tour brings us at last to the Botanic Garden. Here the worlds match up; the layers are visible one beneath the other. The ancient gate, the stately tree, and the Cherwell flowing past are the same in Lyra's world, in Will's and in our own, and there is the bench where Lyra and Will can meet in spirit briefly every year. Louise Allen, the curator of the actual Botanic Garden in Oxford, confirms that the bench is a popular point of pilgrimage for Pullman fans, "especially around midsummer."[5] Who's to say that if we sit there on Midsummer's Day at midday we won't be as close to Will and Lyra in their separate worlds as they are to each other? Or, as Pullman put it, "A city where South Parade is in the north and North Parade is in the south, where Paradise is lost under a car park . . . is a place where . . . likelihood evaporates" (Pullman

---

[3] Map references to locations that exist in Will's Oxford but not in Lyra's appear as handwritten notes on the Globetrotter map.
[4] Two fine novels involving alternative Oxfords, including ones accessed by time travel, are Connie Willis's *Doomsday Book* and Penelope Lively's *The House in Norham Gardens*.
[5] Allen notes that the black pine mentioned in the final chapter of Pullman's trilogy was also a favorite of J. R. R. Tolkien.

2002). He was referring to the real city when he wrote this, but the fictional Oscar Baedecker says the same thing in the epigraph to *Lyra's Oxford*. Our tour of Lyra's Oxford turns up all the contrasts that make the imaginary city differ from the real one, but it's these differences that make Pullman's fiction attractive and, paradoxically, convincing.

AUTHOR'S NOTE:

Some of ideas presented in this essay were first presented in articles I wrote under the name Elizabeth Gatland for the Friends of the Pitt Rivers Museum Newsletter *as listed in the bibliography.*

The carved ivory sphere mentioned in the final paragraph of this essay, from the Hong Kong region of China, is on display in the ivories case in the court of the Pitt Rivers Museum, Oxford (item no. 1940.12.143).

ELIZABETH WEIN's young adult novels include *The Winter Prince*, *A Coalition of Lions*, and *The Sunbird*, all set in Arthurian Britain and sixth-century Ethiopia. The cycle continues in The Mark of Solomon (Viking), published in two parts as *The Lion Hunter* (2007) and *The Empty Kingdom* (2008). Recent short fiction appears in Datlow and Windling's *Coyote Road Anthology* (Viking 2007).

Elizabeth has a Ph.D. in folklore from the University of Pennsylvania. She and her husband share a passion for maps, and fly small planes. They live in Scotland with their two children. Elizabeth's Web site is www.elizabethwein.com

REFERENCES

Allen, Louise. E-mail to author, 4 June 2007.

Frazer, Sir James George. *The Golden Bough: A Study in Magic and Religion*. 1922. Reprint, New York: Collier Books, 1963.

Postermaps. *A Souvenir Map & Guide to Oxford*. Falmouth, Cornwall:

Postermaps, [1990].

Pullman, Philip. "From Exeter to Jordan," *Oxford Today: The University Magazine* 14, no. 3 (Trinity 2002): http://www.oxfordtoday.ox.ac.uk/2001-02/v14n3/03.shtml. Originally published in *The Exeter College Association Register* (Oxford: Exeter College, [2001]).

Lyra's Oxford. Oxford: David Fickling Books, 2003.

"A Raffish, Amiable World of Horse Dealers and Alchemists," *Guardian Unlimited*, 14 August 2004, http://arts.guardian.co.uk/news/story/0,,1284318,00.html.

"Time Machines," *Friends of the Pitt Rivers Museum Newsletter* 50 (October 2004): 8.

Wein, Elizabeth E. [Elizabeth Gatland]. "Ideas and Objects: The Novelist, the Museum and the Real World," *Friends of the Pitt Rivers Museum Newsletter*, 50 (October 2004): 15.

"Writers Inspired. The Pitt Rivers: A Literary Bibliography," *Friends of the Pitt Rivers Museum Newsletter*, 47 (Janurary 2004): 7.

Wood, Felicity. E-mail to author, 31 August 1998. E-mail to author, 30 May 2007.

Every religion has its own Hell—or Hells. Surely an author as broadly read as Philip Pullman, constructing a mythology as rich as His Dark Materials, must have taken his underworldly inspiration from somewhere. Brennan explores a range of afterlives, seeking the source of Pullman's fictional Hell.

A SHORT HISTORY OF HELL AND THE CRABBY OLD GOD WHO SENDS YOU THERE

HERBIE BRENNAN

We discovered Hell 6,000 years ago. At that time it was called *kur-nu-gi-a*, the Land of No Return, but it was Hell all right. The dead lived in darkness, fed on clay, and were "clothed like birds with wings"—presumably that means feathers—according to the ancient histories of the world's first civilization (Budge).

The world's first civilization sprang up in what's now southern Iraq, an area of the Middle East often referred to as the Fertile Crescent. It was a pleasant place to live: sunny, warm, and (since we'd now invented farming) with enough food for everyone. Dying was a change for the worse that left most people bitter. Those who managed to get out of Hell—fortunately very few by all accounts—expressed their resentment by eating the living.

Once it occurs to you, Hell is one of those ideas that's very hard to shift. Certainly it hadn't shifted much by the time the Greek civilization arose. By then we'd decided Hell was a gloomy underworld populated by insubstantial shades with nothing much to do except pine for the good old days. Essentially, the same idea was prevalent in Ancient Rome: Hell was a gloomy shadow-land reached by a one-way crossing of the River Styx.

The old Norsemen were the first to call this miserable realm Hell—or, more accurately, Hel, after its miserable ruler. Same old place (a gloomy, subterranean hall inhabited by shivering, shadowy Specters), but by now we were adding some of the more interesting details. The roof of the hall was made from snakes, which dripped poison on those wading through rivers of blood below. If the poison and the wading made them

189

thirsty, all they got to drink was goat's piss.

But it served them right—the only people condemned to Hel were oath-breakers and those wimps who died of disease or old age. Heroes ended up in Valhalla with the gods, fighting happily amongst themselves by day before enjoying a communal feast of pork and mead by night.

You'll notice descriptions of Hell were fairly consistent up to this point. It was subterranean, gloomy, and chill (much as Philip Pullman described it in the last book of his trilogy, in fact, all dingy mist and listless, shivering dead; we'll come back to Philip Pullman later). But all that was about to change. The people who changed it were the Jews.

Officially, early Judaism didn't seem to have a Hell, or any afterlife at all for that matter. Scripture (specifically Ecclesiastes 9:5) says bluntly, "The dead know nothing and they have no more reward." But whatever the scriptural position, the people themselves clearly believed in survival. King Saul banned necromancy—raising the dead by magic—a piece of legislation that suggests a) necromancy must have been widely practiced and b) if you were calling up the dead, there had to be somewhere they could be called up *from*.

The place where the Judaic dead existed at that time seems to have been *Sheol*, a realm of shades much like the other underworlds we've been examining. You wandered listlessly down there, cold and bored, with nothing to look forward to except the outside possibility some necromancer might take a fancy to you. (Sounds a lot like Pullman's version, actually—except the best his dead had to look forward to for most of history was, if they were lucky, a lost philosopher with a few missing fingers and a knife.)

But Sheol didn't stay that way. As Jewish guilt began to take hold, the idea of judgment crept in and the place was divided into three compartments in order to house, respectively, the good, the bad, and the irredeemably mediocre. The place that housed the bad was called Gehenna.

How Gehenna got its name is interesting. Back here on Earth, the Valley of Hinnom (*Ge Hennom* in Hebrew) had a particularly gruesome history. In the bad old days, it had been a favorite spot for child sacrifice to a singularly unpleasant deity called Moloch. Oddly enough, Jerusalem was established quite close by. As the settlement turned into a thriving town, the rubbish had to be burned somewhere. The authorities decided Ge Hennom would do very nicely.

So the valley became a wasteland of perpetual smoke, flame, and stench, an ideal model for Gehenna, where it suddenly seemed fitting for the wicked to be tortured endlessly by fire. For the first time in human history, Hell started to warm up.

Although the Jews got there first, the idea of a hot Hell appealed so much to the Buddhists that they invented eight of them to balance out eight cold Hells that also welcomed sinners. The hot spots were, respectively:

Sañjva: a Hell where the ground was made from iron, heated by an immense fire. There you were attacked by your fellow inmates, who were equipped with iron claws, when you weren't being attacked by the Hell king's minions and their fiery weapons. If that failed to teach you whatever lesson you were supposed to learn, you had molten metal dropped on you before being sliced to pieces.

Klastra: often known as the black thread Hell because it was the place where black lines were drawn on your body so the king's servants could cut along them with fiery saws and sharp axes.

Saghta: a crushing Hell where the hot iron ground was surrounded by masses of rock that smashed together to crush you to a bloody pulp — before withdrawing so you could revive in time for the whole process to start all over again.

Raurava: a particularly tricky Hell where the ground burned so fiercely that you ran around desperately looking for somewhere to cool your feet. There were refuges built in, but if you were unwary enough to enter one of them, the door locked automatically behind you and the place caught fire. Raurava was known as the Screaming Hell. You can see why.

Mahraurava: known as the Great Screaming Hell because it was almost a mirror image of Raurava except that the pain level was higher.

Tapana: a Hell where the Hell king's servants impaled you on a fiery spear until flames came out of your nose and mouth.

Pratpana: a Hell that makes you suspect the early Buddhists were beginning to suffer from a failure of the imagination. It was more or less the same sort of place as Tapana except you were pierced by a trident instead of a spear. But I expect a trident must be three times as painful as a spear.

Avci: the only Hell I've come across that consists entirely of a single (admittedly enormous) oven. Guess who it was designed to roast? You're right — it was designed to roast you . . . over and over again.

As in the other traditions, the hot Buddhist Hells were all located underground.

Five hundred years after the birth of the Buddha, a new religion sprang up, with fresh predictions of what happens to you when you die. Before St. Paul got his hands on it, Christianity was largely a reform movement of established Judaism, re-emphasizing some aspects of the original creed, playing down others.

One aspect it re-emphasized was an extraordinary development that had occurred about the fifth century B.C.E. That was when somebody produced the Book of Isaiah. This work is a compilation of the sayings of an eighth-century B.C.E. prophet who proclaimed that "the dead shall live, their bodies shall rise"—the first recorded instance of a belief in resurrection. To ensure there would be no misunderstandings about what he was saying, Isaiah described corpses as "dwellers in the dust" and announced that they would "awake and sing" (26:19).

You wouldn't imagine singing corpses would have any great appeal, but Pauline Christianity seized the idea with both hands and linked it to the Second Coming of Christ. Surprising though it may sound, early Christians had no expectation of Heaven or Hell when they died. Rather, they looked forward to a patient wait for their Messiah, whose Second Coming would herald a Final Judgment designed to sort the good, who accepted Christ's salvation, from the bad, who didn't. Only then was there any question of where you would end up—alongside Christ up in Heaven, or cast down as pitchfork fodder for Satan in Hell.

At first the assumption was that Jesus, who had, of course, conquered death himself, would return in glory during the lifetime of his disciples. When the last of his disciples died, the remaining followers hoped that the Second Coming would happen soon, then increasingly settled for the possibility that it would happen eventually.

Meanwhile, the notion of a widespread resurrection remained as potent as ever—and not just among Christians. Resurrection remained an article of the Jewish faith. In the Eighteen Benedictions recited daily, God was addressed as "the One who resurrects the dead," while the Sanhedrin warned that anyone claiming there was no resurrection would be debarred forever from the world to come.

The Emperor Hadrian (117 to 138 C.E.) was so intrigued that he called on Rabbi Joshua ben Chanin to explain exactly how this resurrection would be done. The wise Rabbi told him God would use an indestructible bone called *luz*, located in everybody's spinal column just below the eighteenth vertebra. Joshua just happened to have an old *luz* with him and used it to demonstrate that when the bone was pounded with a blacksmith's hammer, the anvil shattered but the *luz* itself remained intact. (Belief in the *luz* survived until a Flemish physician, Andreas Vesalius, proved conclusively in the sixteenth century that it didn't exist.)

As the years rolled on and Christians began to think they'd have to wait a thousand years for the Second Coming, a degree of impatience started to creep in. While the idea of a mass Judgment Day had huge emotional appeal, it also had certain problems. One was that it seemed unfair to postpone a believer's well-earned trip to Paradise—and even more so to postpone the well-deserved brutalities a loving God would want to impose on sinners as soon as possible. Another was the difficulty in believing that between the day of your death and the day of your eventual resurrection, all you did was lie there quietly and rot.

An early attempt to solve the latter problem (put forward by the Church Father Tertullian) was the concept of "Abraham's Bosom," which lay somewhere a bit below Heaven and a bit above Hell. There you could rest and refresh yourself after death with no worries except, perhaps, for nagging doubts about your fate on Judgment Day. This sounded like such a great idea that the Byzantine Church made it part of its official doctrine.

Not to be outdone, the Roman Catholic Church came up with a rather more wide-ranging solution. This was its medieval doctrine of limbo, a borderland between Heaven and Hell. Limbo was a way-station just like Abraham's Bosom, but a lot less comfortable (think Pullman's suburbs of the dead). Catholicism then (as now) was convinced that more or less everybody died a sinner, so in limbo penances were available to let you scrub your soul a little cleaner *before* the Final Judgment fell on you.

But penances or not, limbo didn't prove enough. The desire to punish sinners was so strong that Church authorities decided, in the thirteenth century, that unbaptized babies went straight to Hell because of their burden of Original Sin, which you automatically inherit from Adam because of that business about forbidden fruit in the Garden of Eden. But mercifully, the poor little mites were given lighter punishments than the rest of us. Despite this, the idea that you might well end up in Hell before the Day of Judgment was so firmly implanted that many, if not most, Christians believe it even now.

In the seventh century C.E., the Prophet Muhammad founded a new religion with its own visions of Hell. After death, you face an examination on the tenets of Islam carried out by two angels. If you pass, your tomb is expanded as far as the eye can see. If you don't, your tomb contracts to crush you before a door opens and the smoke and heat of Hell pour in. But this is only a foretaste of things to come. Both saints and sinners are resurrected in physical bodies to face a Final Judgment. This sends believers to the well-watered gardens of Paradise and the wicked to a Hell where they put on garments of fire and have boiling water poured over their heads. New skin replaces any that is burned away so you don't miss out on pain.

The really dreadful thing is that you can't escape Hell by changing your religion. We've already seen that Buddhism has a fine collection of Hells. Hinduism, if anything, does even better, with as many as 136 of them, some with facilities for burning you alive, boiling you in oil, and having you eaten by hungry birds. The Parsees look forward to Hell (and its own presiding Devil) with as much enthusiasm as the rest of us. The Jains have eight Hells, which apparently get worse (and, for once, colder) the deeper down you go. In Confucian Hell, you're likely to have your eyes dug out of their sockets or be bound to a heated pillar while ox-headed demons flay the skin from your face and cook your hands to an unbearable crisp. Taoist Hells number somewhere between three and ten, depending on who you listen to, and tailor their tortures to your particular sin. If you've been really bad you might be sawn in half, thrown into a cess-pit, or forced to climb a tree studded with sharp blades.

Pullman's Hell, of course, skips the physical torture. Instead, he has harpies whisper in the ears of the dead, keeping them awake by reminding them of past sins. There's no fire or axes or blade-studded trees. Mostly there's a whole lot of nothing—which can be a particularly brutal kind of torture all on its own.

All of which brings us neatly to the philosophical discussion that has plagued theologians for centuries: How in Heaven could a just and loving God possibly sanction perpetual torture as a fitting punishment for the piddling little sins most of us manage to commit? There isn't a court in the civilized world that would consider it a reasonable sentence even for Hannibal Lecter.

(And if you're in the mood for tricky questions, how come the dev-ils—who are much more wicked than the rest of us—get to have the fun of poking us with pitchforks in a fiery environment that doesn't seem to inconvenience them at all?)

The question of how a loving God could sanction perpetual torment has no relevance in the Orient, where most religions teach it isn't God who sends you to Hell, but yourself. In a process known as *karma*, the sum total of your actions during your life determines the degree of dis-comfort you experience after death. Furthermore, Oriental Hells tend to be temporary. You might have to stay several million years, but at least you'll get out (usually to reincarnate) some day.

It's a very different story in the West. Here God serves as judge, jury, and jailer—with access to a dungeon that lasts forever. How can He bear to do the job? Writers like Timothy Findley and Philip Pullman (Findley in his acclaimed bestseller *Not Wanted on the Voyage*, and Pullman in the final volume of the His Dark Materials trilogy) have come up with an interesting answer to the conundrum. They present us with the vision of a God who's gone a bit senile.

I've gone a bit senile myself these days and I can tell you it's no fun. You don't *feel* any different. Inside, you're stuck around the age of eight-een or maybe just a little older, but your body won't behave the way it did back then. You chase a bus or a girl and they both get away without leaving first gear. You *think* you can dance all night, but you're lucky to last until the band tunes up. It'll happen to you one day and you'll find it frustrating. So much so, it may well make you bitter.

Pullman's imagined God is very bitter: quite possibly bitter enough, confused enough, bad-tempered enough, to send the whole world straight to Hell. (We know he's at least bitter enough to task a bunch of harpies with making the dead as miserable as possible. He doesn't even care whether the dead were good or bad when they were alive.) But is that a feasible picture of our dear, kind old Judeo-Christian deity? Surely God is God—eternal and unchanging?

Well actually, no. A careful reading of Scripture will quickly convince you that God has changed a lot. In his initial manifestation as Yahweh, he began as the tribal deity of Abraham's descendants, far more concerned with the welfare of his Chosen People than with the remainder of humanity.

But fortunately for the rest of us, he didn't stay that way. After early demands for sacrifice (both animal and human), He began to take an interest in morality and, while He failed to follow all His own Commandments (*thou* shalt not kill, but *He* did with depressing frequency), He did at least take time to work out rules for humanity's guidance. Then, after teaching the Children of Israel how to build the most potent weapon of mass destruction in the ancient world—the Ark of the Covenant—He eventually changed His emphasis from conquest to peace.

While my history teacher once remarked that the God of the Old Testament routinely behaved in ways no decent human being would behave, by the time you reach New Testament times He had transformed into quite a nice old boy—loving, caring, and concerned with truth and justice. In other words, He was growing up. But if you can grow up, you can also grow old.

So can we safely say a crabby old God is the explanation for Hell? Well, maybe. But I still have doubts. It struck me a long time ago that Hell had more to do with human imagination and ambition than with God. The ingenious tortures you find listed for so many Hells remind me irresistibly of a game we used to play in school called "Gross Out."

The thrust of this game was to devise an either/or question that would utterly gross out your fellow players. Would you rather be shot or strangled? Would you rather be burned at the stake or eaten slowly by a crocodile? Would you rather have your skin peeled off or your guts pulled out? And so on with increasingly repulsive options until your opponents give up in disgust and admit they just can't choose.

The game clearly satisfies a deep-seated human need, since most people continue to play it when they're grown up. Would you rather vote Republican or Democrat? Do you prefer New Labour or the Old Conservatives? Perhaps God likes to play it, too, so we have the choice of what will happen to us when we get to Hell. Would you rather be boiled in oil or sawed in half? Would you rather have your hands burned off or your eyes gouged out?

Or perhaps it isn't God who's playing the game at all, but God's faithful priesthood. Historically, they've shown themselves to have the imagination—just look at the tortures cooked up by the Inquisition—and they certainly have the motive. Belief in Hell once earned the Church a fortune in indulgences, and even now can underpin the respect paid to priests in the world's less-sophisticated cultures.

So my bright idea is that while Hell certainly exists (usually in some quiet corner of God's good green Earth), visiting it after you die is only an ecclesiastical scare story designed to give your betters additional authority—a bit like our current War on Terror.

HERBIE BRENNAN has a well-established career writing for the children's market—from picture books to teenage fiction, from game books to school curriculum non-fiction. He has produced more than 100 books, many of them international bestsellers, including his GrailQuest series and the teen novel *Faerie Wars*, which was a *New York Times* bestseller along with achieving bestseller status in more than twenty overseas editions.

REFERENCES

Budge, E. A. *Cuneiform Texts from Babylonian Tablets*, &c. in the British Museum. London: Harrison and Sons, 1896.

With all the kerfuffle about Pullman's anti-religiousness, perhaps his real crime remains unprosecuted: His Dark Materials is a deeply unhappy read. Heaven is a sham, parents treat their children abominably, young lovers are left sundered, and an array of likable characters are shot, stabbed, and soul-severed. Now, at long last—and with a little help from her friends—Johnson puts Pullman on trial for dereliction of duty with regard to fictional happiness.

PHILIP PULLMAN
AND THE LOSS OF JOY
Truth and Reconciliation (Or Not)

KATHLEEN JEFFRIE JOHNSON

The case of Joyfulness vs. Philip Pullman begins. The complainants, claiming crimes against contentment, will testify before a Judge of the Court as to the damage caused by Philip Pullman and his trilogy, His Dark Materials, to their well-being, in the hope of gaining apology and reparation.

THE FIRST WITNESS IS CALLED: THE BLUEBIRD OF HAPPINESS

It is true that some thought me overdone. Saccharine. Many laughed at the mere sight of me—a small bird the color of bluebells—chirping and singing, hopping merrily from branch to branch, grateful for each sun-kissed leaf and blossom.

Yes, that was me, Your Honor, fluttering, preening my feathers. Promising to any and all who would take the time to look and listen the freedom of innocence, the possibility of rebirth, the joy of perpetual spring.

Mr. Pullman, perhaps you are one of those who thought me a joke?

I wasn't. Being happy, being a harbinger of sweet contentment—that was my job. It is what I lived to do, and it fulfilled me. You could say it was my fate. If so, it was one that did not need to be altered.

Even you, Mr. Pullman, toy with the notion of fate, of predetermination. Does not your own Serafina Pekkala say, in *The Golden Compass*, "'We are all subject to the fates. But we must all act as if we are not . . . or die of despair'" (*TGC* 271).

That is a statement not only of predetermination, but one that can be made only after the loss of innocence. Almost all your characters—the ones most deserving of happiness, of me—lose their innocence, even forfeit their lives, all at your hands. And because of that, the world darkens.

Do not think you are the only one who knows about the myriad universes that so lightly touch our own. Your trilogy, His Dark Materials, has been the subject of intense scrutiny in the natural world. The animals, the plants, even the rocks—all of us—are in deep discussion. Any work of art delving deeply into belief and mythology that purports to explain the nature of the world, of us all, of our hopes and dreams and expectations, affects us enormously and gets our full attention, because what happens to humanity happens to all of us. Not because you are superior, but simply because you are stronger, having mustered enormous machines of industry.

Now, thanks to your book, I, too, have lost my innocence; I have come to know darkness.

From you, I have learned that the entire notion of perpetual spring is false. I don't refer here to the actual season of spring, which does come back year to year, though that too is apparently in jeopardy today from your machines. I mean the spring of hope and joy that lives in our hearts. Ours *and* yours. According to you, there is no rebirth—during life or after—because there is nothing to birth again but our own sorry selves, which seek corruption, destruction, and death. According to your Lord Asriel, "Human beings can't see anything without wanting to destroy it. . . . *That's* original sin" (*TGC* 331). And so our inner darkness rises to defeat light. Our true partners, as described in this world you have invented, are malevolence and death. Thank you for that.

I cannot recall any of your characters who end up happy, except the ghosts, whose momentary happiness at the end springs from their dissipation into—*nothingness*. Instead of coming back to visit the living, in loving remembrance, they are lost forever. And perhaps those strange creatures, the *mulefa*, are happy at the end, when their world is restored. I must say, while I have often in the past been called ridiculous, I was never quite so unrealistic as they.

That is just a quibble, though. We are all peculiar in our own way. My point is: why should the *mulefa* be accorded wisdom and respect when I, who chirped for *you*, am not?

No, you have taught me that life is cruel; nothing exists after death except atoms drifting off into space with other atoms, and that's that. Flowers curl up, turn brown, and fall off. *The End.* Don't call me naïve any longer. I am not.

I confess that, before your books, I really believed that happiness was not only possible but a fact of life; that we crave happiness, all of us. That we crave a belief in something more than sorrow. The most mordantly depressed among us struggle, in part, only because happiness has been so deeply denied to them. It is my belief that suicides are not only cruelly, if temporarily, separated from all joy, they are also deeply angry about it. If the depressives would only listen to me—yes, *me*, dressed in cheery blue, pecking merrily at their windows, singing my happy song—if those in such premature mourning could see that life is waiting for them with a glad smile and a gentle hug, then my work would be done.

What, Mr. Pullman, have you done about sorrow, except increase it?

Good vs. evil. Light vs. dark. It is true that before, I only saw goodness and light. I experienced it every morning when the sun came up and I found myself alive. Now I am tempered. I am the bluebird of despair, and it's all your doing.

THE SECOND WITNESS IS CALLED: CUPID

Yo, here. I know when people hear my name they expect a baby wearing wings and a diaper, carrying a bow and arrow, but that's a pile. I guarantee there's no baby hiding under *these* threads.

I work as a hair cutter. As a *stylist*, okay? Women, men—I do them all. Let's just say I know my way around the human body, and make *everybody* look good. Shampoo, cut, maybe a highlight or two, a little scent spritzed on the important parts. It's about believing you're hot, and it fits right in with my other line of work. Face it, I live in the twenty-first century now, I have to pay rent. This is one dude who isn't gonna starve, I promise you that.

Being Cupid is all about the *luv*, of course. Bringing all kinds of couples together, without them realizing I've orchestrated the entire thing. Introductions. Suggestions for where to go on the first date. Fashion tips. I mean, by the time they leave my shop, my work is halfway done, right?

I tell you, though, it's the other half of my job—the half that people don't even know about—that's the real pisser. What you could call the department of *complaints*. And don't people ever. About love gone sour. Jealousy. Disappointment after the fact. Betrayal. It goes on and on.

And I hear about it every which way that exists. It used to be just the occasional run-in with an unhappy customer at the village well, but today it's all *electronic*. Voicemail, e-mail. Blogs. Vlogs. Text messages. I'm, like, impressed—now leave me alone, okay? It never ends, and it's the reason I'm here today, testifying against Mr. P.

Sometime 'round about the year 2000, I started getting a lot more complaints than usual. At first, I just responded with my usual: *Blah blah blah, I'm sorry. . . . Better luck next time. . . . The right girl will come along. . . . He just wasn't that into you. . . .*

Yawn me a brick. But it's called Good Customer Service, so I do it.

Then I started noticing that the complaints weren't actually about the senders themselves, but about this one couple, Lyra and Will. Who, I thought, are they? They'd never been in my shop. I'd certainly had nothing to do with them coming *together*. As hard as it is to believe, I'm not actually involved in every coupling. Some people just go off on their own and do it, show some enterprise about the whole thing. I say great, it makes my job a lot easier.

Anyway, I finally figured out that people were not upset about the coming together of this Lyra and Will, but about—

Your Honor, might I suggest, to those in the court room who don't know the ending of Mr. P's. *oeuvre*, that they should leave? It's not pretty. . . .

So, okay. Everybody was all upset about the harsh *parting* of Lyra and Will. *Hello*, people. It's not exactly the first time it's happened. I hate to break the news, but some couples—lots of them—just don't make it. Still, the complaints became a whole lot of too much, so I decided I'd better do some research. Get this—it turns out that Lyra and Will are actually *characters* created by Mr. P. for his trilogy. Well, frost me some highlights. It's the first time I've dealt with *that*. So I decided I'd better read the freakin' thing.

The books aren't bad, I'll give you that. Witches, dæmons, talking bears. I'm more of a suspense guy, but whatever. I was pulled in pretty quick. Lyra was what they call a real plucky little girl; Will, strong and virtuous. Having been in the business as long as I have, I could see what was coming: *Lyra and Will were meant to be together.* I know, cliché time. But this relationship had *winner* written all over it. Will actually says it straight out, talking to that head witch—what's her name?—right, Serafina Pekkala. "'I love her more than anyone has ever been loved'" (*TAS* 456). I think that just about nails it, and so, okay, I fell for it. Call me Stupid Cupid. *Guilty as charged.* Love Story 101, and I was the biggest sucker in the room.

I say *sucker*, because what I could not foresee, Your Honor, was what came at the end of book three, the event that sent me into a tailspin and almost landed me in the hospital with nervous exhaustion and depression, forcing me to close the shop for a week and lose customers: the complete and utter destruction of Will and Lyra's relationship.

Not destroyed because one or both of them fell ill and died. Not ended because love died. Please. I see that all the time. No, ended merely because it suited the purpose of Mr. P's book. It was a destruction of *convenience.*

We know life isn't fair, okay? We get that. We know about the dark impulses of man and beast, the chicanery of politics and religion, of the seekers of power and destruction. *Check check check*, they're all on our list. So why, I ask, did Mr. P. have to destroy the one good and *lasting* thing in his book, the incredibly hot love story of Lyra and Will, if but to rub despair into our faces? Into my face? And, hey, I'm *Cupid*!

I mean, I got all the reasons *why* they had to be separated. That only by sealing off the openings between their worlds forever could the different worlds survive and thrive. That only by this harsh separation could *they* survive and thrive. *Blah blah blah.* It was all laid out very logically. I got it.

But. . . .

Writers do all sorts of things in their books, don't they, Mr. P.? If you could create the different worlds that you did, why couldn't you have gone on creating them a while longer, finding a way for Will and Lyra to be together? Is that too much to ask for? Hey, you're the genius in the room. Use it.

I still get complaints about Lyra and Will. Lots of them. I have to tell you, people all over the world are crying. *Weeping.* I've had to clear everything out of all the closets in my shop just to have space to store the raw grief that spills into my life now. That's what my job has become: the management of grief.

Mr. P., what's with you, dude?

THE THIRD WITNESS IS CALLED: THE LITTLE LOST PUPPY

Can Roger come out and play? Can he? Huh? Huh? I want him to throw a stick so I can chase it! I'm thirsty. Where's Hester? I love nose kisses! Can she come out? Huh? Lee Scoresby, please take me for a riiiiiiide in your balloon! Where are you? I'm *hungry*. Why isn't anyone coming out to play? I'm cold. Baruch? Can he come out? Can he, huh? He might bring me a vanilla cooookie. My favorite! Uh oh, it's starting to rain. I'm wet! Is Balthamos here? Huh? My paws hurt. Can Balthamos—

What? Huh? They're all *dead*? Mr. Pullman *killed* them?

Unh-h-h-h-h-h-h-h-h-h-h-h-h-h-h-h-h-h.

No! He wouldn't do that! Mr. Pullman is nice. He gave me my *friends*!

Your Honor, can you come out and play with me? Huh? I don't have any place to go. It's dark. I'm cold and wet and hungry! Mr. Pullman, can you come out? *Please*? I'm *looooonely*.

THE FOURTH WITNESS IS CALLED: HIS HOLY GHOSTLING, THE . . . XXXIII

Thank you, Your Honor, for being so kind as to let me speak. And yes, thank you, too, Mr. Pullman, for giving us such an interesting piece of work in your trilogy. In Heaven, you see, we like to keep up with youngsters such as yourself. Your books have proven quite the conversation starter. And, I might add, stopper. But we in the Kingdom are, of course, used to controversy and have withstood worse.

I am sorry you have a cold and have lost your voice, and will not be able to respond to us directly. Your representative will do just fine, I am sure. I, of course, am also speaking for Another, albeit indirectly. His Eminence, His Light—whatever you feel most comfortable calling Him. Higher Power is popular these days, but God will do just fine. I am but a far, distant relation, of course—seventy-fifth cousin, one billion thirty-three times removed, from the Most Holy Ghost Himself—but will do my very best to represent a small segment of Heaven's concerns.

His Dark Materials. Such a fascinating title! I see that it is taken from a section of John Milton's epic poem, *Paradise Lost*, which you have sensibly quoted at the front of *The Golden Compass*. Ah, Milton. Not a happy sort, was he? Quite obsessed with Heaven and Hell, that sort of thing. The poets are always so *distressed*. It's a pity, really. You want so much to help them, but sadly there is nothing to be done. The anguish just has to wear off on its own.

Paradise Lost, you see, while no doubt an excellent piece of writing, conjures up such a frightful sense of danger and mayhem, does it not? Wars, bloody battles; winners, losers. Frankly, these days we're all about peace up here in Heaven, but the poets have yet to catch on. Perhaps if you had chosen a different title—maybe something a little lighter?— Heaven and Earth would be well on their way to reconciliation, in much the same way this hearing strives to set things right between those who have been robbed of hope and happiness and faith, and the robber. Who, Mr. Pullman, I am sorry to report is you.

So—forgive me for asking what must seem to you a simplistic question—in quoting Milton's lines, just whose materials are you referring to? The poem suggests that these dark materials are the raw parts of God's great machinery, but because the "wary fiend" has crept in so closely, the reader cannot help but conflate God and—who? Lucifer? Their big struggle between good and evil, at any rate. A worthy topic, of course. One you take up quite admirably, if trickily, in your book.

However, I must point out that while God and Lucifer form a nice front—a pleasant deception, if you will—the true "His" of His Dark Materials is no one but yourself. Are you not the creator, the "God," if you will, of your various worlds? The *Authority*, which you so disparage in your books? Of course you are. And yet, interestingly, you eschew the existence of God. As the Bluebird of Happiness pointed out earlier, you posit that life is nothing more than atoms that bind to one another for a time, forming a concrete, living whole, only to then drift apart at death. Realizing this is, somehow, supposed to make your fellow beings happy. But can it be that the man who says there is no God actually lives as one himself, through his books?

Well, it is just a thought. An obvious one at that, you might say. All writers "create" their works. Fair enough.

The thought does, however, lead me to a second one.

You can no doubt appreciate the uproar your books have caused in Heaven. We, quite naturally, do not like to see God pulled off His right- ful throne. Once more, at the instigation of a writer, we are accused of being the cause of all misery, not only on Earth but on every other planet—"world," to you—in the universe. You have not only labeled us criminals, you have killed God, and set the angels running amuck. Really, we have more discipline than that.

But to my point. You are a clever man, Mr. Pullman. A deceptive one, but clever. God, in your books, is revealed to be false—a mere angel *posing* as God—and is destroyed. It is a matter of what you might call *angelic* deception. God is false; therefore, according to your philosophy, God does not exist.

Well, this is where the atheists start singing hosannas, isn't it? However, a close reading reveals that while you *seem* to kill God, you actually do not. A deceiving angel might fall—and indeed, should—but God does not fall, ever. In fact, you do not touch Him, do you? For God is not an angel. God is, always and forever, God. Therefore, when true, good angels and true, good humans alike bewail what you have done, I tell them all the same thing: Mr. Pullman has destroyed only a false idol. Mr. Pullman has left God alone.

You have put so much effort, Mr. Pullman, into this deception, into creating so much despair. Why? A man of your prodigious talent could have done so much more.

I look forward to your response.

THE COMPLAINANTS HAVE MADE THEIR CASE. NOW A REPRESENTATIVE FOR THE DEFENDANT, MR. PULLMAN, IS CALLED: MAXINE GLOT

Your Honor, of course I hurried right over when I heard that our dear, dear Philip was in trouble. We at Muse-for-You, Inc., take our jobs very seriously. I, myself, have been an Executive Muse for eons now, serving many fine authors, men and women, and have responded to more intellectual freedom issues than I can remember.

Intellectual freedom *is* what we're talking about, is it not?

You see, I know you think my job is to only, ah, *prop up* the writer, by providing inspiration. We do, indeed, do that. (And, just for the record, that bit about 1 percent inspiration, 99 percent hard work—well, not true. We at Muse-for-You earn our keep, I assure you.)

So, in that capacity, when Philip first groped his way toward something new, something big—toward, actually, the monumental magnificence that became His Dark Materials—I was there. Picture, if you will, a drop of water slowly reaching full volume, trembling at the brink of gravity. It was I who provided the final push, the intellectual moisture, if you will, that was necessary for that drop to fall. And fall it did, though not—no offense intended, Mr. Ghostling—into moral ruin.

No, as much as humans like to think that art springs wholly from some great swell of emotion—love, hate, pride, rage—to be captured, endowed, and preserved for all time by a writer's pen, the intellect is also involved. The *mind*. What you might call humanity's IQ. Would you have us not utilize this amazing capability?

See, people assume that it's only about love and sex between the artist and the muse. Well, we all have our little secrets, don't we? But we do so much more. We are the instruments of intellectual achievement. Even Mr. Milton found our services useful.

While I am sympathetic to the distress you have all displayed—can someone *please* find the Little Lost Puppy a home?—your anguish is a manifestation of only half the thought process. Emotion, you have in spades. But had one of you used intellect as well, you would have found the solution to your own distress.

Mr. Bluebird, you have fallen into despair because, you contend, Philip has shown you the darkness inherent in life. But, my fine blue friend, has not darkness always been with us? Before His Dark Materials, you focused only on joy and its many possibilities. Was that realistic? I think not. As for the rebirth of spring—of life itself—where, I ask, is that guaranteed for anyone, anywhere? And by whom?

I see the alarm in your face, Mr. Ghostling. I will get to you shortly.

Mr. Bluebird, you have badly used Philip's work. The darkness we all face should make you *more* responsive to joy, not less. You have a unique song; why should you stop singing it just because you now own a larger truth?

As for you, Cupid—Your Honor, perhaps I should mention that Cupid and I have had previous dealings, in what you could call the realm of *little secrets*? Shall I proceed nonetheless? Very well.

Cupid, you agonize over the eternal separation of Lyra and Will. Ah, so do I. I worked closely with Philip on this. I urged him to find a solution for them, a way to keep them together—but in the end I came to fully support his side. His books, after all, are about real life, the way it truly is. And separation is a part of it. Someone once said to me that we eventually say goodbye to everyone we love. That is true, Your Honor. Painful but true.

Cupid, you have long had a realistic understanding of the nature of love, and the possibility of its loss. Instead of succumbing to anger and despair, I suggest instead that you find a way to ameliorate it. Perhaps by setting up a small business on the side? A Will-and-Lyra-inspired hair care line, perhaps, celebrating the deep dare and risk that is inherent in every affair of the heart. And head. Be brave, my friend. Brave.

Ah, Little Lost Puppy. Yes, when Hester and Lee Scoresby died, I cried as much as you. I thought I could not go on. Moreover, it was I who whispered into Philip's ear, telling him of the deep love between Baruch and Balthamos. So you can imagine my chagrin when he killed them off—I even briefly considered canceling my contract with him. But again, reality, Little Lost Puppy. Reality. Life and death are intertwined, one will always conquer the other, and there is always a new friend waiting for you. Your job is to find him. Though—as a matter of practicality—I strongly suggest, as you embark on this new quest, that you steer clear of Philip's books.

Your Holy Ghostling. I come to you with a sorry heart, for I know you do not approve of me or Philip one bit. I know that our relationship, to you, is a scandal. But as much as life and death happen, so does love.

I find your suggestion that Philip does not destroy God to be specious. God is whatever the artist decides He is. His name is whatever the artist gives Him. If Philip calls an angel God, then that angel, as far His Dark Materials is concerned, is God. Your contention that God exists above and beyond all the worlds, including Philip's—that God cannot be touched—well, you cannot prove that, can you? That is *your* story, is it not? The one you tell about Heaven. And if God is the All and Everything you say He is, how can He be so concerned—in all the worlds' universes—with the work of one author?

It may distress you to know this, but in my long career I have also been with many religious writers, and while with them, I also believed in and loved God. Does that surprise you? I love my clients, you see. All of them. I love what they love. From St. Augustine to Martin Luther to John Donne to C. S. Lewis, I helped the religious writers the same as I helped Philip, urging them toward the sweet release of artistry.

It seems to me that both the religious faithful and the atheist are reaching toward a sublimity of *comprehension*—a view of the world that is whole and just and meaningful—trying to understand how life comes into being and how it departs. Really, is that not Heaven enough for us?

Your Honor, I have defended Philip Pullman against these charges to the best of my ability. I trust you will settle this matter in a fair and just way.

HERE FORTHWITH IS THE DECISION RENDERED BY THE PRESIDING JUDGE: PENELOPE

A tired, old woman. That is what I am. Once young and lovely, but now—

Let me explain that I am here before you because of my own long existence in this world. I believe it can honestly be said that I have seen life and death in all their varied guises. I have known multitudes of men, women, and gods—all their scheming, all their sorrows. Their wickedness, goodness, beliefs, and betrayals. All their lost innocence and determined faith. And I can tell you that nothing ever changes. Ever.

I once thought that when my husband, Odysseus, came home, my sorrow and endless weaving would stop. But men and women have made the two of us into heroes. Into what you might call *icons*—beings not so very different from all of you who have testified here today. They have made us live forever, you see, reborn, perpetually, into story. They pursue, without stopping, my beloved husband's strength of purpose, his honor, his wile, and even his foibles. They chase him down, again and again, on his very journey into danger.

As for me, they desire, always, my beauty—wanting to touch me, to know how I endure, how I have the strength to remain so loving and patient for so long. And why. Today, they ask why. So I weave on through age after age, each night undoing what I have completed, waiting for my dear husband, Odysseus, to return from his journey—again and again and again. I have gained a wisdom I wish I had not, but I use it humbly, to do my best for all you gathered here today.

I have listened carefully. All parties to this case have made pertinent arguments. Every one of you is right in much the same way that every one of you is wrong. I am sorry; it is complicated. The entirety of truth, you see, cannot be fully understood or revealed. Simply put, it cannot be unraveled. Therefore, I am unable to grant, to any of you, a final verdict.

For the plaintiffs, I suggest that you each find joy in your own way—much as I have done through the study and application of justice. I will give you a hint, though. It takes courage to thrive in the dark, and it is hard. Myself, I look forward to my last stitch, to cessation. To Odysseus' final homecoming. To when we can at last lie down together in death.

Mr. Pullman, I render against you a single judgment: Remove that dog at once. The Little Lost Puppy is yours.

KATHLEEN JEFFRIE JOHNSON is the author of five novels for young adults: *Gone*, *Dumb Love*, *A Fast and Brutal Wing*, *Target*, and *The Parallel Universe of Liars*. She has lived in the suburbs of Washington, D.C., her entire life—which has been ghoulishly long—and this, the experts feel, is why she writes such bleak realistic novels and such weird speculative ones. On the upside, she is developing a promising picture book series about baby politicians.